REDISCOVERING

NANCY
DREW

REDISCOVERING
NANCY
DREW

Edited by

Carolyn Stewart Dyer

and

Nancy Tillman Romalov

Ψ University of Iowa Press
Iowa City

University of Iowa Press, Iowa City 52242

Printed on acid-free paper

Library of Congress Cataloging-in-Publication Data
Rediscovering Nancy Drew / edited by Carolyn Stewart Dyer and
Nancy Tillman Romalov.
p.   cm.
Includes bibliographical references and index.
ISBN 0-87745-500-7, ISBN 0-87745-501-5 (pbk.)
1. Wirt, Mildred A. (Mildred Augustine), 1905–   —Characters—
Nancy Drew.   2. Detective and mystery stories, American—History
and criticism.   3. Feminism and literature—United States—History—
20th century.   4. Women and literature—United States—History—
20th century.   5. Children's stories, American—History and criticism.
6. Children's literature in series—Bibliography.   7. Children—United
States—Books and reading.   8. Drew, Nancy (Fictitious character).
9. Stratemeyer, Edward, 1862–1930.   10. Children's stories—Publishing.   11. Girls in literature.   I. Dyer, Carolyn Stewart.   II. Romalov,
Nancy Tillman.
PS3545.I774Z87   1995   95-8514
813'.52—dc20   CIP

01 00 99 98 97 96 95 C 5 4 3 2 1
01 00 99 98 97   P 5 4 3 2

FOR SUE LAFKY,
a friend, colleague, and catalyst whose
commitment to public recognition
of women's work led the way
to rediscovery

CONTENTS

Acknowledgments

The Nancy Drew Conference at the University of Iowa, April 16–18, 1993, was one part of the Nancy Drew Project, which included adult reading groups at two public libraries, an essay contest for Iowa schoolchildren, solve-a-mystery dinners for young adults, and a reading by mystery writer Linda Barnes that was broadcast on public radio.

The Nancy Drew Project was funded in part by the Iowa Humanities Board and a challenge grant from the National Endowment for the Humanities. It was sponsored by many departments and programs at the University of Iowa, the Cedar Rapids, Coralville, and Iowa City, Iowa, public libraries, and Friends of the Coralville Public Library. Other sponsors included the Iowa Newspaper Association and Quill & Scroll and many generous individuals and businesses. Funds to transcribe the tapes of the conference, edit the manuscript for this book, and manage the correspondence came from the Office of the Provost of the University of Iowa, the School of Journalism and Mass Communication, and the sale of conference T-shirts and posters (which are no longer available).

Despite the financial support we received, raising enough money for the project was a difficult task, in part because the focus was a *girl* sleuth whom some potential sponsors would not take seriously. (It is tempting to name those who turned us down.) Many people who supported the project have told us that they took a professional risk in associating themselves with a subject that might be seen as silly nostalgia. For most their involvement was vindicated by the success of the project.

In this context, it is important to recognize the support of Kenneth Starck, director of the School of Journalism and Mass Communication at the University of Iowa. He enthusiastically backed the project from the moment the idea popped up in the middle of an administrative staff meeting and made many resources available. Elizabeth Altmaier, first as associate dean of the College of Education and later as associate provost of the University of Iowa, demonstrated the courage of her convictions and the pull of childhood memories in finding funds for both the conference and research assistance for the book.

The project was planned and the work was carried out by a committee of faculty, graduate students, staff, librarians, a public school district administrator, and interested citizens in the community who met nearly weekly for more than a year. Members of the committee were Mary Arnold, Diana Beeson, Esther Green Bierbaum, Susan Birrell, Barbara Black, Bonnie Brennen, Patricia Cain, Carolyn Stewart Dyer, Kay Graber, Michelle Grace, James Hamilton, Hanno Hardt, Sue Lafky, Karen M. Mason, Robert McCown, Judy Polumbaum, Nancy Tillman Romalov, Jeffery Smith, Joan Soucek, Kenneth Starck, Mary Helen Stefaniak, Serena Stier, and Bonnie S. Sunstein.

The work of the staff of the School of Journalism and Mass Communication was invaluable. Joan Soucek, a secretary and receptionist, fielded most of the hundreds of phone calls and much of the mail the project generated over several years. Susan Redfern, whose discovery of Mildred Wirt Benson was the catalyst for the entire project, kept track of the news coverage it generated. Maynard Cuppy handled many of the word processing and desktop publishing chores, and Nancy Parizek worried about the money and kept track of the budget when funds did materialize. Doug Allaire took charge of the audio and videotaping of the conference on which much of this book is based. Mary Arnold managed registration and then, with the help of research assistant Margaret Duffy, generated the data used in this book to describe the fans and readers of Nancy Drew. James Hamilton was the project assistant during the year of the conference.

The Nancy Drew Conference and this book would have been pale shadows of what they turned out to be if not for the considerable assistance of Anne Greenberg, the current editor of the Nancy Drew series at Pocket Books.

Perhaps most important to the project was the cooperation of Mildred Wirt Benson, who says we "blew her cover." Despite the long overdue recognition the conference has brought her, the consequences were an overwhelming number of letters and phone calls and the loss of the privacy her anonymity protected.

The Nancy Drew Conference would have passed away in crumbling newspaper clippings, faded videotapes, and aging memories if Holly Carver hadn't roused herself early on a Saturday morning to hear Carolyn Heilbrun's keynote address. Carver, the assistant director of the University of Iowa Press, suggested that we transform the record of the conference into a book and encouraged us in each stage of its development.

Radhika Parameswaran, who read Nancy Drew as a schoolgirl in India, helped us get the text on the page with as few errors as humanly possible, always working under nearly impossible deadlines. We take responsibility for any errors that remain.

The Nancy Drew Phenomenon: Rediscovering Nancy Drew in Iowa

Carolyn Stewart Dyer

L ike all jobs, being undergraduate secretary in the School of Journalism and Mass Communication at the University of Iowa has its slow moments, especially in the summer. Susan Redfern was new to the job in the summer of 1991. She anticipated that slow moments might turn into endless days, so she assigned herself the task of cleaning the alumni files to make room for more.

Being the granddaughter of the first person to teach journalism full-time at the university and having a desk right under the portrait of George Gallup, founder of the Gallup Poll and the first member of the school's Hall of Fame, Redfern felt a little proprietary about the school's history.

Taking the alphabetical approach, Redfern began with the As. Reading through every file she put its contents in order, discarded duplicate materials and other ephemera, and made note of alums with unusual histories—a man who became a millionaire by inventing plastic book covers, another who was married briefly to singer Connie Francis. During breaks she entertained the staff with stories from the files.

Not long into the task Redfern made her most important discovery, the file of Augustine, Mildred, M.A. 1927, the first person to earn a master's degree in journalism at Iowa. Like the founder of the Gallup Poll, Augustine had been a student of Redfern's grandfather, William Maulsby. And she, too, had left a big imprint on American

1

culture. Mildred Augustine Wirt, writing under the pseudonym Carolyn Keene, was the original writer of the most memorable books from Redfern's childhood, the Nancy Drew mysteries. In 1991 Mildred Wirt Benson was a reporter and columnist in Ohio for the *Toledo Blade*, where she had worked for almost fifty years.

First Redfern told the staff about Mildred Benson, and they recounted their Nancy Drew memories. Then, as they came into the office over the next few days, she told the women faculty. Sue Lafky, an assistant professor, immediately recognized an oversight: Mildred Benson was missing from the Hall of Fame. That wasn't surprising; very few women had been recognized. Most of the luminaries held much more visible positions than Benson. She was an author of children's books, for heaven's sakes, her identity had been obscured behind pseudonyms, and she was then an everyday journalist at a regional newspaper in Ohio. Hardly the profile of a person to hold a banquet for, invite the university president to meet, and enshrine in a portrait gallery. Or so the traditionalists thought.

But the women knew better. Nancy Drews were no ordinary children's books. Reading Nancy Drew was a pivotal childhood experience for millions of girls. More than eighty million copies had been sold since 1930, and new books were still coming out every month in what may be the longest running continuously published series of children's books.

Through the fall and winter, Susan Redfern fantasized misogynist and elitist conspiracy theories to try to understand why Mildred Benson had never been recognized by the journalism school or university, while virtually every Iowa Citian could list the pantheon of famous writers who had passed through the Iowa Writers' Workshop. Sue Lafky simply resolved to get Mildred Benson into the journalism school Hall of Fame.

The Hall of Fame selection process is a little mysterious. At some point every year, a memo is circulated to journalism faculty soliciting nominations to add to those left over from the previous year. Most of the nominees are older men—famous or semifamous journalists, journalism educators, or public relations practitioners. A few are younger alumni who have won distinguished awards or risen to highly visible places at an early age. Often the obituaries of the previous year remind the faculty to add someone forgotten and overlooked in the nomination process.

After the nominations are taken, the faculty members rank their choices on another ballot. The actual votes are not announced. The director of the School of Journalism and Mass Communication just announces who will be added to the Hall of Fame at the annual awards banquet, and the sun sets in the west as usual.

Relatively new to the faculty, Lafky took a direct, public approach to her Benson for Hall of Fame campaign. She prepared herself with facts about Benson's career. She talked to nearly everyone on the journalism faculty. Among the men, she targeted those whose wives, partners, or daughters might have read Benson's books and suggested they ask about Nancy Drew. Then she went outside journalism, enlisting moral support from women in other departments. Those women told others, and the word spread and spread. Soon we were stopped on the street, cornered at parties, called late at night. Everyone had a story about reading Nancy Drew, and this was just the beginning. The Hall of Fame nomination ballot hadn't even been circulated.

Needless to say, Benson made the final ballot. Lafky and the office staff urged faculty to vote early and often. And, by whatever count, Benson was elected to the Hall of Fame.[1] When the election and honors banquet were announced publicly, the phone began to ring. Nancy's fans wanted to attend the banquet, to meet Benson, to request information, or simply to relive a memory. Whatever the purpose of the call, nearly every one of these readers told journalism school receptionist Joan Soucek a story about reading Nancy Drew.

In journalistic terms, there seemed to be a story in this Nancy Drew phenomenon, and we began to dig into it. Searching in a news database, we found references to Nancy Drew in hundreds of stories from sports pages to business reports, and they turned up nearly weekly in profiles of girls and women in the news, who usually said Nancy Drew inspired them to persevere, to achieve, to ask questions and find answers.

Nancy Romalov, one of the women cheering Sue Lafky on in the Benson for Hall of Fame campaign, was researching series books for girls and teaching a women's studies course on the subject. She introduced us to the scholarship on Nancy Drew in fields ranging from education and library science to American studies and even geography and to the world of series book collectors. There were controversies over whether children should read them and whether libraries should buy them and mysteries surrounding the authorship of the books. But most of all, a remarkable passion for Nancy Drew seemed to span a wide spectrum of American society. And so the idea of the Nancy Drew Conference developed, to explore the phenomenon in its many dimensions.

We had several objectives in mind for the conference. The first was to examine Nancy Drew as a part of American popular culture through an exploration of the history of the series. We wanted to make known the important part Mildred Wirt Benson played in the development of this memorable character. We wanted to dig into the controversies and address the impact of these books on both the lifetime reading habits of the devotees and their senses of themselves.

As we introduced the idea of a conference, first to colleagues in the university, then to public librarians, and continually to friends, family, and acquaintances, we heard what came to be a predictable response. Conversation would stop momentarily as the listener probed her store of memories. Then she would ask if we really meant Nancy Drew, the girl sleuth of her childhood. Finally, she would exclaim, "I read *all* the Nancy Drew books!" And she would tell a story. For those like Susan Redfern who hadn't thought about Nancy Drew in years, this was a moment of rediscovery.

Although many individual women and men reconnected only recently with their memories of Nancy Drew, this was merely a revival of interests that had sparked and then burned out on the University of Iowa campus several times before. What Susan Redfern rediscovered in Mildred Augustine's file in 1991 were copies of several articles from university publications in which the true identity of the original Carolyn Keene had been revealed.[2] In addition there had been occasional news stories about the ghostwriter of Nancy Drew ever since the 1930s. The University of Iowa Libraries Special Collections Department had been aware of Benson's contribution to children's literature for at least forty years, and copies of most of her 130-some books were in its Iowa Authors Collection.

What was billed as the first-ever Nancy Drew Conference was an extraordinary event that seemed to stimulate everyone's imagination. It attracted about 500 people ranging in age from four to ninety, about 15 percent of them boys and men. The participants were a diverse group including avid collectors and scholars, librarians and teachers, and a broad range of people in the general public, most of whom fondly remember reading Nancy Drew.

When word of the conference reached the media, it spread from one news organization to another. The result was probably more news coverage than any other University of Iowa event except the participation of its football teams in the Rose Bowl ever attracted. Mildred Wirt Benson was the Person of the Week on ABC-TV News the night the conference began, and Benson and the conference were featured on most of the other U.S. and Canadian radio and television networks as well. Feature stories appeared on page one or section fronts of many major American newspapers and in hundreds of other papers in the United States and abroad. The conference led a number of magazines for girls and women to rediscover Nancy Drew in the months that followed.

News stories and word of mouth about the conference and the renewed interest in Nancy Drew continued long after the event and followed its organizers and participants around the world. The coordinator was asked to lecture on the conference in Sweden and Norway. A woman wearing a conference T-shirt was grilled for details in the Australian outback. Mildred Wirt Benson was named to both the Ohio and Iowa Women's Halls of Fame and selected for a Distinguished Alumni Award by the University of Iowa in the year following the conference.

So why did Nancy Drew break through to widespread popular consciousness this time? What had changed? And what does this Nancy Drew phenomenon mean?

Most of what's written and said about American popular culture in both the mass media and academic works has focused on the passions of boys and men, while the memorable childhood experiences of girls have been largely ignored. Think of the aggrandizement of sports and adventure comic heroes, for example: reveries of baseball games or seasons gone by. With the rise of feminism has come some recent attention to popular culture aimed at adult women—romance novels and soap operas, in particular—but the underlying objective of many studies, such as those by Janice Radway (1984) and Tania Modleski (1982), and mass media accounts seems to have been to demean these genres or to find out what is *wrong* with women who like them. The pastimes of girlhood still have been largely neglected.

The women who were perhaps most affected by the experience of reading about an independent, self-confident, successful girl were those who grew up in the late 1940s and 1950s in the United States, when there was great pressure on girls and women to devote themselves to preparing to be perfect wives and mothers. Many of the women who were affected by this reading are just now coming into considerable responsibility, respected for their professional judgment. And some of them are now in positions of authority in the news media. That seems to help explain why now, rather than earlier, the news media were so taken by the story about a conference on Nancy Drew and the recognition of Mildred Wirt Benson, the woman journalist who wrote the original stories. Many of the journalists who assigned or produced newspaper, magazine, or television stories about the conference or Mildred Benson were such women. In other news organizations where there were no such editors or producers journalists who badly wanted to cover the conference failed to convince their superiors to send them to Iowa City.

Most compelling of the many elements in the stories women told us about reading Nancy Drew were the accounts of how, as girls, they saw in Nancy an alternative to conventional notions of what a woman could be. Women in many occupations told of learning from Nancy to see adventure in solving problems and the joy of self-reliance. These qualities, they said, led them to the futures they chose as lawyers, researchers, librarians, and detectives, among other roles.

This phenomenon of looking to popular literature as a guide to life reminded us of Carolyn G. Heilbrun's insightful book *Writing a Woman's Life* (1988). A pioneer feminist literary critic, Heilbrun wrote that fiction, biography, autobiography, and real life itself offer opportunities for women to invent themselves, the chance to depart from roles society has prescribed. Heilbrun's account of her own adoption of the pseudonym Amanda Cross to create Kate Fansler as the protagonist in one of the first contemporary American mystery series by and about a woman parallels in some respects the life and work of Mildred Wirt Benson and Carolyn Keene. Both Heilbrun and Benson have said they wrote mysteries they would like to have been able to read and created characters who could live more adventurous lives than they thought they could lead early in their careers. And Kate Fansler, who is an independent woman and amateur sleuth, has been referred to as a "grown-up Nancy Drew."

Unlike many literary scholars, Heilbrun has written accessible work that has offered the discoveries and ideas of feminist scholars to women who look to books for clues on how to construct a satisfying and adventurous life. Therefore she seemed to be the ideal person to open the Nancy Drew Conference, which attracted many women who had found in Nancy Drew different ideas about what in the world a woman could do. In her introductory essay for this book, she provides a cultural context for understanding the Nancy Drew books in time and place that perhaps no other scholar could provide. In fact, one reviewer of her conference presentation suggested that Heilbrun's professional career helped make the Nancy Drew Conference possible.

Although Nancy Drews were written and published for girls, boys read them, too, and the time seemed just as ripe for them to reflect on their memories. Many of the most avid and prominent collectors are men, including several we asked to speak at the conference. As women got caught up in their memories of days with Nancy Drew, they found, often to their great surprise, that their brothers admitted to secretly reading their Nancy Drews or that their husbands or partners had done the same with their sisters' books. A Swedish woman told of discovering that her grandfather had stayed up late during summer holidays at a cabin in the woods reading his granddaughters' Swedish Kitty Drew books after they had gone to sleep. And some of the journalists most interested by the story of Mildred Wirt Benson and the Nancy Drew Conference were men.

However familiar the stories adults tell, their rediscovered childhood passions are refracted by time and subsequent events in their lives. The haze of nostalgia, the power of the researcher's magnifying lens and theories of interpretation, and the material interests of the collector all make something different of the objects of their attention, whether they are baseball cards or Nancy Drew books. Rarely are children consulted as the contemporary authorities on their own experiences.

Since Nancy Drew books have been passed on to several generations and new books continue to appear, we decided to ask children for their own accounts of reading Nancy Drew. We invited Iowa students in grades five through eight to submit essays on the theme "Keen Friends, Stouthearted Chums: Nancy Drew and the American Girl," drawn from the quaint language of the early books.

The submissions ranged from children's original Nancy Drew mysteries to textual analyses by budding literary scholars. As the titles and quotations from Nancy Drews they mentioned in their essays revealed, contemporary children read Nancy Drews from every era, from the blue-cover originals through the yellow-spine rewrites, to the latest Nancy Drew Files and SuperMysteries. We have included excerpts from the four winning essays on the title pages of the parts of this book.

For those who did not attend, this book represents an effort to capture in print the varied menu and rich flavor of that conference. The conference was divided into two programs: the public conference, planned for a broad general audience of adults and children, and the scholars' conference, intended for scholars and students of Nancy Drew and children's literature. This book draws primarily from presentations at the public conference.[3] Our version of the public conference, like the *Congressional Record*, is a revised, corrected, annotated, supplemented, and updated account of much, but not all, of the scheduled talk and some of the spontaneous discussion in the formal sessions. To provide some context for the essays that follow, we continue the narrative about the conference in introductions to the four parts of the book that follow Carolyn Heilbrun's keynote.

NOTES

1. To remedy another oversight, the school chose the late Frank Luther Mott, Pulitzer Prize–winning journalism historian, first director of the School of Journalism at Iowa, and, we learned later, one of Mildred Wirt Benson's teachers, to share the honor with Benson in 1992. Interestingly, the only other time two people were selected was 1953, when the first woman was chosen. That was Beatrice Blackmar Gould, then longtime editor of the *Ladies' Home Journal*. Gould, who helped transform the magazine into an advocate for women's rights, was paired with Theodore Koop, who ended a long journalism career as vice-president of CBS in Washington.

2. Frank Paluka, head of the Special Collections Department of the University of Iowa Libraries in 1965, published a comprehensive list of Benson's publications in a bibliography of Iowa authors. In 1973 Benson wrote her only published autobiographical essay for the library's publication *Books at Iowa* (reprinted in this book as chapter 6). The *Iowa Alumni Review* published a feature on Benson in 1985, "The Se-

cret of the Ghost(writer) of Ladora." In 1989 Geoffrey Lapin, who had devoted years to unmasking Carolyn Keene, wrote an article on his search in *Books at Iowa*.

3. Papers from the scholars' conference as well as other articles appeared in a special Nancy Drew issue of the children's literature journal the *Lion and the Unicorn* 18: 1 (June 1994).

CHAPTER 1

Nancy Drew: A Moment in Feminist History

Carolyn G. Heilbrun

N ancy Drew—the original Nancy Drew, written by that active woman Mildred Benson—is a moment in the history of feminism. Almost all the critics writing about Nancy Drew have read the later novels, not written by Mildred Benson, and the revisions of the early novels Benson did write. The clue here is that they all refer to Nancy as eighteen, and she was sixteen through all of Benson's accounts of her adventures. The reasons for this age change are unclear: partly, it is said, to conform to new driver's license regulations. Far more likely was the attempt to make her more grown up, more a "lady," more likely to act on her own. The point is that it was the sixteen-year-old Nancy Drew, born at age sixteen in 1930, who was a vital but alas solitary moment.

To understand her significance we must look at her as she appeared in 1930 and the years immediately following, and not as we look back on her now with all our newfound sensibilities and critical sophistications. Frankly, to read *The Bungalow Mystery*, published in 1930, as I have recently done, is to see something incredibly clear and, at the same time, terribly flawed to our current vision. I want to offer a few gems from *The Bungalow Mystery*, but not without a tribute and thanks to Professor Donna Perry, who saved almost all these early editions from her childhood and kindly lent some of them to me in preparation for the Nancy Drew Conference. Yet even Donna Perry had only the dimmest memories of Nancy Drew.

And this dim memory was the first astonishing fact I learned about Nancy Drew when, because of the conference, I began mentioning her. Everybody perks up at her name, stands up and salutes as it were. At the same time, nobody can remember a thing about the plots of the books, nor do they have any of the facts about her in very good order. One and all they glow with fond memories: she is their favorite childhood character. But when asked what they remember—if they have not reread the books since their childhood—they mention the roadster, and perhaps her friends Bess and George; a certain number, to my surprise, remembered that she was blond. In short, they remember more a sensation of pleasure than any of the particular components of that pleasure. And that pleasure came, I wish to assert, from the adventures of a sixteen-year-old girl who took events into her own hands. Certainly the plots have long since faded into gossamer, but Nancy Drew's autonomy has not.

Scholarly critics like Ellen Brown of Virginia Polytechnic, in an interesting essay on Nancy Drew, ask significant and profound questions about the books. But critics like Brown have reread them. So when Brown asks: "What did Nancy Drew teach me?" she is mediating between her fourth-grade self and Nancy Drew with a sophisticated feminist, multicultural, and lit crit consciousness. She is not reading Nancy Drew as we first read *A Room of One's Own* or *Jane Eyre*, with a wild sense of recognition and discovery. She is not reading the Nancy Drew of the 1930s.

Now I have one memory many who are younger cannot have— a memory of the first, heady, hopeful, exciting, and, yes, as Adrienne Rich has said, erotic days of feminism in the early seventies. The astonishing fact about those original Nancy Drews written by Mildred Benson is that Nancy Drew sounds just as we did, flinging about the same daring challenges we offered to each other in those early years. I was in my forties, I had waited a long time for feminism, and if I had been reading Nancy Drew in her original form at that moment I would have suspected she was a contemporary.

What I would also have suspected more forcibly than do her younger critics of today was her connection to the mysteries that comprised the so-called Golden Age of detective fiction.

Read Patricia Craig and Mary Cadogan in *The Lady Investigates*, because much as I admire them and their critical work on the detective story, I think they're wrong here in a particularly contemporary way. Craig and Cadogan say:

> Every one of the rules laid down for adult detective fiction during the period known as the Golden Age is infringed in the Nancy Drew stories. There is no mystery about the identity of the criminals; plots and subplots are welded together by a series of preposterous coincidences; the triumphant conclusions are not presented as a result of logic or even of plausible chance. . . . The girl can spot a wrongdoer at first sight. Her unreasonable assumptions are invariably correct. She sees connections where none could possibly exist. She's helped, too, by clues in the form of strange messages which drop out of the air. (155)

Now Nancy Drew may commit all of the above sins, but so did many of the detectives of the Golden Age apart from Agatha Christie's. Golden Age detectives used intuition, as does Nancy Drew, and they used, furthermore, the contingency that often makes that intuition possible. In all work, I would like to claim, there comes a moment when intuition leaps to the fore, and when, as happens in comic strips, a light suddenly gleams. On this subject, I have the word of no less monumental an authority than Stephen Jay Gould, and he, furthermore, knows that intuition is how science works and that it is how literary detectives work also. But he begins with Nobel Prize winner Barbara McClintock to make his point:

> McClintock does not follow the style of logical and sequential thinking often taken as a canonical mode of reasoning in science. She works by a kind of global, intuitive insight. If she is stuck on a problem, she will not set it out in rigorous order, write down the deduced consequences and work her way through step by step, but will take a long walk or sit down in the woods and try to think of something else, utterly confident that a solution will eventually come to her. This procedure makes scientists suspicious.
>
> [This procedure] is a common practice, though perhaps rare in science. It is neither mystical nor, in another vulgar misrepresentation, feminine as opposed to masculine in character. . . . I am particularly sensitive to its denigration because I happen to

work in the same way. (I am hopeless at deductive sequencing and can never work out the simplest Agatha Christie or Sherlock Holmes plot.) . . .

I think the best description of this style was presented not by a psychologist or neurologist, but by another mystery writer, Dorothy Sayers, who, I am convinced, worked this way herself and established Lord Peter Wimsey as a conscious antidote to the Sherlock Holmes tradition of logical deduction. Now Wimsey was no intellectual slouch, but he solved his cases by integrative insight (and those I usually figure out). (165–166)

Having defended intuition, I now shall proceed further to defend Nancy Drew as a Golden Age detective. I return, and indeed you must have wondered how far I meant to wander from it, to *The Bungalow Mystery* as published in 1930. The story begins, you may remember, with Nancy and her friend Helen overtaken by a storm while out on the lake in a motorboat. The boat capsizes; Helen cannot swim:

> "Hold your breath when you see a wave coming," Nancy instructed. "Don't be afraid. I won't let loose of you."
>
> She knew that Helen would soon wear her out unless she overcame her fear and remained quiet. Already Nancy was short of breath, and for a swimmer far from shore that was a fatal warning. Yet never for a moment did she consider abandoning Helen, although by doing so she might save her own life. (10)

On to Dorothy Sayers, Golden Age exemplar. Peter Wimsey has got himself and Bunter stuck in a bog.

> "Wish you'd keep away, Bunter," said Lord Peter peevishly. "Where's the sense of both of us . . . ?" He squelched and floundered again.
>
> "Don't do that, my lord," cried the man entreatingly. "You'll sink farther in." . . .
>
> "Get out while there's time," said Peter. "I'm up to my waist. Lord! This is rather a beastly way to peg out."
>
> "You won't peg out," grunted Bunter. (*Clouds of Witness*, 200–201)

Back to Nancy Drew in *The Bungalow Mystery*:

> "Oh, what shall I do, Nancy?" Laura cried desperately. "I can't go back! . . . I have no place to hide. I am without friends."
> "You mustn't forget that I am your friend," Nancy returned quickly. "I'll do everything in my power to help you." (68–69)

Back to Sayers: Harriet Vane: "It seems very probable that I shall not survive. . . . People have been wrongly condemned before now." Peter Wimsey: "Exactly; simply because I wasn't there" (*Strong Poison*, 46).

I'm not suggesting that Nancy Drew and Peter Wimsey are equals as detectives. I am suggesting that Nancy Drew is not as far from her predecessors as some contemporary critics would like us to believe. And when Laura, in *The Bungalow Mystery*, complains that her guardian "doesn't keep a single servant" (65), we are to remember, while getting ourselves into a modern, anticlassist frenzy, that Lord Peter might have noted the same thing about someone with that income at that time.

Let us return to Nancy Drew, resembling a newly minted feminist from the seventies in *The Bungalow Mystery*: "She had talent for unearthing mysteries" (11). "Certainly, Nancy Drew never missed an opportunity for a thrilling adventure" (12). "If I get through, I must depend upon my own initiative" (54). But later she has learned some lessons we learned in the later seventies: "It was with difficulty that Nancy controlled her anger as she saw the man. . . . She longed to fly out at him and accuse him face to face. However, she was far too wise to allow herself to be governed by a mad impulse. She must bide her time" (102). The narrator says of her, which is more than could be said of many of us back then, "Although courageous, she was not foolhardy" (95). But we are reassured that "to think was to act with Nancy Drew" (110). Or, as Nancy sums it up near the conclusion, "I seem to have a way of getting into the thick of things" (203).

In an article called "The Mystery of Nancy Drew," in the new *Ms.*, Jackie Vivelo testifies to the changes which the revisions in the Nancy Drew mysteries have instituted. Contemporary adult, socially enlightened critics of Nancy Drew have probably read the revisions of the early Benson novels. All the changes point to the original Nancy Drew as a true feminist adventurer, while her more recent avatar makes her more of a Barbie doll conforming to that ideal of femininity dear to the radical right. A few examples: official positions originally filled by women are now given to men. Where Nancy drove policemen in her car, they now drive her. At camp, in the new versions, the girls are supervised by a chaperon. What Nancy once did for herself is done by her boyfriend Ned in the revised version, or else she is carried off by him to rest after combat.

Although Vivelo does not say so, I'm fairly certain that Bess and George are also not so subtly transformed. These two girl cousins, friends of Nancy's, don't appear until the fifth of the original books. Here is how they are introduced at the beginning of *The Secret at Shadow Ranch*:

> "Alice is pretty as a picture," George supplied. "Not at all like me."
>
> "Why, you're not a bit homely," Nancy assured her promptly. "I think you're quite distinctive looking myself."
>
> "You base flatterer! Look at this straight hair and my pug nose! And everyone says I'm irresponsible and terribly boyish."
>
> "Well, you sort of pride yourself on being boyish, don't you? Your personality fits in with your name, you will admit."
>
> "I do like my name," George admitted. (3–4)

George's cousin Bess is "noted for always doing the correct thing at the correct time. Though she lacked the dash and vivacity of her cousin, she was better looking and dressed with more care and taste" (4). Surely it is not too wildly difficult to guess which cousin Mildred Benson most admired and resembled, but, alas, the revisions make Nancy more like Bess and less like a union of the two of them, each representing an authentic side of her. As Bobbie Ann Mason puts it:

Not only is Nancy perfect, but she possesses the ideal qualities of each age and sex: child, girl, teenager, boy, and adult. She has made a daring stride into adulthood, and she also trespasses into male territory. . . . Nancy's two sidekicks, squeamish Bess and tomboy George, emphasize this ambivalence. Bess Marvin is "dainty" and "feminine," and George Fayne, her cousin, is boyish and says "Hypers" a lot. George wears her hair short and scoffs at Bess's romantic ideas. (Mason, 53)

Nancy, if not boyish, is allowed the efficiency reserved in more stereotypical times for boys. So she skillfully backs a car out of a tight corner in *The Bungalow Mystery*, having no trouble reversing. But Jan Morris, who, you will remember, underwent as James Morris a sex change operation, reports in her book *Conundrum* that, after her sex change operation: "I did not particularly want to be good at reversing cars, and did not in the least mind being patronized by illiterate garage-men" (150). Men convinced they must become women by the most extreme surgical means may long, of course, for stereotypical femininity. Nancy, the early Nancy, eschewed it.

But, from World War II on, through the terrible fifties and early sixties, only boys were allowed to be daring and to be proud of a gift for "getting in the thick of things." I was reminded of this some time ago during a bout of house cleaning. As those who have grown children well know, getting them to leave home is child's play compared to getting them to take their possessions with them. After a decade of storing objects about which children feel sentimental enough to keep in your space but not sentimental enough to store in their own, most parents rebel. "Come and get it," they say, "or out it goes." Some time ago, as most of the accumulation was going out, I rescued two paperbacks originally published in 1940 and 1964 entitled *The Boys' Book of Great Detective Stories* and *The Boys' Second Book of Great Detective Stories*, both edited by Howard Haycraft. (These were the years in which Mildred Benson wrote fewer Nancy Drew mysteries; after 1959 the revisions were underway.) Haycraft's preface to the first volume began thus: "This is a book for modern boys in their teens—for those active, growing, adventurous young minds that demand more robust fare than 'children's books.' At such an age boys turn naturally to the detective story" (vii). The collection begins with Poe and ends with Sayers, including Agatha Christie in between. Haycraft no doubt believed then what movie makers believe today, that girls will reverberate to stories about boys, but not vice versa. But that girls and boys are not always so different is witnessed by the Nancy Drew books.

Having identified Nancy Drew as the model for early second-wave feminists, I might add a few of the other requisites for that identification. Most important is that blue roadster. She can not only back it up out of tight places, she can get into it and go any time she wants. She has freedom and the means to exercise it. That blue roadster was certainly for me, in my childhood, the mark of independence and autonomy; the means to get up and go.

Even more important than the roadster, Nancy Drew has no mother, no female mentor from the patriarchy to tell her to cool it, be nice, let the boys win, don't say what you mean. Mothers have long been and were, in Nancy Drew's day and before, those who prepare their daughters to take their proper place in the patriarchy, which is why in so many novels with interesting women heroes, whether by Charlotte Brontë or Mildred Benson, the female heroes are motherless. The lack of a mother bestows possibility on a young girl, at least in fiction. No mother, a roadster, and a father who is quite simply proud of you—it is an adolescent girl's dream. Bobbie Ann Mason suggests that the mystery Nancy Drew is really about for her young readers is the mystery of sex (63). Maybe, but it's also the mystery of overcoming gender expectations and *doing* something in the world.

The roadster, the lack of a female trainer in patriarchy, and the sheer gutsiness are what make the original Nancy Drew a moment in feminist history. Her class and the fact of her ready money and upper-middle-class WASP assumptions are what make her an embarrassment today. The question is, should we therefore dismiss her as predominantly an embarrassment, a moment in the history of feminism of which we are now ashamed?

The issue is joined as Ellen Brown, whose thoughtful essay I have already mentioned, writes (quoting Judith Fetterley): "nothing less than our sanity and survival is at stake in the issue of what we read" (10). Who can argue with that? But it is on this principle that Brown wishes to discount Nancy Drew's contribution to our sanity and survival. "Many women," she writes, "will continue to lead the wasting lives of Nancy Drew, doomed forever to be eighteen, sexually frozen, unmothered and unmothering, married to the masculine world of order and reason, with avocation but no vocation, dependent on the Great White Father for economic security and permission, driving around in Daddy's car" (10).

I think this is an example of how we deprive ourselves of active female fictional characters because they do not fit our highly developed, and highly defensible, contemporary criticisms of society. Sara

Paretsky has noted in her introduction to *The Secret of the Old Clock*: "The books we relished as children dished up some dreadful racial attitudes." Indeed they did, and reading them today makes one's teeth tremble. Jean Rhys, when she wrote *The Wide Sargasso Sea*, awakened us all to the racism and patriarchal abuses of Rochester's first wife in *Jane Eyre*. But for all that, the words of Jane Eyre, unique in all of nineteenth-century literature, pleading for liberty and adventure, still stand as a rare boost to the "sanity and survival" of unhappily restricted girls and women. And Nancy Drew, in her lesser genre, did the same.

I have made my living from literary criticism, feminist theory, and the close analysis of texts. I am not about to disassociate myself from these disciplines. But there is a danger that we critics, with our close analytical machinery and our explorations of social and economic conditions, will damage the original Nancy Drew books, just as the revisions have damaged them, looking for things they do not and cannot offer, while failing to see and praise their real qualities. It is worth noting that novelist Sara Paretsky, while recognizing the racism in Nancy Drew, can remark: "It is easy to poke fun at the girl detective" and still claim her as important to us, just as so many of us have claimed the richer, snottier Peter Wimsey.

Bobbie Ann Mason points out that "Nancy Drew, as girl detective, gets to be adult without sacrificing [her] right to adventure. . . . In the role of girl sleuth, Nancy, always eighteen [sixteen], escapes time and enjoys the best of all worlds. She doesn't have to confront feminist anxieties" (74). I think we have to be double-minded enough to celebrate Nancy Drew and hang on to our feminist anxieties. Mason goes on to ask what Nancy Drew would become in real life: the answer is she would be with us now, as she helped to make us possible. The point about Nancy Drew we must hold on to is that she did not commit the cardinal sin: to see herself as more intelligent than other women while conforming to the conventions of female lives. Nancy Drew is neither confined to conventional femininity nor considers herself exceptional, and therefore not really belonging to her sex. That was the trick of many accomplished women throughout history. It is one social sin Nancy Drew avoids, and the only one we need bless her for and emulate her in.

Or, to put this in the elegant words of my friend, colleague, and fellow editor Nancy K. Miller:

The deepest vein of inspiration in the 1970s came from the desire to pose a massive challenge to the regime of the universal subject. It was imperative to expose that regime as particularized: the universal subject, it turned out, was merely a man. It was irresistible to insist on a female universal subject. The 1980s revealed that the universal female subject could be just as oppressive as her counterpart; and under accusations of imperialism and essentialism her reign was quickly dismantled (Miller).

By the 1990s we have learned that no woman can speak for all women. Certainly Nancy Drew cannot speak for women of color or poor women. Yet if we put her today up against the women we see in films and on television, I think she comes out pretty well. She has a gun, but she doesn't shoot it, she risks danger, she survives without falling into any man's arms. She never says, "Reader, I married him," and she avoids romance.

Of course, there are attractions other than feminist ones. The genre of detective fiction is a popular one because we know it is going to end well and that the major character will not, like major people in our quotidian lives, be hideously snuffed out. Today women detectives age: V. I. Warshawski is contemplating forty. But unless Paretsky wants to pull a Reichenbach Falls, we do not fear for Warshawski's life. And Nancy Drew, like V. I. Warshawski, allows a female to contemplate a destiny almost inevitably assigned to males. That, believe me, is a heady moment.

Arthur Prager, in his article "The Secret of Nancy Drew," recalled his daughter (he was a single parent) reading Nancy Drew. Being a man, and not a broad-minded contemporary feminist critic, he also came to some wrong conclusions. "A parent who tries to fathom the secret of Nancy's success," he wrote, "is doomed to failure, because, strictly speaking, Nancy is a terrible square. Apparently there is a rock-ribbed streak of conservatism in the nine-to-eleven group. They will participate in outlandish fads for the sake of show, but they like things simple, basic, well-organized" (18). Nancy is not terribly square: that is just his word for what she is, a young woman who refuses to be a romance-obsessed sex object, and who takes risks on behalf of those in need of help. She reassures the girl reader about the ephemerality of the "outlandish fads." She says a life of adventure is possible, and even noble. To Prager, that seemed square; to his daughter, it must have seemed strangely promising.

You may know that I have created a woman detective not unlike Nancy Drew. Her name is Kate Fansler: she is rich, white, born to the establishment, and protected by her father's money, conveniently inherited at his death. When I invented her in 1963, I didn't think of any of the social problems we now know to be of the utmost importance. Perhaps because I was born twenty-one years after Mildred Benson, I was aware of the evils of racism. It was sexism that haunted me. It was the horror of the expected and restricted woman's life we all lived after World War II and in the terrible fifties. I was afraid we women were too brainwashed, that we had too completely internalized the patriarchy's rules about women for there to be any hope for us. So I decided to invent a woman who had it all, and to see if she could do anything with it. Of course I wouldn't create such a character today; over the years I have tried to make her grow as she aged, and I hope she has changed, in all but her drinking and smoking, sins which, perhaps along with a few other habits, make her more grown up than Nancy Drew.

I think that what stirred me in 1963 was not very different from what stirred Mildred Benson in 1930; the desire to take a female without domestic burdens and let her battle mostly on her own against the mean, selfish, criminal people. I have no doubt that either of us, setting out today to create such a female detective, would do it very differently. But as I said when I began, Nancy Drew belongs to a moment in feminist history; it is a moment, I suggest, that we celebrate, allowing ourselves the satisfaction of praising her for what she dared and forgiving her for what she failed to undertake or understand.

PART I

Creating and Publishing Nancy Drew

*One of my keenest friends lives in a book. She travels
in my school bag in our car. She has gone with me to
Texas and to Illinois. And even though she is a girl, she
spends a lot of time in my room. Her name is Nancy
Drew. I met her after I read my way through all of Frank
and Joe Hardy's adventures. Nancy Drew has grown to
be one of my most cherished friends because of her
courage, her detective skills, her quick thinking, and
her independence.*

*If I could ever get over the fright, I would like to be a
detective. My good friend Nancy Drew taught me that.
Mildred Benson told me that Nancy Drew was a lot like
her. I think everyone who reads her stories would like
to be a lot like Nancy.*

—MIKE MEFFORD,

AGE 13, GRADE 8,

PEKIN MIDDLE SCHOOL,

PACKWOOD, IOWA

Nancy Drew was the last creation of Edward Stratemeyer, who perfected the process of developing, mass producing, and marketing exceptionally popular children's series books. Signing writers to contracts that bound them to secrecy about their part in the process, he shrouded the business in mystery his successors have perpetuated. But as in all mysteries, clues have been left along the way enticing collectors and scholars alike to piece together answers to questions about exactly how the books were produced and what the roles of writers, editors, and marketers have been in making the series a success.

The history of Nancy Drew as a product of the Stratemeyer Syndicate is far more complex than the relative simplicity of the genre books would suggest. For example, six different series of Nancy Drews are being published today, each with its own publication history. The first Nancy Drew Mystery Stories were published in several blue-covered editions until 1961. Then many of them were rewritten and new ones were added in a series with yellow spines. Both series were published by Grosset & Dunlap, which still publishes the revised and original yellow-spine editions. Simon & Schuster began publishing new stories in paperback editions of the Nancy Drew Mystery Stories series in 1979 and added a new series for older children, the Nancy Drew Files, in 1986. Nancy Drew joined forces with the Hardy Boys in a new series of SuperMysteries begun in 1988. Applewood Books published facsimile editions of the first three Nancy Drews in 1991 and added two more in 1994. Nancy's origins as an eight-year-old sleuth are the focus of the Nancy Drew Notebooks series begun in 1994 for second to fourth graders. "Nancy Drew Titles, 1930–1994" lists these books.

A clearer picture of the Stratemeyer history has quite recently begun to emerge as collectors of children's books and scholars of children's literature and popular culture have mined a rather limited store of available source materials and discovered the identity of some of the living writers of the early books. The essays in this section are primarily firsthand accounts of the history of the publication of Nancy Drew books. They offer glimpses into the production of the books from several unique and original perspectives ranging over the 65-year history of the books from the first editions to the current paperback series and recent reprints of the originals. The emphasis in the essays is on how the work has been done from the vantage point of those who have written, edited, and marketed the books and others who have devoted their professional and leisure time to solving the mysteries laid out by the syndicate.

How the Nancy Drew stories were assigned, refined, packaged, and marketed is the subject of the essays and discussion in this section. Chapter 2, a historical essay by Deidre Johnson, a specialist in children's literature, illustrates how the stories were solicited and manuscripts edited to prepare Stratemeyer children's books for the market.

Johnson is both the leading academic scholar on the work of the Stratemeyer Syndicate and a collector of series books who has worked with excerpts taken primarily from the few manuscripts that have circulated in the collectors' community. For want of access to the company's extensive files of manuscripts and correspondence, Johnson relies on examples drawn from both Nancy Drew books and other Stratemeyer series to show how the ghostwriters worked with the editors in producing the original books. Her essay also provides a vivid illustration of the corporate principles and practices that guided Edward Stratemeyer and his successors.

Phil Zuckerman is president of Applewood Books, which in 1991 published facsimile editions of the first three Nancy Drew and Hardy Boys books for a "nostalgia" audience of adults in their thirties and forties or older who fondly remembered the experience of reading the original series. The enthusiastic reception of the facsimiles was one milestone in the rediscovery of Nancy Drew. Zuckerman's essay, chapter 3, about his recognition of a new market for the original Nancy Drews and negotiation of a place for his books in it reveals a good deal about both the early publishing history of the series and the complex business it has evolved into.

While both Johnson and Zuckerman portrayed the production of Stratemeyer books as a corporate process which obscured the creative efforts of individuals, their audience revealed in their questions a special interest in the contribution of the individual writers and their business and professional relationships with the syndicate. In addition to Johnson and Zuckerman, Esther Green Bierbaum, whose essay appears as chapter 19, joined in responding to questions presented in chapter 4.

Collectors, scholars, and librarians have known for a long time that the Nancy Drew books were ghostwritten by a series of writers whose work was solicited by the Stratemeyer Syndicate and edited to fit an established mold. Nevertheless, the personal appeal of Nancy Drew and the mystery surrounding the identity of the "author" have sent scholars, collectors, and ordinary readers in search of the *real* Carolyn Keene, the individual creative mind in the manufacturing process. Most persistent of these seekers is Geoffrey S. Lapin, a cellist with the Indianapolis Symphony Orchestra and series book collector. Lapin's account in chapter 5 of his quest to find Carolyn Keene and then bring recognition to Mildred Wirt Benson, the woman he credits with creating Nancy Drew as we know her, reveals still more about the corporate practices of the Stratemeyer Syndicate to protect the identity of the fictional author.

As Mildred Wirt Benson tells her story, writing Nancy Drew—and more than 100 other adventure stories for children—was a job, a way for a woman who always wanted to be a writer to make a living and later to supplement her income as a newspaper reporter. For her, writing Nancy Drew on contract was less satisfying than creating her own favorite teenage sleuth, Penny Parker. Chapter 6 is a 1973 autobiographical essay from *Books at Iowa* in which Benson disclosed her identity as Carolyn Keene. Benson recounts her relationship with the Stratemeyers, completing a picture of how the early books were written. "Books by Mildred Wirt Benson" lists all of her books and the pseudonyms under which she wrote them.

One of the most frequent topics of news features and academic papers on Nancy Drew is how the books have been changed over the years—from the originals, to the rewrites of the 1960s, to the new books now being published. Invariably, the writers find their favorite old series—which might be either the blue-cover originals or the yellow-spine rewrites—superior to those that came later and the newer Nancy to be a pale reflection of the truly independent teenage sleuth they remember. Avid young readers today seem to read from each of the series quite indiscriminately, however, and they often name both old and new books as their favorites. There is, then, both continuity and change in the history of Nancy Drew.

To bring the story of the production of Nancy Drew up to date, we wanted to provide a firsthand account of the production of contemporary series, to let those involved speak for themselves, to explain how and why the series have developed as they have. Anne

Greenberg, who has served as executive editor at Simon & Schuster Pocket Books for the current series almost since the beginning, tells about the development of the modern Nancy Drew and how new books are produced through a collaboration of writer, editor, and book packager.

In planning for the session, we came to know half a dozen recent "Carolyn Keenes," each of whom was eager to appear on the conference program. Ultimately, Anne Greenberg selected one experienced Nancy Drew writer to appear under her own name and Simon & Schuster waived her confidentiality agreement for three days. For this book, however, she was required to put the mask back on, to carry on the mystery. Greenberg and Keene's essays in chapters 7 and 8 give a detailed picture of the current concerns of the heirs to the Stratemeyer Syndicate. As was evident in conversations we have had with other Carolyn Keenes, these essays reveal that those who write and edit Nancy Drew books know they bear a special cultural responsibility akin to safeguarding family heirlooms.

Writing is part of the everyday culture of Iowa City, where the Writers' Workshop was invented and a writer lives on nearly every block. It was not surprising, then, that one group of participants in the discussion of the new books presented in chapter 9 posed quite technical questions about the art and craft of writing and editing the new Nancy Drews.

There was electricity in the air during parts of the discussion on the new Nancy Drews as both scholars and collectors challenged Anne Greenberg as a representative of Simon & Schuster, the keeper of the mysteries Edward Stratemeyer first propounded. In particular, the interchange in chapter 9 reveals their eagerness for access to the historical records of the Stratemeyer Syndicate and their conviction that Mildred Wirt Benson should be publicly acknowledged as the first writer of the Nancy Drew series.

Within a few months of the conference, Simon & Schuster gave the Stratemeyer Syndicate records to the New York Public Library, where they will eventually be open to researchers, and the current publishers of Nancy Drew agreed to acknowledge Mildred Wirt Benson's role in the history of the series whenever her books are reprinted in any language. Since Benson's identity as Carolyn Keene was no longer secret, she was finally permitted in 1994 to write introductions for the Applewood reprints of the fourth and fifth books in the series.

CHAPTER 2

From Paragraphs to Pages:
The Writing and Development
of the Stratemeyer Syndicate Series

Deidre Johnson

For almost a century Edward Stratemeyer and the syndicate he created have been turning out successful series, enthralling millions of readers. Born in 1862, Stratemeyer started writing boys' stories in the 1880s under various pseudonyms. About 1905 he realized he had so many ideas that he couldn't write them all, so he decided to form a "literary syndicate," the Stratemeyer Syndicate. Stratemeyer would come up with ideas for books, outline them, and hire others to write them. By 1930, the year he died, he had created close to 100 different series, including 19 girls' series, the last of which was Nancy Drew. Stratemeyer's two daughters, Edna Stratemeyer and Harriet Stratemeyer Adams, then assumed control of the syndicate, continuing Nancy Drew and even trying a few more series with female sleuths, none of which achieved Nancy's success. In 1984 Simon & Schuster purchased the syndicate and still publishes several successful series, including four featuring the indomitable Nancy Drew. In all, Stratemeyer and the syndicate have been responsible for close to 1,400 titles. Over 390 of these are in girls' series, and over one-third of them are about Nancy Drew.

Although the published Stratemeyer Syndicate series and even the syndicate's use of ghostwriters are well known, one aspect of the series books remains shrouded in mystery—the actual methods by which they are created. Through the years, as the syndicate changed management, so, too, has the writing process for the series changed.

Currently, only limited materials are available to researchers, and none show the evolution of a series or take an entire book through the process. Hypothesizing about the process thus means imitating Nancy Drew, piecing together clues from diverse sources and examining bits and pieces of the process which people associated with the syndicate shared with various researchers and institutions.

In Stratemeyer's day, one of the first steps in creating a series involved submitting titles and ideas to the publisher for approval. Stratemeyer would write brief paragraphs highlighting the plot of the book, such as the following, for *Tom Swift and His Sky Racer; or, The Quickest Flight on Record* (1911):

> Tom and Aero Managers talk about meet—a great prize for the swiftest aeroplane—Tom and father invent the Humming Bird, little but oh my! Trial trip—Mr. Swigt [sic] very ill, but wants Tom to go in race anyway—Rivals try to damage the sky racer, foiled, various adventures—Mr. Swigt [sic] worse—the consultation, must have an operation, want noted doctor—the flood has damaged railroad, cannot get there—Tom's [illegible: great(?)] flight with the [illegible: nervy(?)] specialist—the operation— "will he live?" Time will tell, a week perhaps—Tom's anxiety— the great race—Won: the operation successful.[1]

After the publisher approved the idea, Stratemeyer would expand it into a synopsis, usually two or three pages long, and relay it to a writer. Howard Garis wrote most of the Tom Swifts, and Stratemeyer's daughter remembers the two men getting together in the Stratemeyer living room to discuss plots and even act out scenes ("Tom, Jr.," 26–27).

Later writers described outlines in more detail. Leslie McFarlane, the ghostwriter for many early Hardy Boys and some other syndicate series, started with the syndicate about 1926. He wrote to Stratemeyer in response to an advertisement in *Editor and Publisher* and received books from two series to read. He was asked to choose one then was mailed an outline. McFarlane submitted two sample chapters, which were approved, and completed the book from the outline (McFarlane, 10–12, 23–24, 31–32). At this stage, the outlines for each chapter were short paragraphs, almost as long as the entire proposal for the Tom Swift title, and the outline ran for several pages. In his autobiography, McFarlane reconstructed a typical outline from memory, using *Dave Fearless under the Ocean* (1926), part of a boys' adventure series, as an example.

> CHAP 1—Dave and Bob cruising off Long Island in launch Amos run into fog—mention first and second volumes of series [this was a favorite tactic for advertising previous volumes]—engine fails—ring reminds Bob of adventures on Volcano Island [another book in the series]—mention other volumes—boys discuss Lem and Bart Hankers, believed dead—sound of foghorn is heard—ocean liner looms out of fog—collision seems inevitable. (McFarlane, 22)

The writer would build from this framework. In the case of Dave Fearless, the chapter begins:

> Dave Fearless looked out over the rolling waves and frowned as he saw a greasy cloud rolling in from the horizon.
> "There's a fog coming up, Bob."
> "Looks like it. Do you think we had better turn back?"
> (McFarlane, 23)

The chapter then continues, summarizing previous volumes and introducing the crisis, as Dave announces, "The engine is dead and a fog is coming up"—leading to an appropriate cliffhanger:

> Suddenly [Dave and Bob] heard the booming of a foghorn, alarmingly close at hand. . . .
> A great dark shape loomed out of the fog.
> "We're done for!" gasped Dave.
> Like a mountain, the ship bore down on them through the dense mist.
> They were right in its path. (McFarlane, 24–25)

But don't worry—the beginning of the outline for chapter two shows that the ship "veers off in the nick of time" (McFarlane, 22).

One possible reason for the detailed outlines is that, unlike the Garises, many of the ghostwriters didn't live near Stratemeyer. McFarlane moved to Canada shortly after he began working for the syndicate, so he would receive an outline by mail and ship back the finished product, without being able to consult Stratemeyer as he wrote. Mildred Wirt Benson, who worked on many Nancy Drews, lived in Iowa and Ohio during her years with the syndicate.

When a ghostwriter had completed the work, he or she was asked to sign a release, assigning all rights to the book, the character, and the pseudonym to the Stratemeyer Syndicate. This release, from Howard Garis (for the first Tom Swift book), shows the extent to which Stratemeyer controlled the series:

> For and in consideration of the sum of seventy-five dollars and other good and valuable considerations, the receipt of which are hereby acknowledged, I hereby sell, transfer and set aside to Edward Stratemeyer, of Newark, N.J., all my right, title and interest in a certain story written by me on a plot and title furnished by said Edward Stratemeyer, title of story being, Tom Swift and His Motor Cycle.
>
> In making this transfer I affirm that my work on the story is new, and I hereby give to Edward Stratemeyer full right to print under a trademark pen name belonging to him or his publishers, or both, and I agree not to claim any right in such pen name or attempt to make use of the same in any form whatsoever. [signed] Howard Garis (Dizer 1992, 9)[2]

Writers received a flat fee for their manuscript and, if their work was suitable, the opportunity to write more. No matter how many copies were sold, the writer received only that one payment. Stratemeyer picked up this technique from his dime novel days, when he'd had to sign over his rights to publishers and saw his stories reprinted three to four times each, with all profits going to the publisher.

The releases for the first two Tom Swift titles are dated February 17 and March 10—less than a month between the two (Dizer 1992, 9). Generally, ghostwriters say they took four to six weeks to write a book, though some were done as quickly as three weeks and others took a little longer.

After that, Stratemeyer would edit the manuscript, then send it to the publisher, who would send galleys back to him for final approval.

Two portions of the corrected galleys for *The Blythe Girls:*

Snowbound in Camp; or, The Mystery at Elk Lodge (Grosset & Dunlap, 1929) by Laura Lee Hope, a volume in a girls' career series, show the types of revisions at this stage. Most alterations were minor, little more than an occasional word change. For example, chapter 1 refers to an art dealer's "profession," which Stratemeyer changed to "business."

One of the most extensive corrections on the Blythe Girls galleys appeared late in the story. After a snowstorm, the Blythe girls are getting directions from a local woman. She tells them, "After a while, you'll come to a hill and on the other side o' that hill is Bailey's shack. You can't miss it. It's got a roof painted bright red." An alert copy editor wrote in the margin: "Wouldn't the roof be covered with snow?" Stratemeyer (or an editor) then added another sentence, so it now reads: "It's got a roof painted bright red. It's a high peaked one, so's it'll be swept clean of snow by the wind," making the directions quite logical (Stratemeyer-Adams Collection).[3]

After Stratemeyer's death the outlines changed. Mildred Wirt Benson, who started working for the syndicate about 1927 and stayed with it off and on until 1953, witnessed many of these changes. She discussed them over fifty years later, in 1980, while testifying in a lawsuit involving the Stratemeyer Syndicate, Simon & Schuster, and Grosset & Dunlap. (In 1978 the Stratemeyer Syndicate had switched publishers for new books from Grosset & Dunlap to Simon & Schuster; Grosset & Dunlap sued, trying to prevent the change. Part of the trial concerned how the books were actually written.)

During the trial, Benson described syndicate writing practices under Stratemeyer's management. A typical outline "was two or three pages, and it was all written together. The characters' names were given, but they were all run in. There was no cast of characters" (that is, no separate list), and the outline apparently wasn't divided into chapters as McFarlane's reconstruction was (*Grosset & Dunlap v. Gulf & Western* transcript, 94, 95).[4] Benson characterized Stratemeyer's approach to the books, observing, "He only gave me one direction at the time that I was hired. He said you can snap your fingers at literary content but keep up the suspense" (*Grosset & Dunlap v. Gulf & Western*, 213). This is worth remembering in light of what happened after Stratemeyer's daughters took over.

After Stratemeyer's death, the outlines became more detailed. As Benson explained, "They [Harriet Adams and her sister, Edna

Stratemeyer] began giving me a great deal more material and they began giving me more direction, they began giving me casts of characters. Later on, they built in quite a good deal of filler material . . . background material—if it's a jade ring story, it's about what jade is, and so on and so forth" (*Grosset & Dunlap v. Gulf & Western*, 218). She recalled that "in the later years, the outlines did definitely have chapter endings, each one would be chaptered off to 25 chapters." There were apparently separate lists of characters, with background information, plus factual information (*Grosset & Dunlap v. Gulf & Western*, 218–219).

The bit about the "filler material"—the jade—is instructive. When Stratemeyer first started writing boys' books, he did many works of historical fiction. They thus had to contain some factual information. In an interview about 1904, Stratemeyer stated that children needed lively stories with "a fair proportion of legitimate excitement, and with this a judicious dose of pleasantly prepared information" ("Newark Author," 76). Somewhere along the line it appears that Harriet Adams seized on this idea, but decided that the Stratemeyer Syndicate formula was—to quote Nancy Axelrad, a syndicate partner—"Good mystery and lots of action, with some educational material" (Herz, 8). She seems to have overlooked that in Stratemeyer's day not all syndicate series gave this dose of information—some just told good stories to entertain. But later stories under Adams almost invariably work in a lesson. Her stories try to find one element connected with the plot—like the jade—where they can insert "educational material" for the sake of inserting it.

One example of this approach can be seen in a letter the syndicate sent to Benson while she was working on a Kay Tracey title, *The Sacred Feather* (1940), part of a girls' mystery series from the 1930s and 1940s. At one point, Edna Stratemeyer, who wrote the letter, explains, "In this outline, a certain amount of it is fact regarding the sacred ibis in Egypt, so make this information authentic wherever it is used in the tale." She also instructed Benson to "be sure to add poetry in the story, quoting from the Egyptian wherever possible" (Stratemeyer to Wirt, February 8, 1940).[5] (Presumably, the syndicate had sent the poetry along with the outline.)

The same syndicate letter also showed its increasing control over the story. Another passage mentions the cast of characters: "On the cast of characters, the second cousins of Hassan Iran are set forth mostly for your benefit, rather than using them continually in the manuscript." In short, even for minor characters, the syndicate is now handling the names and relationships; it doesn't allow the writer even that much freedom.

At the trial, Benson pointed out one problem with the more detailed, chaptered outlines: some confused detail with action, making it difficult to write a smooth story while adhering to the outline. She explained, "There's a difference between detail and action. You can write a page and say chapter 1 and it might run only a page of copy[,] while you may take another chapter and have four or five or six exciting scenes in it, each one of which should be a separate chapter, perhaps" (*Grosset & Dunlap v. Gulf & Western*, 221–222).

A later letter from the syndicate, this time written by Harriet Adams, illustrated another problem with the longer, more specific outlines. In it, Adams told Benson she was enclosing only the first eight chapters of what would become the Nancy Drew mystery *The Ghost of Blackwood Hall* (1948) (Adams to Wirt, May 23, 1947).[6] Because the outlines were more detailed, they took more time to write. This one came in two stages, which created problems for Benson: when the second part of the outline arrived a month later, Benson discovered that some of the early scenes had been misleading, and she had to double back and revise them.

The syndicate's May 1947 letter to Benson also showed other elements that affected the series while Stratemeyer's daughters controlled the syndicate. Adams had her own approach to writing, which is evident in the letter. The second paragraph begins, "What I have missed, and trust that you will make every effort to put into this story, is characterization; not only of the new characters, but of the old ones as well. . . . Throughout the story will you use adjectives, adverbs and short phrases to make Nancy keen but diplomatic; George boyish, blunt, and astute; Bess feminine, fearful, but willing to go along." This was her idea of characterization—two or three key traits, reiterated throughout the book. The letter also indicated the syndicate's responsiveness to its audience, for Adams writes, "A number of fans have been asking what became of Nancy's little dog Togo . . . so you might bring him in now and then when Nancy is at home, and even introduce a scene where she talks over the mystery with him."

Eventually, the differences between the Stratemeyer Syndicate and Benson became great enough that she stopped writing for them, though not until she'd done close to fifty books in various series.

Before moving on, it's also instructive to see how the character of Nancy Drew evolved, again because of the different personalities in the syndicate. The first three Nancy Drews were written while Stratemeyer was still alive, and during the 1980 trial Benson described his reaction:

> I remember [Stratemeyer's response] very vividly because I was rather crushed. He wrote that he thought I had departed from the pattern of the old series books that had been written. . . .
>
> He said the character in particular was too—too flip, she was too vivacious—she was not the namby-pamby type of heroine that had been dominating series books for many, many years. . . .
>
> He said I had missed it and he did not think that the publishers would probably either want it or care for it. (*Grosset & Dunlap v. Gulf & Western*, 117)

But even though he felt this way, Stratemeyer submitted her manuscript to the publisher instead of rewriting it, as Adams later would. Benson told the court what happened next: "He wrote back and said they were enthusiastic, that he had given it to the reader and they [*sic*] liked it and that he was ordering more" (*Grosset & Dunlap v. Gulf & Western*, 117). So part of the character of the original Nancy Drew really came from Benson and an unknown reader at Grosset & Dunlap.

After Harriet Adams took over, she had her own ideas about Nancy Drew. During the trial, Benson was asked about the syndicate's criticisms of her writing. She gave her opinion of the differences, commenting, "Two writers have two different styles. I imagine the things that I wrote in there did not hit Mrs. Adams as Nancy" (*Grosset & Dunlap v. Gulf & Western*, 225). She explained that as time went on she'd see that some manuscripts had been rewritten more and more extensively, summarizing the situation:

> I think the whole thing here, there was a beginning conflict in what is Nancy. Mrs. Adams was an entirely different person; she was more cultured and more refined. I was probably a rough and

tumble newspaper person who had to earn a living, and I was out in the world. That was my type of Nancy.

Nancy was making her way in life and trying to compete and have fun along the way. We just had two different kinds of Nancys. . . .

The Nancy of today would not be the Nancy of my—my Nancy. (*Grosset & Dunlap v. Gulf & Western*, 232)

Lest this seem too harsh a treatment of Harriet Adams, there are good things to be said for her influence. There's a tendency to criticize Adams for changes she made, but if she hadn't taken over there would have been no Nancy Drew beyond the first few books. Adams also introduced some elements that we now think of as standard in the series. Initially, Nancy worked alone and her relationship with Hannah Gruen, the housekeeper, was that of employer to servant—courteous, but without any special closeness. It was Adams who decided Nancy needed companions and was responsible for introducing her two good friends, Bess and George—and for Nancy's boyfriend, Ned Nickerson. It was also Adams who decided Hannah should be like a surrogate mother and that there should be a special bond between the two (Felder, 31).

After Benson left, the method for writing Nancy Drew titles underwent more changes. During the 1950s the syndicate appears to have continued—and even increased—its practice of extensively revising manuscripts. Ernie Kelly, a researcher who interviewed many former syndicate employees, concluded that "it would not have been unusual for . . . five or more persons [to contribute] to and/or [edit] a draft series book at any one time." He noted that one unnamed author called the process "a sausage factory" (Kelly, December 1988, 5).

As the years went on, the outlines seem to have become even more detailed, although after a certain point it's hard to determine for whom they were prepared. The one outline available is for *The Double Jinx Mystery*, a Nancy Drew title that came out in 1973. By then, Adams was apparently writing some volumes in the series herself, so this was probably for her own use. If it was for a ghostwriter, it had reached the point where the syndicate left almost nothing to the writer's creativity.

The outline for the beginning of chapter 1 is an incredibly detailed page and a half that was almost typeset as written, complete with dialogue and descriptions. The story starts with Nancy introducing the current mystery to Bess and George. Oscar Thurston owns an aviary, and the town council is trying to rezone the land to build condominiums, which would force Thurston to close down. While the girls are talking, they hear a knock at the door, but when Nancy answers, no one is in sight. She sees a stuffed bird—a wryneck woodpecker—on the lawn. Nancy calls her father, who asks the girls to look around the Thurston place. They meet Mr. and Mrs. Thurston and learn that Kamenka, a "Eurasian" girl who lives with the Thurstons, owns a live wryneck. Nancy wonders if there's a connection.

The chapter 3 outline picks up from there: "N[ancy] inquires about Petra, the wryneck. Kamenka has always had one for a pet. Says it brings her GOOD luck. She is taking courses at nearby Harper University in ornithology. In return for her board she helps Oscar. He invites the visitor to wait for her and Mrs. Thurston serves tea" (Stratemeyer-Adams Collection).[7]

As the chapter progresses, there's an incredible level of detail, again including dialogue. For example, the third paragraph reads:

> Bess asks her [Kamenka], "In your country do people use wrynecks to cast spells on others?" The Eurasian girl clams up, doesn't answer, & excuses herself. Bess aghast but Mrs. Thurston says, Kammy is moody. "Kamenka is very psychic." Mrs. T laughs. "She can tell you from the stars exactly what's going to happen to you." N asks, "Does she predict the outcome of the land deal?" "Oh yes. She says we'll win out but there's danger ahead."

In the published version, this passage becomes:

> [Bess] turned to Kammy. "In your country do some people use wrynecks to cast spells on other persons?"
>
> Suddenly Kammy's happy expression became sullen. She too arose and put down her teacup.
>
> Without answering Bess's question, she said, "Will you all please excuse me? I'd like to go to my room." She picked up her handbag and the books she had brought with her, and left the room.

"Oh dear![”] said Bess. "I'm afraid I hurt Kammy's feelings but I didn't mean to."

Mrs. Thurston spoke up. "Don't worry about it. Kammy is moody. By the way, she's also very psychic—knows a lot about astrology."

Oscar laughed. "At least my wife thinks she does. She insists that Kammy can tell from the stars exactly what's going to happen to you."

Nancy smiled and said to him, "Has Kammy predicted the outcome of the land deal?" (23)

As can be seen, some passages are used almost verbatim, while other material needs only a few details added. The handwritten outline runs over thirty pages.

The outline also includes a page with information about birds and omens and another page describing the characters in detail: for example, "Oscar Thurston, 50, robust, jolly, greying hair and beard." It also has a list of the town councilmen, noting their position on preserving the aviary.

In 1982 Harriet Adams died, and the remaining partners and some of her children managed the syndicate for a while, before selling it to Simon & Schuster in 1984. None too surprisingly, methods of writing for the series again changed, as did the series itself.

In August 1986, in an effort to reach a wider audience, Simon & Schuster launched a second Nancy Drew series. The digest-size Nancy Drew Mysteries were aimed at eight- to twelve-year-olds and continued the original. The Nancy Drew Files, mass market paperbacks targeted at ten- to fourteen-year-olds, introduced a trendier Nancy Drew, one who appeared to have finally discovered adolescence, complete with an interest in fashion, rock music, and boys.[8] Currently, Mega-Books of New York packages both lines. Like Stratemeyer and Adams, Simon & Schuster and Mega-Books prefer to keep much of the writing process for the series a secret, and information about ghostwriters, outlines, and similar materials is considered confidential. Someday, future researchers may reveal the inner workings of this period in the syndicate's history.

Planning a syndicate series book has come a long way since Stratemeyer's one-paragraph proposals of 1911 and 1912. It has moved from loose syndicate control of the plot to highly structured syndicate control of everything from plot to minor details. The only thing that hasn't changed is the syndicate's ability to turn out successful series.

NOTES

1. Quoted in Keeline, November/December 1992. Reprinted by permission of Pocket Books, a division of Simon & Schuster. Anne Greenberg, the current editor of Nancy Drew, explained the function of the paragraphs in a conversation, April 17, 1993.

2. Dizer received the releases from Brooks Garis, one of Howard Garis's grandchildren.

3. Reprinted by permission of the University of Oregon Library and Pocket Books, a division of Simon & Schuster.

4. The transcript was provided by Geoffrey S. Lapin and David Farah.

5. Letter provided by Geoffrey S. Lapin. Reprinted by permission of Pocket Books, a division of Simon & Schuster.

6. Provided by Geoffrey S. Lapin. Reprinted by permission of Pocket Books, a division of Simon & Schuster.

7. Reprinted by permission of the University of Oregon Library and Pocket Books, a division of Simon & Schuster.

8. The Nancy Drew & Hardy Boys SuperMysteries and the Nancy Drew Notebooks series were started later.

CHAPTER 3

Publishing the Applewood Reprints

Phil Zuckerman

This is about what happens at the sausage factory,[1] how Applewood Books came to reissue the original Nancy Drew books and the processes we went through to bring them out.

Applewood Books was founded in 1976. Since 1981 it has been reissuing books from the past that people are interested in today, a variety of popular culture from George Washington's *Rules of Civility and Decent Behavior* to Mickey Mouse books. We were most proud to be able to publish the Nancy Drews.

In the winter of 1990 I was reading *The Mystery of Cabin Island*, a Hardy Boys book, with my oldest son, who was six at the time. This was a book I wanted to read because it had been pivotal to me. It was the first book that I recall reading by myself, without parental advice. It felt great and I remember the experience. The boys go out on a lake in an iceboat and I remember the atmosphere as being so incredibly palpable that I froze to death in my room as I was reading it. So I picked up a copy of the blue-cover *The Mystery of Cabin Island* at my local used bookstore and brought it home and was delighted to be able to read this to my son. I read it to him, and he liked it all right, but something was missing for me. It didn't seem like the same book. I thought, "Well, that's growing up; you just lose those things that were so precious to you when you are a kid." But then I discovered that the book had, in fact, been rewritten since the time when I had read it. And I went back and got a copy of

41

the original *The Mystery of Cabin Island* and read *that* to my son and I was delighted to find that it was exactly as I had remembered it. And so off I went to see if there was a way to right a wrong I felt existed.

One of the things that one *must* do as a publisher is figure out the marketplace before even attempting to publish a book. My approach to this is to talk to as many people as I can. Specifically, I talk to people who are in marketing and people who are the gatekeepers of information in the publishing business. One of the people that I happened to talk to was Judy Applebaum, the paperback columnist for the *New York Times*. Judy, who is a guru for me, said, "That's nice, Phil, but you need to do Nancy Drew. The Hardy Boys were characters, but Nancy Drew was a role model." I heard that then from every woman I talked to: "Yeah, I read Hardy Boys books," they would say, "but Nancy Drew is *important*."

So in the spring of 1990 I began to search around to find out how I might be able to publish the books. In the beginning I thought that these books were in the public domain, but I learned otherwise. I contacted Louise Bates, the rights and permissions person at Putnam,[2] who informed me that I would have to contact Simon & Schuster.[3] I was referred to Olga Vezaris, the rights and permissions person at Simon & Schuster Pocket Books, who in turn informed me that in order to proceed with reissuing the books it was necessary that Simon & Schuster get permission from Putnam. I think that everyone was so amazed that we would actually pay money in advance to do these books that they thought, "This crazy guy, let's let him do it." So we signed a contract to do the first three Nancy Drews and the first three Hardy Boys with an option to do an additional four of each.

The next stage after obtaining a contract is to start to sell a book. Applewood is an unusual publishing company in that it receives working capital, or financing, from another publishing company which, at that time, invested in all the titles that we did. This company was also our distributor. Although it allowed us to do anything we wanted, carte blanche, it was still necessary to sell the book to the powers that be at the company. I began talking to the marketing manager of our distributor, Globe Pequot Press, which was owned by the *Boston Globe*. The marketing manager was astonished that we wanted to reissue books that everyone believed already existed. And I began the process that I would repeat again and again over the next two years: trying to communicate the fact that what existed was not the original and that there was a marketplace for these original books. They didn't think so, and they advised me that although heretofore they had invested in everything we'd done they would not, in fact, invest in this title. So we decided to publish it ourselves with our own working capital.

We began to try to educate people. I decided to send up a trial balloon and see what kind of response we would get in the marketplace to a book like this. So in our spring list for 1991 we advertised *The Tower Treasure*, the first of the Hardy Boys books, just to see what would happen. We figured we would roll out the breeders[4]— the first three of each book—to see if there seemed to be a marketplace, or we would just forget about it if there didn't seem to be.

There didn't seem to be anything we could do with the books when we announced *The Tower Treasure*. I went to a sales conference and stood up there and said, "This is important." I showed them the original texts and I showed them rewritten texts, and they looked at me and said, "We can't sell this. You're asking people to pay $12.95 for something they can buy for $4.50?" And I said, "No, they're different books; they're different audiences. This is for a nostalgia audience, people who want to return to their earlier days."

There was a tremendous amount of resistance, so we began to compile all the ways the marketplace was going to resist. We learned that price was going to be an issue. We learned that we needed to clarify to buyers, rights people, to anyone who is involved in making a book work before it ever gets to bookstores, what the differences were between our books and the rewritten versions. We needed to say why the originals were better.

One of the first people I convinced on this subject was Cullen Murphy, an editor at the *Atlantic*. Cullen was taken with this and surprised to know that the books had been rewritten and decided to put together a piece that would appear in the *Atlantic* (Murphy).

I decided that the only way to convince people that this was different was to create a taste test and to allow people to try out these different things and collect responses and then publish those results. I decided to set up a taste test modeled after a Pepsi and Coke test I had once seen. I called the Pepsi-Cola people and got all of their information about how this process worked. And we modeled our test exactly after theirs, using all the blind procedures we could to make this reasonable.

We created two plastic cards with original text on one card and the rewritten text on the other card to use at the annual American Booksellers Association (ABA) meeting which is held for booksellers from all over the country. The idea was to test out booksellers and see which they preferred, the originals or the rewritten versions. The cards were placed in front of the respondents so that the original text was sometimes placed on the left, sometimes on the right. We interviewed 250 booksellers. After careful study and a great response, we determined that 88 percent of the people who responded preferred the original books. And this was 88 percent of booksellers. It was for me a great moment because I had the information—semi-scientific—I needed to go ahead and convince people to do this.

That American Booksellers Association meeting was a very important moment in the books' history. At that ABA was Marilyn Stasio, a friend of mine who is the mystery reviewer at the *New York Times*. Marilyn was all abuzz about the fact that we were reissuing these books. She cornered me at a party and said, "I've got people to introduce this book." I said, "Well, I think I know who I want to introduce them," and she said, "Oh, well, okay, but you need Sara Paretsky and you need some Sisters in Crime to introduce this book."[5] She also introduced me to an editor of *People* magazine who was very interested in doing a piece on Nancy Drew, which ultimately came out and was a great force in helping the books move along through the system ("Hardy Once Again").

During that summer we requested permission to have introductions by both Leslie McFarlane and Mildred Wirt Benson in the books. We were allowed to use Leslie McFarlane's introduction, but not to use Mrs. Benson's introduction. So we went to find other introducers and found mystery writers Sara Paretsky, Nancy Pickard, and P. M. Carlson.

We began to get the books ready for publication. The *People* magazine piece ("Hardy Once Again") came out and a slew of other things began to happen. There was a lot of radio coverage and a lot of other media coverage to let people know that these books were now available. The letters started coming when the books arrived at the bookstores. We began to get two to three letters a day. These were from people who remembered the books and who thanked us for bringing them out. They were absolutely wonderful. They came from people in all walks of life; from the old, from the young, from the middle-aged. It was delightful.

We decided that it was important to continue the series. When we asked to exercise that option to print more books, permission was denied. The complication of the arrangement is that two publishers had to agree to allow us to continue. It was the feeling of the folks at Grosset & Dunlap that our books were competitive with theirs and were eroding the marketplace for their books. I continued to request that we be allowed to publish the books and I hoped that someday we would be able to go on with the series. At the time of the conference, that didn't look like a possibility.

The books continued to sell. In November 1992 *Ms.* magazine did a piece on Nancy Drew which created a new awareness of the books (Vivelo). That December our sales skyrocketed, and close to a thousand copies a month were sold over the next three months. I expected that would continue. We printed about 25,000 of each title, and most of those were in the publishing pipeline at distributors or booksellers.

It's been a fabulous ride and it's been great to be associated with it. Our future goal at the time of the conference was to find a way to be able to acknowledge Mrs. Benson's role in the publication of these books. That, we thought, would be really fabulous. We would like to publish the first seven of the series at least, perhaps beyond that.[6]

NOTES

1. The Stratemeyer Syndicate book publishing process has been referred to as a sausage factory (Kelly, December 1988, 5).

2. The Putnam Group is the parent company of which Grosset & Dunlap, the original publisher of Nancy Drew, is a part. The company publishes the yellow-spine editions, most of which are revisions of the original books, and holds rights to publish the originals.

3. Simon & Schuster acquired the Stratemeyer Syndicate and publishes the new Nancy Drews in the Nancy Drew Mystery Stories and Nancy Drew Files, Nancy Drew & Hardy Boys SuperMysteries, and Nancy Drew Notebooks series.

4. The standard practice of the Stratemeyer Syndicate was to publish a "breeder set," three volumes of a new series at once to test the market.

5. Sisters in Crime is an organization of mystery writers and readers, primarily women.

6. In 1994 Applewood received permission to publish additional Nancy Drews and Mildred Wirt Benson was permitted to write introductions to them. Those volumes are no. 4, *The Mystery at Lilac Inn*, and no. 5, *The Secret at Shadow Ranch*.

CHAPTER 4

The History of the Stratemeyer Books:
Questions and Answers

*Deidre Johnson, Phil Zuckerman, and
Esther Green Bierbaum*

*Didn't Mildred Wirt Benson sign away her rights to authorship? And
if she did, how is she now able to state that she was the original author of Nancy Drew?*
ZUCKERMAN: Technically, she can't. It is true that she did sign away
her rights and that's a matter of commerce, I think. But what's happened is that Nancy Drew has become more than commerce. It has
become something that is now interesting historically. So it's time to
rewrite history and correct the record.[1]

*Why do the publishers give Leslie McFarlane credit for writing the
Hardy Boys when he signed the same release at approximately the
same time as Benson?*
BIERBAUM: Even though McFarlane signed the same papers, he broke
that contract when he wrote his autobiography, *Ghost of the Hardy
Boys*, in 1976. Apparently the syndicate decided to let that record
stand. As an issue of scholarship one would think it is time to correct the bibliographic record regarding Mildred Benson.

*Mr. Zuckerman, when Grosset & Dunlap and Simon & Schuster gave
you permission to print the McFarlane introduction, what reason did
they give for not allowing Mildred Wirt Benson to introduce her work?*
ZUCKERMAN: Well, there was really no explanation. I really didn't
seek an explanation per se. I discussed it, I talked about it, I said it

was something we really wanted to do, but beyond that a "no" is a "no" and it was not within my right to use it.[2]

What records did the Grosset & Dunlap and Simon & Schuster people allow you to review when you were putting together the reprints?
ZUCKERMAN: I didn't really ask them for permission to review any of their records. One of the first people I went to was Didi [Deidre] Johnson and she forwarded me to Gil O'Gara [editor of *Yellowback Library*], who spread the news within the collectors' community. That's where we went to get all the information we could about the books. It seemed the collectors knew a lot more than anyone else about the books. Not to say that the Stratemeyer Syndicate does not know about it, but I think there is more information floating around within the realm of collectors.

How many of the records from the Stratemeyer Syndicate are still in existence? Do we know who did the rewriting of the Nancy Drew Books?
JOHNSON: We don't know exactly what records have survived.[3] As far as authorship of the rewrites is concerned, it's been very fuzzy. Some people in the syndicate did them. The syndicate had staff writers and some of them did the rewrites, but beyond that, at least at present, we don't know. Harriet Adams said she wrote them, but it's hard to know how much was wishful thinking and how much really happened.

As a buyer, how can I tell if I have one of the modified editions?
JOHNSON: The revised texts always have a formula: 180 pages and 20 chapters. The original ones tended to have 25 chapters—although there are variations to that—and they are closer to 214 pages on the average. Watch the copyright dates; they began to revise them in 1959. If you have an early copyright date on the first 34 volumes of the Nancy Drew series, that is, before 1959, then you probably have the original story.

Mr. Zuckerman, from your perspective, don't you find it a little odd that Grosset & Dunlap feels threatened by your books, when you're essentially selling an entirely different product?
ZUCKERMAN: The odd thing that I feel is that it was so difficult in the beginning to make people understand what these books were and

then finally it was understood and they got out into the marketplace and now it's a threat. It's like hitting your head against the wall to make it work and then hitting your head against the wall to try to make it work not so much so you get to do more. It's a very bizarre situation.

Will Grosset & Dunlap take your idea and do it themselves?
ZUCKERMAN: I don't think so. I'm not sure they have the right to do that. I don't know all the legal aspects of this, but the result is that neither company publishes them.

When you were reprinting the original books, did you get criticized for bringing back racist books?
ZUCKERMAN: This was of tremendous concern to me. When you reissue books from the past you have to live with what existed back then and you can't look at things retrospectively. You must understand that this is the way it was and that there were good things and there were bad things and that you can at least talk to your children about the bad things and explain them. But if you don't see bad things in the past and you just see things as totally good then you're blinding yourself to the reality of our time. The fact is that we have good things and bad things about our present. The bad thing in our present is the amount of violence in our society. The good thing about these early books is the lack of violence in them. So it's a balance and it's not that this is good and that's bad. To be considered a racist in publishing these books, I felt, was an interesting and unfair accusation. But cynically, from a marketing point of view the controversy has been fabulous. My opinion about publishing history is that you do not change history.

Are your reprints being marketed to adults or to children?
ZUCKERMAN: Our whole line is really children's books for adults. However, I did take them to the classroom and we did a taste test there to see what the response would be. The result was that about 55 to 60 percent of the kids preferred the original books. So they do like them and we do get letters from kids.

You talked about a trial. Could you tell us about that?
JOHNSON: The trial took place in 1980. The syndicate was fed up with Grosset & Dunlap, who had been cutting back on royalties and,

the syndicate felt, was not doing a good job on advertising. So they went over to Simon & Schuster where they could market paperbacks. Grosset & Dunlap said in essence, "You can't do that, you've published with us forever and will publish with us from now until eternity." They tried to claim that they owned the characters since the books weren't really written by Stratemeyer but by hired writers who had created and shaped the characters. That's why they brought in Mildred Wirt Benson, so she could talk about how she created characters. Fortunately the judge did not lock the syndicate into a publisher and they were able to go to Simon & Schuster. But the other fortunate thing was that since Mildred Wirt Benson got to testify we do have testimony, under oath, that she said she wrote those books and Harriet Adams sat there and could not say she didn't. That made it official.

Is there hard evidence which proves how much Harriet did write of the Nancy Drew books, after Mildred left?[4]

JOHNSON: The only information I've seen is from an interview by Ernie Kelly with the syndicate and he seems to support the idea that Harriet Adams was actually writing. But what went on at the syndicate during a lot of that period is very fuzzy. So far only the syndicate knows. If she created the outline, in one sense she wrote Nancy Drew. She didn't write the whole story, but she shaped the basic outline. It is confusing.

A woman in the audience has a letter on a Carolyn Keene letterhead that was sent to her daughter from the syndicate in 1965. In it they say, "Carolyn Keene is a pen name the author uses because she carries on other types of work in the literary field." They give some background information: "She was born in and still lives in the United States, presently just outside of New York City. She attended one of the large women's colleges in the country." That is basically the background of Adams. Although a secretary wrote it, the letterhead says "Carolyn Keene."

I've known people who are just devastated when they learn there is no Carolyn Keene, because in the past Carolyn Keene actually wrote to them. Harriet Adams was interviewed on National Public Radio and made several tours and was quoted in numerous newspapers saying that she was Carolyn Keene. And the syndicate was very defensive about this. Adams's explanation was that she would

have had to mention a cast of thousands, and besides, she was pro-
tecting the children. One does have to be a little bit kind to her.

Could you talk about the situation with Walter Karig?
JOHNSON: I know that he stepped in for a couple of years and wrote
three Nancy Drew books.[5] I gather that Harriet Adams was quite
upset because Karig had announced that he had written Nancy
Drews and consequently the Library of Congress has him listed as
one of the ghostwriters.[6] He went on to write many things after that,
but not for the syndicate.

NOTES

1. Following the Nancy Drew Conference, in the summer of 1993,
Mildred Wirt Benson reached an agreement with the publishers under
which she was to be given credit for writing the original stories. She was
to be acknowledged in all forthcoming printings of the books she wrote,
including the translations. They were to insert the following statement
on the copyright page: "Acknowledgement is made to Mildred Wirt Benson, who, writing under the pen name Carolyn Keene, wrote the original NANCY DREW books." She may also identify herself as the writer.
2. In 1994 Applewood was permitted to publish two reprints with
introductions by Mildred Wirt Benson.
3. Simon & Schuster contributed 150 boxes of Stratemeyer Syndicate papers and 7,000 first editions to the New York Public Library in
August 1993. The materials were expected to take three years to
process before being opened for use by researchers. Nancy Axelrad, a
partner in the syndicate for many years, has contributed papers to the
Beinecke Manuscript Collection at Yale University, which include her
recollections of who wrote, revised, and edited which volumes through
1985. James D. Keeline compiled the information for publication in
Yellowback Library (Keeline, 1995).
4. Adams is cited as writer, reviser, and editor of a number of volumes in the information compiled by Keeline (1995).
5. Karig wrote *Nancy's Mysterious Letter* (1932), *The Sign of the
Twisted Candles* (1933), and *Password to Larkspur Lane* (1933). His
other work included the television scripts for the series *Victory at Sea.*
6. See the text of a letter regarding Walter Karig from Harriet
Stratemeyer Adams to Mildred Wirt, May 23, 1950, in chapter 5.

CHAPTER 5

Searching for Carolyn Keene

Geoffrey S. Lapin

The Nancy Drew Conference brought to an end a very long chapter of my life and the conclusion of a dream I've had for almost thirty years. It's a story with many parts, but I'm going to focus on the part I played in solving the mystery of Carolyn Keene.

I first became intrigued by the ambiguous authorship of the Nancy Drew Mystery Stories in 1963 when I was a high school student vacationing with my family in Atlantic City, New Jersey. In those days, Atlantic City was the grand queen of sea towns, where families stayed at Victorian hotels and had wonderful times on the beach and the boardwalk. My family was fortunate to have a summer home there. Because I didn't like the beach I hung out at the public library, where for years I spent every day all summer as a volunteer. Since the library catered to the needs of vacationing families, it boasted a large collection of children's books, including the Hardy Boys and Nancy Drew mystery stories.

While I was doing some cataloging, I discovered that next to the author's name for the Nancy Drew books was the italicized word "*pseud.*" I had to look up the word in the dictionary and when I learned that it meant "pseudonym" I was baffled. As had millions of other readers, I had always assumed that there really was a Ms. Keene, regularly churning out the exploits of the teenage sleuth. Knowing the thoroughness with which librarians catalog information, I was surprised that the authorship information simply stopped with the word "pseudonym," particularly since I had found that authors other than Keene had their real names listed along with their pseudonyms. I became intrigued. Inquiries to the library staff were of no help; no one even seemed to care. During the next three years the only printed fact I found was a notation in an author catalog: "Carolyn Keene, *real name unknown.*"

My first big lead came in my home town, in the reference department in Baltimore's Enoch Pratt Free Library. While looking through an old volume of the *Cumulative Book Index*, I found that someone had put an asterisk in pencil next to the name Carolyn Keene and had written, "see Wirt, Mildred A.," and had listed a reference book to refer to. I located the book and learned that Wirt was the author under her own name of many non-Drew titles including *Carolina Castle* (1936), *Sky Racers* (1935), *Through the Moon-Gate Door* (1938), *The Shadow Stone* (1937), and *The Runaway Caravan* (1937). Pseudonyms listed for Wirt included Dorothy West, Joan Clark, Frances K. Judd, and Carolyn Keene.

Returning to the *Cumulative Book Index* I found under Wirt's name the additional pen names of Frank Bell and Don Palmer. Checking under these names and her other pseudonyms, I was able to compile a list of over fifty titles she wrote, not including the Nancy Drew books.

When I first discovered the name Wirt I started going to used bookstores and buying everything she had written. The next step was to start reading them. Even though author and character names were different, everything else seemed quite familiar; not just plot lines and situations, but colorful descriptions of country roads, dark passageways, and the like all had a pleasant readable flow, a certain rhythm: one word leads to a phrase, a sentence into a paragraph, a paragraph into a chapter. It all progresses at a certain speed that keeps your attention. This is her gift.

It is well known that Edward Stratemeyer created the idea and the outline for the stories, and it is commonly believed that the formula is all that was needed to write a series book; one just followed a certain recipe and one had a book. Anybody can come up with a plot such as: "There's a guy named Josiah Crowley and he dies and nobody knows where his will is. His family is fighting over it and there are these poor people who took care of him."[1] But the important thing is what was done with this outline, this formula. Mildred Wirt was able to come up with a way to write these books that has sustained Nancy Drew for all these years. None of the other series that Stratemeyer outlined—the Motor Boys, the Outdoor Girls, the Motion Picture Boys, Ruth Fielding,[2] and many others—are with us today. There must be an explanation, and I think a good part of it is found in Mildred Wirt's writing style and characterizations.

In 1969 I was finally able to track down Mildred Wirt—by then Mrs. Benson—in Toledo, Ohio, where she was working as courthouse reporter for the *Toledo Blade*. I had written to her requesting an interview because of an article that appeared in the *Saturday Review* in 1969. In "The Secret of Nancy Drew," Arthur Prager told of the "grandmotherly lady" who was author of the Nancy Drew Mystery Stories. Prager wrote that Harriet S. Adams, daughter of Edward Stratemeyer, had been writing that popular series since its inception in 1930, as well as hundreds of other books. Having read the majority of books written under the name of Wirt and her pseudonyms, I was convinced that she indeed was Carolyn Keene. So why was this Adams woman being touted as the author of those books?

Mrs. Benson invited me to meet her at the *Toledo Blade* office. We went into the city room where she had her desk. As she opened a drawer to put away her scarf I caught a glimpse of that particular issue of the *Saturday Review*. I knew then that I was onto something. We talked about how the series came to be written and about the work that she had done for the Stratemeyer Syndicate. I asked her why she wasn't given credit for what she had done and why Harriet Adams was claiming authorship. She told me about what is now common knowledge regarding the way the syndicate worked: the ghostwriters were required to sign a release relinquishing all claims to authorship, character names, and plot lines for the books in exchange for $125.

From what I can gather from the different ghosts I've talked to through the years, Edward Stratemeyer was a gentleman. He was also a fine businessman. It appears that when he passed away the operation of the syndicate became quite secretive, which is why it's taken so long for Mildred Wirt Benson to get the credit she is finally receiving for writing the Nancy Drew books.

I was fortunate to have been invited to be a possible witness for the 1980 trial involving a lawsuit between Grosset & Dunlap and the Stratemeyer Syndicate. Also present at the trial was Grosset & Dunlap's principal witness, Mildred Wirt Benson. In return for my lending them all my first-edition Nancy Drew books for evidence— Grosset & Dunlap no longer had copies—I was allowed to photocopy many of the documents which were used as evidence during the trial. I want to share some of those documents to demonstrate how the secrecy surrounding Nancy Drew's authorship was maintained for so long.

While on the witness stand, Benson was presented with numerous documents and letters which had been subpoenaed by the Grosset & Dunlap attorneys. She was able to identify and verify all work releases she signed as well as numerous documents that proved the truth about her claims to authorship. Letters submitted included one from 1938, sent to Harriet Adams from attorneys for Warner Brothers Pictures. It seemed that their 1930s series of movies about Nancy Drew could not be made unless Wirt signed a release of movie rights for the books she had written.[3]

The letter says: "Dear Mrs. Adams, Regarding Nancy Drew Stories, I'm enclosing herewith two copies of form letters to be signed by Mrs. Wirt and Walter Karig." (Karig wrote three Nancy Drew titles—*Nancy's Mysterious Letter, Password to Larkspur Lane*, and *The Sign of the Twisted Candles*—when Wirt refused to write them after they cut her salary from $125 to $75 during the Depression.) The letter continues: "I also suggest that you be sure you list in the assignments all the stories involved. I understand from the assignments that you have given me that the stories written by Mrs. Wirt are as follows . . ." (Morris Eisenstein to Adams, March 4, 1938,4).[4]

By signing this form she was relinquishing any rights to the movies (*Nancy Drew, Detective*, 1938; *Nancy Drew, Reporter*, 1939; *Nancy Drew, Trouble Shooter*, 1939; *Nancy Drew and the Hidden Staircase*, 1939), thus ensuring the continued protection of secrecy.

A letter written to Mildred Wirt from Harriet Stratemeyer Adams in 1947 is further evidence of Wirt's authorship of the Nancy Drew books. It's a proposal for a book, in which Adams makes her expectations known: "What I have missed, and trust that you will make every effort to put into this story, is characterization; not only of the new characters, but of the old ones as well. With new readers we are apt to forget that new readers are not acquainted with Nancy and her family and friends." Adams then outlines each major character's traits and continues: "Please bring out the fondness of Mr. Drew for Nancy and the reliance of both of them on Hannah's good sense and faithfulness" (Adams to Wirt, May 23, 1947).[5]

Another letter submitted as evidence during the trial addresses the issue of authorship. In the 1970s Nancy Drew stories made their way to television, which prompted Mildred Benson to write to the producers, Dan Curtis Enterprises, claiming some right to the TV series. Shortly thereafter she received a letter from the Stratemeyer Syndicate attorney, stating: "I'm writing you on behalf of my client the Stratemeyer Syndicate. . . . the statements you made [claiming authorship rights] in the letters I have seen are completely untrue, false and in the nature of a trade libel of the Stratemeyer Syndicate." He then "reminds" her that should she make any claim to the Drew character, "legal or equitable action including an action for damages" would be taken against her (Dixon Q. Dern to Benson, November 4, 1975).[6]

A final letter is from Harriet Adams to Mildred Wirt in 1950. Walter Karig had written to the Library of Congress asking to have his authorship of some of the Nancy Drew books officially and bibliographically recognized. Harriet Adams's reaction is recorded in her letter to Wirt: "How many times has the Stratemeyer Syndicate rued the day that Walter Karig wrote any books for it. . . . If it were possible to make any claim to the pseudonym of Carolyn Keene, you naturally would have more right to it than Mr. Karig . . ." (Adams to Wirt, May 23, 1950).[7] So here we have more documentation that Mildred Wirt wrote the books.

The 1980 United States District Court case of *Grosset & Dunlap v. Gulf & Western Corp.* (the parent company of Simon & Schuster at the time) and the Stratemeyer Syndicate was decided in favor of the syndicate. The publicity surrounding the trial was quickly eclipsed by another event—Nancy Drew's fiftieth birthday party in 1980. Harriet Adams and Simon & Schuster were in the spotlight. The festivities received coverage in *Time* ("People") and the *New York Times* ("Jubilee for Nancy Drew"). Adams was interviewed on National Public Radio. The National Endowment for the Arts sponsored a documentary made by Harriet Adams's grandson, because she was a "national treasure." Mildred Wirt Benson was never mentioned.

My own attempts to correct the record have been incredibly

frustrating. When I wrote to the *Saturday Review* to explain Mildred's part in writing the books, I received a form letter saying, "Thank you very much for your interest in our publication." After *TV Guide* ran a story by Harriet Adams about herself and the Nancy Drew books (Adams 1977), I wrote to them. In response I received a postcard saying, "Thank you for sending us information about the authors of Nancy Drew. Our editors are interested in hearing from our readers and we pass it along to them for their attention." That was the end of it. I wrote to National Public Radio about a story they did on Harriet Adams (August 25, 1981) and got the same response: "Thank you for your interest in our show."

Mildred Wirt Benson is the author who made the formula work. She took what could have been another stereotypical character and set her up to last for years. That's why Nancy Drew is still around; that's why we have not only Nancy but the Boxcar Children, the Babysitters Club, and other series. And the Nancy Drew books were not the best books that Mildred Wirt Benson wrote. Her Penny Parker stories show what Nancy Drew could have become if she had not been constrained by the formula of the Stratemeyer Syndicate.[8] It's unfortunate that Penny Parker could never effectively compete with Nancy, because I believe they could survive and do well alongside Nancy Drew in today's market. The Penny Parker publisher—Cupples and Leon, Grosset & Dunlap's heartiest competitor—just couldn't keep up.

It's wonderful that Mildred Wirt Benson is finally being honored; official recognition of her role in the creation of the Nancy Drew series has been long overdue.

NOTES

1. This is a description of the plot of the first Nancy Drew, *The Secret of the Old Clock* (1930).

2. Mildred Augustine began her career with the Stratemeyer Syndicate in 1927 by writing several Ruth Fielding books under the pseudonym Alice B. Emerson.

3. The films are discussed in chapter 23.

4. Reprinted with permission of Warner Brothers.

5. Other parts of this letter are included in chapter 2. Reprinted with permission of Pocket Books, a division of Simon & Schuster.

6. Reprinted with permission of Pocket Books, a division of Simon & Schuster.

7. Reprinted with permission of Pocket Books, a division of Simon & Schuster.

8. Mildred A. Wirt wrote seventeen Penny Parker Mystery Stories under her own name between 1939 and 1947. They featured a girl sleuth who worked for her father's newspaper.

CHAPTER 6

Fulfilling a Quest for Adventure

Mildred Wirt Benson

"Fog" was the bob-tailed title of the short story printed in *Lutheran Young Folks* in 1935 (Wirt). My eye fell upon the yellowing issue as it tumbled from an old filing cabinet. The story bore my name, Mildred Augustine Wirt, a Ladora, Iowa, graduate of the University of Iowa School of Journalism. Certainly I had written that story and nearly one hundred others at a previous or slightly later date, yet blessedly all memory of this tale of aviation's early day had been erased from my mind. Scanning it, I winced at a few aeronautical inaccuracies; yet it did seem to carry suspense and imagination, particularly the latter, for in the 1930s my nearest approach to flight had been a brief ride taken as a child with a Cedar Rapids pilot who barnstormed Iowa towns in an old jenny. Reviewing "Fog," it dawned upon me that my style as a writer of action books for young people already had been set, a style which possibly evolved from extensive childhood reading of *St. Nicholas Magazine*.

Not style, however, but content snagged my attention. In this tale of a girl who, despite feelings of inadequacy, successfully challenged the skies, did I not detect a long-slumbering personal wish? Until this moment, the motivation which led me, late in life, to become a pilot had gone unrecognized. At an age when wiser persons welcome Social Security, this misguided author took up flying, earned advanced ratings, and functioned as a commercial pilot, reporter, and aviation columnist for a Toledo newspaper.

Significantly, now that I might be better qualified to write aviation fiction, I feel no urge to do so. Facts, I am sure, would fetter my imagination. Scenes which rolled rather smoothly in "Fog" would be rejected as "improbable" by an aeronautical mind. So, too, would the several out-of-print aviation fiction volumes contrived by me for Barse & Co. in the 1930s. *Ruth Darrow in Yucatan* (1931), for example, combined flight with archaeology, of which I then knew nothing.[1] Later the subject became an absorbing hobby, leading to nine trips to Mayan Indian sites in Yucatán and to more remote parts of Central America. However, having savored fascinating reality, I felt no compulsion to make printed use of any material gathered. Glancing over shelves usurped by 120 to 130 volumes of juvenile fiction written by me over a thirty-year span, I cannot avoid the conclusion that much of my writing was based upon an unfulfilled desire for adventure.

Even as a child, a determination to write possessed me. I detested dolls, but played with hundreds of tiny wooden spools, moving them as actors on a stage. "When I grow up I'm going to be a *great* writer," I proclaimed to anyone who would listen. In those uncomplicated days, "prolific" was unknown in my vocabulary. When I was twelve, my first short story appeared in *St. Nicholas Magazine* (Augustine 1919).[2] Others followed, printed primarily in denominational papers.

Soon after obtaining a bachelor's degree in 1925 at the University of Iowa, and working for a year on a Clinton, Iowa, newspaper, I headed for New York City. An anticipated writing job failed to materialize, but I did meet Edward Stratemeyer of East Orange, New Jersey, head of the Stratemeyer Syndicate and author of numerous series books, including the famed Rover Boys. The syndicate, so flourishing later, then consisted of Stratemeyer himself, a secretary, and a few "ghosts" who accepted a brief plot outline, vanished, and returned to the office weeks later with a finished manuscript.

Shortly after my return to Iowa, a letter came from Mr. Stratemeyer, offering me an opportunity to continue the then-faltering Ruth Fielding series. This full-length book was written at my parents' home in Ladora, Iowa, and it fought me on every page, as I could gain no kinship with the main character. A second volume, *Ruth Fielding Clearing Her Name* (Cupples & Leon, 1929), came easier. By this time I was brain-deep in graduate work at the University of

Iowa. The story was written on a typewriter in the old journalism school. Fortunately my professors assumed that I was hard at work on a thesis.

Next came a chance to undertake a new series, Nancy Drew, one destined to dominate the popular market for more than thirty years. Mr. Stratemeyer died soon after it was launched. But under his two daughters, who took over the syndicate, and at the request of the publisher, I continued writing Nancy books through the first twenty-five, ending with *The Ghost of Blackwood Hall* in 1948.[3] The plots provided me were brief, yet certain hackneyed names and situations could not be bypassed. Therefore I concentrated upon Nancy, trying to make her a departure from the stereotyped heroine commonly encountered in series books of the day. Never was Nancy patterned after a real person, unless as one who interviewed me suggested: "I gain the impression that Nancy was yourself." In writing, I *did* feel as if I were she, but then when I created the Dot and Dash stories for younger children (Cupples & Leon, 1938) I likewise felt as if I were Dot's obnoxious dog, Dash. Not only in the Nancy books, but in others written after my association with the syndicate ceased, "feel" for a situation and presentation of a character with which readers could identify were my goals.

Mr. Stratemeyer expressed bitter disappointment when he received the first manuscript, *The Secret of the Old Clock*, saying the heroine was much too flip and would never be well received. On the contrary, when the first three volumes hit the market they were an immediate cash-register success for the syndicate. By 1969 the series was printed in seventeen languages and, according to a published report, achieved sales of more than 30,000,000 copies (Prager 1969).[4] As "ghost" I received $125 to $250 a story, all rights released.

Analysis is not one of my accomplishments. However, it seems to me that Nancy was popular, and remains so, primarily because she personifies the dream image which exists within most teenagers. Definitely, Nancy had all the qualities lacking in her author. She was good-looking, had an oversupply of college dates, and enjoyed great personal freedom. She never lost an athletic contest and was far smarter than adults with whom she associated. Leisure time was spent living dangerously. She avoided all household tasks and, indeed, might rate as a pioneer of Women's Lib.

Under the name of Wirt, the Penny Parker Mystery Stories (Cupples & Leon) later took shape, with a heroine similar to Nancy, though performing in situations more to my liking. These tales achieved popularity but were plagued by distribution problems and never overtook the fleet-footed Nancy. In addition to many pen names owned by the syndicate, I used at least five of my own, including Don Palmer, Dorothy West, Ann Wirt, Joan Clark, and Frank Bell. Also, I wrote extensively as Mildred A. Wirt and published a few books as Mildred Benson. Usually pen names were selected by the publisher, who wished to avoid glutting the market with too many books by one author. In my most prolific year I turned out thirteen full-length volumes under various pen names, writing the entire list of new books for one publisher.

When I was writing with ease, words fairly flowed from my typewriter. Always I sought for rhythm by word, sentence, paragraph, and ultimately by chapter. If all were achieved, a story seemed to gain suspense—in effect, hooking the reader. As work piled up, writing became increasingly burdensome, physically and mentally. The most trying part for me was the making of a detailed outline. An order would arrive, perhaps several simultaneously. Titles, outlines, and the dates at which manuscripts could be delivered would be requested, all "at earliest convenience." Always panic took possession of me. If only I had an idea! A plot! Three plots! Usually several days of painful concentration would bring the glimmer of an idea upon which one could build. First, the story's opening problem and the climax were plotted. If these were sufficiently strong, and the basic complications were satisfactory, then interior chapters fell into place.

Selection of a title normally preceded the plot, preferably a short one, easily understood and lending itself to illustration. Often a title immediately suggested its own story, so that an outline readily took shape. Titles in this category included *Whispering Walls* (1946), *The Shadow Stone* (1937), *Through the Moon-Gate Door* (1938), and *The Clock Strikes Thirteen* (1942). However, one can be betrayed by closeness to a subject. In the first individual mystery story written by me for Cupples & Leon in 1935, this misguided author proudly called her masterpiece *The Gimmal Ring*. Publisher Arthur Leon wisely suggested the *The Twin Ring Mystery* (1935). This change, plus the fact that my loyal mother purchased fifty copies, I'm sure was a vital factor in launching me as a writer.

Few of my books ever rated display on librarians' shelves. An exception was *Pirate Brig* (Scribner's, 1950), an ambitious attempt at a boys' historical yarn. Many months of labor went into this book, compared to a few weeks spent on more popular-type material. Other volumes which found a place on public library shelves included *Dangerous Deadline* (1957), winner of the 1957 *Boys' Life*–Dodd Mead contest, and *Quarry Ghost* (1959), written for the same publisher. *Dangerous Deadline* was based upon newspaper experiences mostly gleaned from others, including William Maulsby, one of my journalism teachers at Iowa City.

Rarely, if ever, is Iowa mentioned by name in any of my stories, but different localities from Iowa nevertheless appear in numerous book scenes. For example, in *Ghost Gables* (Cupples & Leon, 1939) the first chapter carries a brief description of a college-town boat landing which could be no other than the old Iowa City canoe dock of the twenties on the Iowa River. Vermont figured in many of my tales for children, but only as reflected through stories told me as a child by my pioneer grandfather. As I turn to such volumes as *Dot and Dash at the Maple Sugar Camp* (1938, by Dorothy West) rich memories come flooding back. This story and others which intermingle Vermont and Iowa life include antics of a mischievous dog once owned by my husband and recollections of fascinating automobile

trips made through the countryside with my father, a Ladora, Iowa, doctor. In particular, a visit to the home of a farm lady with a peacock seems to have left a lifelong impression. Long after these books appeared, a genealogy tour of Vermont confirmed that my grandfather had accurately described maple-sugar mountain country and passed down its true flavor. The trip was most delightful, but I do not recall that I ever again made use of Vermont in my writing.

Quite suddenly, creative activity ceased. Personal loss came into my life. At the same time, a large backlog of published books was wiped away when the Girl Scout organization objected to any writing use of the word "scout." In one swoop, my Cub Scout, Girl Scout, Boy Scout Explorer, and Brownie Scout books went down the drain. "Why write?" I asked myself. Obligingly, ideas took themselves elsewhere. In the 1970s an editor, after coming upon out-of-print Penny Parker books, wrote that his firm planned to launch a modern series for teenagers based upon drug abuse and other social problems. Would I undertake it in the style of my old mysteries? For a moment, I was tempted. The teenagers for whom I wrote lived in a world far removed from drugs, abortion, divorce, and racial clash. Regretfully, I turned down the offer. Any character I might create would never be attuned to today's social problems. In my style of writing there can be no time concept, no chains binding one to the present.

To be remembered for more than an hour, a tale must ride in a sealed capsule, isolated from everyday living. A presentation should be as true to childhood aspiration in the year 2003 as in 1906. Such sentiments definitely identify an author with a swiftly receding past.

So now it is time for the final chapter, seemingly one destined from the beginning. A fadeout becomes the most difficult of all, for though the story is finished, the reader must be led to believe that the very best lies directly ahead. New worlds to conquer! New horizons to explore!

Ruth Darrow and all the pilots of fantasy suddenly take shape before our eyes, their waggling wings flashing the personal message: "Come fly with me."

Such a challenge cannot be denied. Work forgotten, we hasten to the nearby airport where a small plane awaits its all-too-willing passenger. Eagerly we take off, climbing high above the smog, the petty perplexities of life. The sky is blue . . . the wind blows free. Here at last, far above the earth, age and youth imperceptibly blend, and stern reality dissolves into the ultimate Magnificent Dream.

NOTES

Reprinted in revised form from Mildred Wirt Benson, "The Ghost of Ladora," *Books at Iowa* 19 (November 1973): 24–29. Used with permission of the Friends of the University of Iowa Libraries.

1. A bibliography of Mildred Wirt Benson's books appears at the end of this book.

2. The story was apparently *written* when Benson was twelve. She was thirteen on the publishing date. She won a silver badge in a children's writing contest for the story.

3. Benson also wrote a manuscript for no. 30, *The Clue of the Velvet Mask* (1953), that was substantially revised.

4. In 1994 the estimate was that more than 80,000,000 Nancy Drew books had been sold.

CHAPTER 7

Fashioning the New Nancy Drews

Anne Greenberg

I have the job Nancy Drew fans dream about. I spend hours and hours reading Nancy Drew books *and* I get paid for it.

When I took this dream job, nearly nine years ago, I had no idea what I was getting into. I had vague knowledge of the Stratemeyer Syndicate and was familiar with the names of its most enduring creations, but I hadn't read more than a couple of Nancy Drew mysteries as a child and then only because my sister made me. My sister is still the kind of person who will say, no matter what she is reading, "This is the greatest book ever. You *have* to read it." And that's how I read a couple of Nancy Drews.

When I was a youngster someone whispered something to me that I now know is not entirely true. Someone told me that Carolyn Keene's real name was Harriet Adams. I was thrilled. Something hidden had been revealed, something that adults wanted to keep from kids. Hearing this information was every bit as satisfying as eavesdropping on one of my mother's telephone conversations. I was proud to possess this secret knowledge, and of course I repeated it to anyone who would listen. So maybe I was prepared for Nancy, after all.

Nancy Drew was brought into the world in 1930. Edward Stratemeyer had scored a success with the Hardy Boys, and he thought a mystery series for girls would be a good idea. He outlined the first few books, then suddenly took ill and died. Five books were copyrighted in 1930, and new volumes were published at the rate of one or two a year, until there were fifty-six books in 1979, all published in hardcover by Grosset & Dunlap. In 1979 Simon & Schuster made an agreement with the syndicate to publish new books in the series. In 1982 Harriet Adams, who had carried on her father's work in running the syndicate, died, and in 1984 Simon & Schuster bought the syndicate altogether. We published another twenty-two books (nos. 57–78), and then it was decided to reevaluate the series and how it was being published. Our goal was to appeal to as many readers as possible and make the books as widely available as possible. That meant we would have to decide who the audience was and tailor the editorial content to it. And along with the editorial aspect we had to consider the format and the packaging—what the books should look like on the outside. The format would also determine where the books could be sold.

Who was our audience? Of course we knew it was almost exclusively girls. But what age? The readers seemed to be getting younger. By the time they were eleven or twelve we were losing them. But the format we had been publishing in—a larger, digest-size paperback—was perfect for readers eight years old and up. We decided to continue the "classic" series, but we designed a new cover look and changed artists. We freshened the writing style but stuck to mysteries that often had a gothic tinge—the spooky world of the cobweb-filled attic or the haunted cemetery crypt. Now we publish six new Nancy Drew Mystery Stories each year, and book no. 122 came out in December 1994.

In addition to this audience, we knew there was another, bigger one, capable of and used to making its own purchasing decisions. This is what is called the young adult audience, and the success of the Sweet Valley High series had exploded every publishing preconception of just how big it was.

How were we going to reach this mass audience? The easiest way to let these readers know that Nancy Drew was now being written for them was by publishing books in the smaller, adult-size paperback. Using this format would allow us to distribute the books more widely, particularly to retail outlets whose display space can't accommodate a larger book. Along with the adult-size format, we knew we would need a more sophisticated cover style. When we started the Nancy Drew Files, in 1986, most young adult books had cover art that illustrated a scene from the book. We decided to take a different tack by using a two- or three-plane concept. That meant that Nancy would be up close and personal—a heroic figure—with an action or danger scene and a guy behind her. Most young adult covers at the time had art that went to the edge of the covers, what is called "full bleed." We used a lot of white space. For the final element we commissioned cover copy that had the edge and polish found on adult books.

But a different format and a different cover look might prove to be merely cosmetic. The stories would have to deliver a different reading experience, one that reflected the interests and concerns of the adolescent and preadolescent. In other words, up to a point, Nancy Drew would have to get hormones.

We did not want to tamper with the basic character, though. We wanted Nancy to be the same gutsy, smart, resourceful, independent, and accomplished person she had always been. But we did want to place her in a recognizably contemporary environment, with characters who spoke like today's teens, and in situations the readers were familiar with or hoped to be. One of those situations is boys. Ned Nickerson had been Nancy's boyfriend for many books, but theirs was a chaste and unexamined romance. We thought the readers would like to see more of what goes on between them, so we've explored their relationship a bit. We've even broken them up and then gotten them back together again. In fact, we wanted to look at *all* the characters with fresh eyes. George, that perennial tomboy, we now thought of as being into fitness. Carson Drew, always described as a widower, became in our minds a single parent. We knew, too, that the style of the writing would have to change. The action had to move more quickly, the dialogue would have to sound real, and the crimes and mysteries would have to be more sophisticated.

We knew what we wanted to do, but how were we going to make it happen? I had not yet been hired, and my soon-to-be boss engaged the services of a book packager, Mega-Books of New York. A book packager is an independent literary service that performs editorial work and can supply a finished manuscript. The Stratemeyer Syndicate was a book packager, and Simon & Schuster hired one because in-house staff wasn't immediately available for the ambitious project ahead.

Creating the new Nancy Drew turned out to be—and continues

to be—more challenging than you might expect. You may think, "Dozens of books already existed. Why not just follow the formula?" While we do follow certain mystery conventions, we don't, strictly speaking, have a formula. We don't tell the writers, "This must happen in chapter one; this in chapter five," and so on. We did decide that the books had to start with an intriguing opening line, but that's standard in any kind of fiction writing. And we decided to end each story on an upbeat and usually humorous note. We've found that the stories are more interesting if they have at least three suspects. If the writer can provide a juicy red herring, so much the better. One element we knew we had to have was the cliffhanger. That tried-and-true device of literary manipulation grabs you by the throat and takes you to the edge and doesn't let you go until you have no choice but to turn the page and get yanked into the next chapter with your flashlight batteries running down.

Now we come to the story lines, the plots themselves. The mystery Nancy will solve, the settings, the nonseries characters—all must have young adult appeal. At first it wasn't so hard to come up with situations: in book no. 1 Nancy goes undercover at a high school, the most popular setting in young adult books; in book no. 2 she solves a rock 'n' roll mystery; in book no. 3 she goes skiing; book no. 4 is set at a teen magazine; book no. 5 takes place in Fort Lauderdale during spring break; and so on. But when book no. 83 in the Nancy Drew Files was published, we had plot lines through book no. 100, so there is a challenge. And we publish eighteen all-new books a year—twelve in the Nancy Drew Files and six Nancy Drew Mystery Stories.[1]

With a publishing program this big we can't rely on just a few authors. I doubt that even Edward Stratemeyer at the height of his powers could have coped alone. In such a situation it's an advantage to have to work with many writers and the Mega-Books editorial staff. Different writers provide different areas of expertise. One may know about boating; one may know about the fashion business; one may know about the world of underground dance clubs; and because they live all over the country, they can effectively use their local settings to give us diversity and keep the stories fresh. We rely a lot on the writers to come up with new themes, but all of us involved are constantly on the lookout for plot ideas. Some derive from aspects of daily life: we've used personal ads, an MTV-like setting, and a comedy club. Newspaper and magazine articles also inspire us: we've done mysteries about illegal immigration and steroid use among high school athletes.

Once we have a premise that we think will make a good story, we ask the writer to populate it with characters that young readers can relate to. Obviously, not all the characters can be teenagers or in their early twenties, but some can, and this is a way to work in more young adult appeal. Does one of the suspects happen to be a good-looking guy who's romantically interested in Bess or George? Great—but how will this affect the girls' friendship? What happens when a young actress decides that only Ned can help her with her lines? These sorts of situations set up a tension between Nancy's head and her heart, and as she works out a resolution the reader is drawn closer to her and gets to know her better. We've also created a new series character, Brenda Carlton, a kind of a bumbling Moriarty to Nancy's Sherlock Holmes. Brenda is the same age as Nancy and aspires to be an investigative reporter. She's indulged in this delusion by her father, who owns a newspaper. The problem is that Brenda thinks she can outsmart Nancy and has the annoying habit of messing with Nancy's investigations, with exasperating and often humorous results.

But no matter what the plot or the setting, Nancy remains Nancy: level-headed, quick-witted, fearless, and not always taken seriously by adults, at least not at first. By the end of the story, though, she has changed their minds and earned their respect.

Now, from my point of view, I'd like to take you through the process of doing a book step by step. Each one begins with a précis, a one-page summary of the story that tells us what the mystery is about, where it takes place, who the suspects are, and who the villain is. About once a month the Mega-Books staff and mine get together to discuss the latest crop of précis. We consider whether they meet our criteria for a good mystery that will appeal to our readers. But I have another concern: is the story similar to any we've done before? If so, in what way and does that matter? For example, I wouldn't want to publish two rock music–related books consecutively; nor would I want to publish consecutively stories in which the person who called Nancy in on the case turns out to be the guilty party, no matter how different the settings. So at this point I look at where a particular story fits into the series as a whole. I also look at how a story relates to books being published in other Stratemeyer series in the same month so that we avoid similarities.

Once a précis is approved with any necessary changes, the writer proceeds to the outline, which to me is the supremely important stage. (In the good old days of the syndicate the outline was rather sketchy. It was two pages, single spaced, and from that a book was written, and written very well.) Chapter by chapter—and ideally in not more than one page per chapter—the writer tells us what is going to happen. Now we can see how the mystery is structured.

At this stage I consider many things. Is the mystery holding my interest? Are there enough characters? Are there enough suspects? Is it obvious too soon who the guilty party is? What does Nancy know, and when does she know it? (She'd better not know too much too soon or we'll lose the reader.) Has the writer used the setting effectively? Does the action derive from the setting or does it seem generic and tacked on? Is the action similar to what we've done before?—any car chase had better be different from the hundreds that have gone before it, thrilling though they were. Over how many days does the story take place? Is there enough action to fill the time? Do all the characters contribute to the story? This is particularly important with Nancy's sidekicks, who could easily just shadow her actions. Could all the nefarious deeds have been done by the people who did them when they did them? Have all the clues and suspicious acts been accounted for? Do we have any scenes where the teen characters engage in teen activities? For example, do they go to the mall, eat pizza, watch a movie on video, go to a party or dance, or just talk?

The outline is also the stage at which we carefully review the cliffhangers. They can be action-oriented or psychological, but they need to be in place. At this stage I also try to make sure that there is a scene that can be illustrated on the cover.

After the outline is delivered to Mega-Books, one of their editors reviews it, writes comments on it, and sends it to me or one of my staff with a cover letter, stating its strong points and what may still need some work. Then I read the outline and letter closely, keeping track of all the elements I just mentioned, and return it to Mega-Books with my comments and a letter. Of course I always hope that very little revision will be needed, but I check carefully because mystery readers are alert, and they're quick to let us know if we've made any sort of mistake. The outline with all the comments is then returned to the writer, who may have to rethink some parts before proceeding to the first draft.

When the first draft comes in, a similar process occurs. The Mega-Books editor reads the manuscript, comments on it, and sends it to me with a cover letter. At this point all the structural problems should have been resolved. However, each stage of the book presents different areas of concern, so while I will check once again to make sure that all clues and suspicious acts have been accounted for, I'm much more interested in the writing. Does the book start off strongly? Is it suspenseful? Does the dialogue sound right? (This is particularly important for young adult books.) Are the motivations convincing? Do the series characters behave recognizably like themselves? Do the cliffhangers work? Do they have the rhythm that makes them dramatically effective and forces the reader to turn the page?

At this point I also note other technical matters, such as staging. Has the writer situated the characters and moved them around so we can visualize the action? Are the characters capable of performing the action as it's described? Is the factual information correct, as far as I can tell? Is the story told from Nancy's point of view? The reader shouldn't know more than she does. Again, anything that needs to be fixed is noted on the manuscript and in a letter, both of which are returned to Mega-Books to send to the writer for the final revision. Then the manuscript comes back to me to be copyedited and typeset.

From start to finish, the process is lengthy, much lengthier than in the old days of the syndicate. It's a very careful process. We take a lot of trouble because it's important to maintain quality when publishing a series. Readers are very quick to notice when a familiar series no longer delivers a satisfying reading experience, and once they lose interest it's almost impossible to win them back. From a publishing point of view, every bit of effort we put into editorial preparation pays off in maintaining the longevity of the series. We're betting that Nancy has a lot of life left.

NOTE

1. The Nancy Drew Notebooks series, inaugurated in 1994, was scheduled to be published every two months.

CHAPTER 8

Assuming the Role:
Writing the New Nancy Drews

Carolyn Keene

The summer I was ten I read nothing but Nancy Drew. The first one I read was a castoff, my cousin's copy of *The Ghost of Blackwood Hall* (1948). I read it because, at that point, ghost stories were my favorite kind of book. I'm not sure I realized that I was getting something very different in a detective story. All I knew was that I was hooked, mostly by the suspense and the atmosphere. As Carolyn Heilbrun pointed out, what I recall now about those early Nancy Drews is a very generalized experience of pleasure—I remember blond-haired, adventurous Nancy, her good chums (as they were called then), Bess and George, her "distinguished" father, Carson Drew, the faithful Hannah Gruen, and, of course, the blue roadster. I know I thought Bess very silly (I was a very serious child, and even at ten I basically had no patience for that sort of female); I thought George was sensible, Ned was boring, and Nancy was perfect. Actually, the only thing I couldn't really fathom about Nancy was her attraction to Ned. I still have trouble with that one. I remember somewhat gothic settings—old spooky houses, eccentric elderly women in distress, and stories that were scary and exciting.

I also had a very clear picture of what Carolyn Keene looked like. She was middle-aged, with short, blond permed hair, blue eyes, and had a penchant for wearing white buttoned blouses with scalloped lace collars. She was also quite buxom and always wore a string of pearls. It never, in my wildest dreams, occurred to me that

I would grow up to be, among other things, Carolyn Keene. When I really think about this part of my identity, I get a mild feeling of disbelief. It increases when I realize that quite a number of my good friends, many of them male, are also Carolyn Keene. We are quite a diverse company, and it's a tribute to the publishers and their editors, but mostly to the power of Nancy herself, that Nancy Drew has passed through so many hands and voices and imaginations and yet remains distinct and consistent through the years.

She's a very specific vision and as such can be difficult to write. I came to the series through publishing. I'd been working in children's books for years as an editor and a writer. Like many editors, I'd started as an editorial assistant, which means doing everything from typing to answering the phone, to weeding through the slush (unsolicited manuscripts), writing copy, and spending many, many hours cursing at the uncooperative copy machines. I graduated from being an assistant to being a manuscript reader, which is where I first met Anne Greenberg (I was doing freelance reading for Bantam, and she was managing editor there). Later I did proofreading, copy editing, and editing, which included developing and managing other middle-grade and young adult series. I'd even written two young adult mysteries for Random House's My Name Is Paris series, which is set in Paris at the turn of the century and follows a sixteen-year-old American girl who takes up sleuthing à la Sherlock Holmes. And so by the time I came to Nancy Drew, I knew many of the basics of what makes a good story. I had a decent handle, I thought, on plot and character development, language, background, pacing, and what it takes to keep young readers interested.

I've now written seven Nancy Drew books, five in the Nancy Drew Mystery Stories series and two Nancy Drew & Hardy Boys SuperMysteries. I've also written for nine other series and rewritten other people's books in countless other series (though I rarely edit now, I still do a great deal of rewriting and salvage work). I can honestly say that writing Nancy Drew is for me the most difficult work of all. I have a few theories as to why this is true.

Part of the problem is specific to me. I am not ideally suited to write mysteries. As a reader, writer, and editor, I'm very character-oriented. At heart I basically agree with Henry James's theory that character *is* plot. This is not a useful definition of plot when approaching Nancy Drew. Nancy needs action, one suspenseful event propelling the next, characters who are always in peril, and villains who provide continuous, compelling danger. One of the tightest constraints the writers are up against is that so many other books in the series are still out there. I remember sending in a plot in which one of my cliffhangers was that the brakes on Nancy's car go out, having been tampered with by the villain. It came back to me with an "Oh God! Not her brakes again!" comment. So much has been done, and so much recently, that it's difficult to come up with situations that feel fresh. (It's also difficult to always have to explain why the police are completely unable to solve a crime without Nancy's help.) Nevertheless we're given a lot of freedom by the publisher. We can put Nancy in virtually any place and any situation, as long as it isn't too similar to another Nancy and works within the boundaries of the series.

Plotting is always the most difficult part, and I think this is because I'm not, by nature, a mystery aficionado. When I read mysteries I read people like Tony Hillerman, Ellis Peters, and Dick Francis; and I read them because I'm fascinated by the worlds they describe. Deep down, I don't really care "who done it." One of the things that came into focus for me when I began writing Nancy Drew was that I'm not someone who likes to have every little detail worked out to the point where all is neat, logical, and comprehensible. On a personal level, I believe very deeply in mystery, the Divine Mystery, if you will—there seem to me to be many things in this world that don't conform to neat, rational, explanations—and when left to my own devices I like to leave a bit of mystery, a little room for the unexplained. This, too, is not useful in writing Nancy Drew.

The way I deal with my limitations is that I often start from either a setting or a situation that intrigues me. I love the fact that you can put Nancy absolutely anywhere. For example, when I wrote my first one, *The Secret at Seven Rocks* (1991), I had recently traveled to the Rockies and was fascinated by the Victorian mining towns, like Cripple Creek, Colorado. And so I created my own little mountain town of Seven Rocks, complete with Gaslight Night, when everyone is decked out in full Victorian regalia. When I co-wrote the Nancy Drew & Hardy Boys SuperMystery *Evil in Amsterdam* (1993), my co-writer and I had been talking about how different Europe is from America, in that the shadow of World War II is still so present there. My collaborator had spent time living in the Netherlands, and so we came up with a mystery set in Amsterdam, and the secret of the story traced back to the Resistance movement in Holland.

Many people say to me, "Oh, Nancy Drew must be so easy to write. It's formula." The formula is, in fact, what makes writing them so difficult. It is not a formula which tells you that you have a theft in chapter 1, a red herring in chapter 2, a car chase in 3, a missing person in 4, and in 16 the bad guy confesses all. Nothing about these books is that simple. What the formula does insist on is that every chapter end in a cliffhanger, that the plot be tightly constructed with adequate clues, red herrings, and a logical, believable solution to the mystery. It also insists that Nancy and the characters in her world remain essentially as they've been from the beginning. When you write these books, you put your own ego aside and surrender to Nancy.

To digress, I think what any good book does is to tell the truth. And so in writing Nancy I try to find the truth of the characters, the situation, whatever. I think this is what makes a story feel real.

Writing these characters is a very different experience from reading them. Bess, whom I outright dismissed when I was ten, is great fun to write. She's the easiest way to inject a bit of humor into the story. We've all met people like her. Bess is into guys, food, and clothing. She's loyal and a sweetie, but she can be completely silly, and she's wonderful to play against George. George is also fairly easy to write, because she's such a convenient co-detective. Like Watson, she asks all the right questions on the reader's behalf, and she can be depended on to help Nancy with the logistics. One can always send George to the library for research and trust that she'll come back with a vital piece of the puzzle. I still find Ned dull and so I have never used him, but I'd like to assure you that other writers have been more sympathetic to him and have written good Ned stories.

Nancy has changed a bit over the years, but she's still essentially perfect, and even when you love doing character, it's hard to write someone who's perfect because she's such a long way from anyone you will ever encounter. She is the definition of wholesome. This is a girl who always does and says the right thing. She rarely internalizes about anything that isn't connected to the case. She almost never gives in to anger or fear or despair, is never awkward or neurotic, never has a "bad hair day," never really suffers from doubt, and

never worries about money. Some days I find it a little hard to identify with all that, to find the truth in it and make it seem real.

On the other hand, Nancy has a pretty good gig. She goes
where she likes, when she likes, and is always surrounded by good
friends. She's friendly, popular, generous with her time and energy,
always ready to help those in need, and able to solve most any problem. The girl gets results. She's basically no one, and therefore everyone, and when we are Nancy (inside that place that is Nancy Drew)
we're in very good shape.

This describes my basic approach to the aesthetics of writing
Nancy. But what about the process of putting together one of these
books? There are four basic stages, each one very closely supervised
by both the packager and Simon & Schuster, meaning you must get
approval on each one.

The first stage is the précis, which is a one-page summary of
characters, suspects, red herrings, crimes, and the plot. The tough
part here is packing a complex plot into one comprehensible page.

Next a detailed chapter-by-chapter outline is submitted. This
usually comes back with numerous queries, all of which need to be
addressed before going into the first draft. Once the outline is approved, the writer is generally given six weeks to complete the first
draft. The first draft is then returned with suggestions for revision
by both the publisher and the packager, and then the final draft is
written. For me, the outline is the critical stage, because it's here
that the complexities of the plot must be worked out. I've found, not
surprisingly, that the stronger the outline, the easier it is to write
the book.

The process changes with a co-writer. I found the Super-
Mystery that I wrote with a collaborator to be the easiest of all the
Nancys I've worked on. This was because he and I were lucky to have
complementary strengths and weaknesses. Plotting is not my forte,
but he came to this project having written fourteen action-adventure
books and several Hardy Boys. He's a dynamite plotter. He also
doesn't care much for writing dialogue. So after a few long, giddy
sessions of staying up late and hammering out the plot and outline,
we divided up the actual scenes according to preference. We were
also careful to see that each of us wound up with fifty percent of
the work. He took almost all the scenes that called for heavy-duty

action—the chases through the canals, the race across Amsterdam's rooftops, etc. I wrote almost everything that depended heavily on dialogue. He then went through the entire thing, sewed the scenes together, and then went through a second time for consistency of language and style. When the book came back to us for revisions, we talked about what needed to be done, and I put in all the revisions and then went over the whole thing again for consistency of style. It was quick, it was fun, and we were both amazed at how much easier it was to write Nancy as a team than to write solo. Simon & Schuster tells me we achieved what we were trying for, which is the feeling that Carolyn Keene, not two collaborators, wrote the book.

I think that if you're interested in writing with another person, what you need to find is another writer whose ideas spark your own, and someone who doesn't have too much ego tied up in the project—someone willing to have their words changed.

Having gone on to other books as a child, I've developed a new respect for Nancy Drew as an adult. I continue to be amazed by how she works on me and has changed my life. (First of all, I never go anywhere without a flashlight.) It was largely contracts to write Nancy Drew that allowed me to escape New York and move to Tucson. The owners of the first house we rented there told us they chose us from among many other potential tenants because they felt good about someone who writes Nancy Drew. Then, in one of her more unexpected turns, she took me to Iowa for the Nancy Drew Conference.

She's been an instant passport to recognition and acceptance. I can't tell you how many people I've met who have said to me, "Nancy Drew saved my life." I've come to see what was evident in so many of the testimonials at the conference.[1] Nancy gets herself and others through difficult times. Whatever her limitations, she's a character of tremendous resonance. So to end, I'd like to acknowledge her enduring power and give my thanks for her presence in my life and the chance to honor it.

NOTE

1. The testimonials are in chapter 10.

CHAPTER 9

The New Nancy Drew Series:
Questions and Answers

Anne Greenberg and Carolyn Keene

How long does it take you to write a book?

KEENE: Actually it really depends on the book. From the time the outline is approved, we're generally given six weeks to get out the first draft. And some of them have gone much more quickly than others. And that generally depends, finally, on how strong the outline is. If you've got a good strong outline, you can write books pretty quickly. If your outline is a mess, it will take you every day of your six weeks or more. And you get faster as you write these things. It's a hard question but I'd say three to six weeks is a good range.

Have you ever pitched a Nancy Drew that didn't get accepted?

KEENE: The very first one I did was set in New Mexico, and it was an idea that really just didn't work, so I let it go and started with something else.

Even after a chapter by chapter pacing, do you ever get in a completed manuscript with surprises that are unwelcome?

GREENBERG: It doesn't happen that much. Often, it's not the events or action that need to be changed but the way they're presented. Here is a good example of how you think you have a good idea for a story and then somehow you're horrified to realize that it probably won't appeal to your readers. We okayed a book about someone stealing very rare civet cats from the local zoo for making perfume. We thought, endangered animals, rare animals—this is popular. Then we realized that we were going to have to talk about glands. We had this awful moment where we said, "My god, where is the kid appeal here? What are we going to do with this book?" Finally what we came up with was that the person behind the thefts was the grand-daughter of someone who had come up with a very famous but now lost perfume formula and needed this natural substance instead of a synthetic substance. So we were able to salvage that book.

Is there a strategy behind your redoing the artwork to the standard Nancy Drew series so frequently?
GREENBERG: Before I came to Simon & Schuster Pocket Books there had been a format and a look which was done under a different kind of publishing sensibility than we have in the mass market end of things. And that format changed before I got there. We're still using the basic type and graphic design; we've changed artists, however, because I wasn't necessarily happy with the way the art was looking. In fact on that classic Nancy Drew series I think we have a wonderful artist and I'm really thrilled with her work.

This is kind of a heavy question. Years ago, I think before you were in charge of the line, I met with an earlier editor. I was going to possibly ghost a book for her in the series. And while we were talking about it, the subject of Mildred Wirt came up. She said she couldn't really talk about it too much. My question is, why hasn't Simon & Schuster jumped on the bandwagon and said, "We own the property; the original ghostwriter has been discovered after all these years." I mean, it would be great press.
GREENBERG: Well, we have confidentiality agreements with other writers. Leslie McFarlane wrote his autobiography and revealed that he had written the Hardy Boys (McFarlane). I believe that Howard Garis wrote revealing that he was really Victor Appleton who wrote Tom Swift. Nevertheless, my advice from my legal department—and none of this is necessarily my decision—is that we have an agreement with Mildred Wirt Benson and we have other agreements, and we should stick to the Stratemeyer tradition of not discussing who actually wrote the books.[1]

COMMENT: Interesting, because since the trial in 1980 everyone knows that Mildred Wirt wrote the original one; it's a matter of public record.

GREENBERG: I know, it's a very difficult question to answer.

With so many books coming out now in the Nancy Drew series, do you anticipate difficulty in the future in keeping so many in print? Or is there difficulty in keeping so many titles in bookstores?

GREENBERG: Yes, it is hard because at some point accounts run out of space. They just can't stock everything. What we do on our digest series is reissue books. In other words, we sell out the stock, they take a little break, we bring them back. That means that every other month we designate a book to be reissued and our sales force actively goes out and solicits orders instead of just going into an account and saying, "Oh, I see you're missing number seventy-six so I'll just send you some." Instead, they go to the bookseller and say, "This month we have this book and we'd like you to take some," which is a more active, aggressive way of getting the books out. We definitely can't keep all the Nancy Drew Files in print and we have retired some of them.

You made mention of certain dialogue that would not appeal to young adults and I'm wondering if you just rely on the instincts of the people who are the decision-makers or if you have a more sophisticated means of surveying young adult tastes in regard to what will work.

GREENBERG: Well, we don't specify, "You have to say this" or "You can't say that" but I will say, though, one thing we don't do is try to be absolutely up to the minute with slang. In fact, we try to avoid slang because it quickly dates a book. And we don't say this is the most popular rock group at the moment because next week it's going to be somebody else. But there is a flavor, and if you listen to kids and if you're familiar with the books written for readers at this age level you internalize what is needed and what sounds right. I feel like I'm going on my gut, but of course it's not my gut; it's many, many books that I've read that have been popular with kids. My former job was with Bantam Books, where they had any number of successful series. Having read many of those books, I really developed a feeling for what would work and what wouldn't, and when you read it, you know. In fact, young adult dialogue is very hard to do and many writers can't do it and many editors can't respond to it. You either have it or you don't have it and it's almost impossible to edit it in. So that's one of the trickiest parts of these books.

There's been a lot of criticism of Nancy in recent years that she has sort of wimped out. Do you want to respond to that?
GREENBERG: Yes, I'd like to respond to that because I get angry a lot when I sit in my office and read these articles. I sometimes wonder which books the writer of the article read because I think very often there is confusion. Is the writer responding to the Grosset & Dunlap revised editions? Is the writer referring to those books I sort of refer to as "the last gasp of the syndicate"? Or is the writer referring to the books that I've been overseeing? I don't think that Nancy has wimped out. Far from it. I don't think that she's any less active than she ever was. I don't see it. Now, maybe I'm wrong. I think what happens very often is that adults going back, reading the books and comparing them, are seeing the books with adult eyes, but they can't read them now and capture the experience they had when they were young and first read the books. They just have to realize that they're not perceiving the books in the same way as when they were younger. I don't think Nancy has wimped out, I really don't.

Do you see a difference between the revised Grosset & Dunlap books and the ones you're now producing?
GREENBERG: Well, I think there has to be a difference. I mean, all these books are written as though they are taking place in the present. The 1990s present sounds a little different from, let's say, the 1960s present or the 1970s present. There's a change perhaps in writing style and language. I think the essence of the character has stayed the same; it's these trappings surrounding the character and the style of writing and the language used that are different.

Do you make a conscious effort to dilute dialogue because you think you need to play it down a little for young adults?
KEENE: It's not a matter of diluting it; it's a matter of trying to make it sound teenage and trying to make it sound like Nancy and George and Bess, who are all very different from other teenage characters I've written. In response to the last question, whether Nancy is

wimpy. I don't think she's wimpy. I think when she first emerged in the 1930s, she was quite radical as a female. And now in today's world she's not at all radical; she's incredibly straight, you know. We're in the 1990s and I think that's part of the difference in the perception of Nancy. And she's hard to write because she is so straight. When I wrote Hardy Boys dialogue, for example, I was amazed that it came so much faster and the reason it came faster is because they are always ribbing each other and being kind of ironic, which Nancy isn't. Nancy doesn't have too much irony in her. She has a sense of humor, but it's very gentle, especially compared to the way kids talk today. So it's not diluting, it's just trying to get Nancy right.

COMMENT: As a parent, I don't see that I talk any differently to my kids than I do to adults. It's just that the subject matter may be a little different, but you're saying there is a conscious effort to put young adult dialogue in?

KEENE: Teenagers, for example, do not always speak directly, in that they'll often cloak something in irony; there will always be a hint of sarcasm in it, which is a defense mechanism against having to identify yourself too strongly with anything you actually say; it's a safety shield. Nancy isn't really like that. She uses irony sometimes but she's quite straightforward as a character. So I do her differently than I would any other teenager, including Bess, who has other concerns. For me it's a matter of trying to be true to the individual character and I don't see it as diluting or talking down.

You talked about confidentiality agreements. As the conference demonstrates, there seems to be more of a willingness for individual authors to talk about their books, about who is actually writing them, or ghosting them. Do we really need the confidentiality agreements, particularly in relation to the older stuff? Do we need to continue this? Is this maybe a thing that is just created by lawyers? As a historian and a librarian I would like to see some of the original documents and materials put out there so that people can do research.

GREENBERG: Well, I'll tell you, this is not the creation of lawyers; it was the creation of Edward Stratemeyer, who devised pseudonyms because it was a way of assuring continuity of the series. Even if one writer left, the same name would be on the cover and the series could continue. He began this practice, and even now, from this perspective, I think he was wise to do so. It's worked very effectively. I personally don't like to tell young readers who write in that there is, in fact, no person behind the name—or no one person, anyway. But he began that practice and the agreements are binding, as far as I know, and we continued it. I should say that many people have written these books. Any one of them could decide to represent himself or herself as speaking for the series or speaking for what we do, and that would not be fair to us. It certainly wouldn't necessarily be accurate. So really it's our publishing effort and we do put a lot of effort into it. "Carolyn Keene" was able to speak at the conference because we agreed to waive the confidentiality for this meeting.[2]

But other names have come out . . .
GREENBERG: Well, listen, I'm not the KGB, I can't squelch everybody, and neither can Simon & Schuster's legal department, but this is a practice of long standing and it's a tradition we've continued.

I'm curious. I know that for many years if you wrote a letter to Carolyn Keene, Carolyn Keene answered. Does Carolyn Keene still answer?
GREENBERG: We deal with the mail in a variety of ways. We have fifth-grade kids who write to us because their teacher has encouraged them to write to their favorite author. You can tell the teacher has done this because you get a whole envelope full of the same questions. And this could be from all across the country. There are certain things that readers want to know. Where do you get your ideas? That's question number one. So in order to handle the volume of mail with a limited staff we devised a form response. For others who have more specific or unusual questions we try to respond in a more personal way. But we do not ever say that we're Carolyn Keene.

I understand that on the shelves at Simon & Schuster there are just boxes and boxes of all sorts of fairly ephemeral materials. Are there any plans to make that available to national archives or otherwise to the public?
GREENBERG: We did acquire all the records that they had: many old books, manuscripts, including setting copy of the first Nancy Drews, which still exists. You'll never get it. Don't even think about how much you can offer me. Sorry.

Will it ever be available for scholars?
GREENBERG: It may, at some point in the future.[3]

You talked about Stratemeyer. Did he live long enough to see Mildred Wirt's manuscripts?
GREENBERG: He didn't live to see them published, I don't think. But it's clear from her testimony in the lawsuit that he was not happy with at least the first manuscript. I actually went looking for this information but was unable to find out what months the books came out. Stratemeyer died in 1930 and I don't know that he actually saw them published. He died very quickly, within a week, I think it was, of pneumonia. It was very fast.

How popular are the new Nancy Drew series, compared to the old?
GREENBERG: The sales are very strong. I can only gauge by our monthly sales, by what we see over a period of time, and from mail we get from readers. And very often they're not writing the letter that the teacher made them write. They're saying, "I read every one of them" or "I read this, this, and this . . . my favorite is this . . ." "I like this situation . . ." "When are Nancy and Ned going to get married?" "Is Nancy ever going to go to college?" or "I think you should kill Ned off." So we do get some mail that indicates that young readers are still plowing right through them all.

In preparation for coming here I read one of the Nancy Drew Files; I don't remember the title, but it's one where Nancy gets engaged to someone else.
GREENBERG: It's called *Till Death Do Us Part* (1988).

It was much better than I expected. I thought I was going to be up in arms about the new Nancy Drews. But I don't think, in essence, this is the same person, that's why I can't be too enthusiastic. But I wonder if it will have any staying power.
GREENBERG: I don't know how I can answer that because I can't say how the readers of today are going to feel down the road when they're adults. They may or they may not. That's going to depend on future events and their changing attitudes.

When do you get your ideas? Before going to bed? Before breakfast?
KEENE: All the time. In fact, the best ideas for me usually come when

I'm drifting off to sleep. That's when I work out something I've been stuck on. So when I sleep I have a little pad and pen right beside the bed so I can wake up and write it down.

What can you say about the other series, such as Tom Swift? How are they doing, what do you think about them? Are you planning on continuing them?
GREENBERG: Tom Swift is disappointing, very disappointing to me. Sometimes it seems like the things I work on the hardest somehow are not quite as successful. Perhaps the time has passed. I mean, I just have to assume that the time has passed for Tom Swift, sadly.

The books that were published by Grosset & Dunlap had a very distinctive look about them. How often do you change that look and why?
GREENBERG: Well, once in a while we talk about it and say, "Maybe it's time for a new format." In mass market you change sometimes simply for the sake of changing. I mean, it makes something look new and fresh and it's sort of a marketing technique, and the booksellers like it: "Oh, this looks a little different." So we've played with the Nancy Drew Files logo a couple of times. The Hardy Boys Casefiles actually we have not changed since we began. We've fiddled with the look of the logo of the SuperMystery, and we probably will again. Very often just for the sake of making it look a little new, a little fresh.

Do you plan any hardcover books?
GREENBERG: There is such a limited market. The best we could hope for is selling some to libraries. There really isn't a retail market for the hardcovers. At one point we did do them in a different imprint, the Wanderer imprint. But the numbers are so small. The readers want them in the paperback format, and the libraries can rebind them so they're sturdier and more durable. It's still cheaper for a library that's really strapped, as everyone is, to take them in paperback.

Since the amount of research in the area of series books has increased so much in the last several years, have you developed a policy regarding individual researchers' requests to see files or asking for interviews with specific authors?
GREENBERG: I have a policy, yes. The material is not accessible. It is

truly not accessible. It is in a warehouse. Much of it is fragile, much of it is not. Actually, in the interest of future research it's a good idea not to have a lot of people handling this material and possibly getting it out of order. I know that a lot of people would like to go through it, but if you think about it, you're one person, but there are probably a lot of other people who would like to go through it and I think it would be, ultimately, damaging to the material. And as I said, it's really not accessible.[4]

I know there were negotiations started between the New York Public Library and Simon & Schuster to make these available. Could you tell us the status of these negotiations?
GREENBERG: We have been approached, but there is nothing firm and definite yet.

Is it possible that it will happen?
GREENBERG: Yes.

NOTES

1. After the conference, the publishers agreed to acknowledge Mildred Wirt Benson's contribution. The agreement is discussed in chapter 4, note 1. The first public recognition of Benson's role came in a letter by Anne Greenberg published in the *New York Times* in May 1993 (Greenberg).

2. Several other ghostwriters of Nancy Drew asked to participate in conference sessions, but they were prevented from doing so by their confidentiality agreements with Simon & Schuster.

3. The 1993 Simon & Schuster contribution of the Stratemeyer Syndicate papers to the New York Public Library was the largest contribution ever made to the library. It included books and archival materials: manuscripts, typescripts, and corrected proofs; business and personal correspondence; and financial records.

4. The New York Public Library expects the Stratemeyer papers to be available to researchers after three years of processing and cataloging.

PART II

Reading Nancy Drew, Reading Stereotypes

Nancy Drew. To me, those words mean a bright, ambitious girl, yearning for an adventure. They mean cuddling up in a warm blanket on a cold winter day, ready to travel to the corners of the world and beyond with my favorite sleuth. They mean seeing the worried look on Hannah's face as she takes one last glimpse of Nancy's car speeding out of sight, off to pursue another adventure-filled mystery. Nancy Drew means being exposed to danger, or even death, wherever you go. Those words mean being chided repeatedly at supper to "PUT THE BOOK DOWN," right when Nancy hears a piercing scream. They mean challenging the mind and body to get Nancy out of an impossible situation, and loving every minute of it.

—RACHEL K. LYLE,

AGE 11, GRADE 6,

HANSEN ELEMENTARY SCHOOL,

CEDAR FALLS, IOWA

I n numerous newspaper and magazine profiles, women of accomplishment have cited their reading "all the Nancy Drew books" as a central experience in their childhood, leading them to understand that their horizons were unlimited and introducing them to the joys of a lifetime of reading. These accounts echo the spontaneous stories we have heard continually since we rediscovered Nancy Drew. And they led us to organize the conference to witness, explore, and examine what this reading has meant to individual readers and its implications for the changing society in which it has occurred.

The essays in this section begin with evocative first-hand accounts by adults of the experience of reading Nancy Drew and continue with an examination of two controversies about that reading. As the call of readers' stories drew us to the idea of a conference, the centerpiece of the conference was an open-mike session at which participants could tell their tales of life with Nancy. To moderate the session and pick up the common threads, we chose Bonnie S. Sunstein, an assistant professor of English and education at the University of Iowa who studies stories people tell about reading and writing. In chapter 10, Sunstein has recreated the testimonial session by weaving a narrative around transcripts of the stories participants told.

Readers had richly colored memories of how and where they got their books, what they looked like, where they read them, and what happened to their books after they outgrew them. Many of the books were passed down from mother to daughter or granddaughter or more often from aunt to niece. Other readers formed their own circulating libraries among their friends. The stories tell of the rich and varied meanings readers found in their childhood encounters with Nancy Drew. They demonstrate the importance of considering the readers' active part in establishing the significance of a text.

Many of the stories about reading Nancy Drew could have been told about reading any books, the pure pleasure of reading a book as a means of finding satisfaction, relief from the stresses of a difficult childhood, a private time all to oneself. But as a series, Nancy Drew books offered the benefit of being predictable, like a reliable friend, an experience to repeat over and over. Indeed, in a survey of people who attended the conference or inquired about it, we found that most people read ten or more Nancy Drew books and nearly every one listed a number of other books or series they read as children.

About 10 percent gave the stock response of eager readers: "I read everything I could get my hands on."

Despite Nancy Drew's popularity for more than half a century, reading Nancy Drew has also been controversial, creating tensions among librarians, educators, and parents, many of whom have been concerned about the impact of reading these formulaic books on the development of reading habits and on the young readers hooked on the compelling stories. Scholars and human rights activists have targeted the racist images of nonwhites and other people at the margins in the early editions and their virtual exclusion from the later books.

To address these tensions, we sought scholars who could put the controversies into historical context and people who could give firsthand experiential accounts of their meaning in everyday reality. The intent in the contextual essays is to present the long view, to demonstrate where these critiques of Nancy Drew and other Stratemeyer books fit into the history of books and reading in American society. Ideally, even devoted Nancy Drew fans can take from these accounts an understanding of how mass production on the one hand and deeply imbedded social attitudes about race and class on the other shape popular culture.

In chapter 11, Nancy Romalov, who studies the history of girls' series books predating Nancy Drew, draws on the professional literature of librarians for her essay. She shows that historical arguments about quality in children's books derive from the objective of assimilating immigrants and the poor into middle-class American culture through provisions of "good" books in free public libraries. In chapters 12 and 13, Barbara Black, who was then a young adult specialist in a public library, and Joel Shoemaker, a media specialist in a middle school, addressed the conflicting pressures on those who select books for the reading public.

The Nancy Drew readers who responded to our survey suggest that reading Nancy Drew as a child is a brief stage in the life history of a person who is then and continues to be a voracious reader. Nearly half of the adults reported reading one to five books a month, and another quarter said they read six to ten books a month. While about half of the Nancy Drew graduates continue to enjoy mysteries as adults, few were attracted to other genre fiction, as the critics of series books would predict. Most read across a spectrum of material.

When the Stratemeyer Syndicate began revising the original

Nancy Drews in 1959, one of the changes was to remove altogether or to modify the stereotyped images of African Americans and other ethnic and racial minorities in the early books. It is not entirely clear what the stimulus for this aspect of the revision project was, as it started before the Civil Rights Movement of the 1960s had come to general public consciousness in middle-class white America. It had the effect, however, of replacing stories peppered with objectionable characterizations of those who were at the margins of American society with stories in which they are invisible. And rarely do nonwhite characters play any roles in the new books now being published.

Since children continue to read Nancy Drews in all her incarnations and many of the adult fans of Nancy Drew read and fondly remember only the original editions, how race has been addressed in the books is as salient an issue now as it has been at any time in the history of the series. Chapters 14–16 address the issue of racism—by stereotype and omission—first in historical and cultural context and then in the firsthand accounts of two women who as children read themselves into the stories despite their being misrepresented or excluded.

Donnarae MacCann, a critical cultural historian of children's literature, traces the belief in white superiority over nonwhites in prevailing attitudes from the nineteenth century up to the time the first Nancy Drews were published. In chapter 14, MacCann takes periodic readings of the cultural climate in which the Stratemeyer Syndicate books were written to help us understand how the representations of African Americans and other ethnic minorities as ignorant and often villainous could seem natural to white readers. As such they served to help perpetuate the myth of white supremacy, as MacCann demonstrates.

For nonwhite readers and others excluded from the text, these books, like much of American popular culture, pose a dilemma leading to a solution that has been referred to as reading in opposition to the text, recreating the stories and characters to fit into their own images of society. An alternative response was alienation from the stories and rejection as JoAnn Castagna, who grew up in a working class Italian-American family, described it in the testimonial session in chapter 10.

To elaborate the experience of reading Nancy Drew from the perspective of those excluded from the narratives we pursued two journalists who had previously told their Nancy Drew stories, unaffected by the later scrutiny these stories would undergo. The objective was not to ask them to represent their racial and ethnic groups but rather to articulate the *experience* of being a child conscious of her race while reading Nancy Drew and attempting to make mainstream popular culture personally meaningful.

Njeri Fuller was an honors student in the journalism school at the University of Iowa when the conference was being planned. Like many others she told a committee member about her passion for Nancy Drew at the mention of the girl sleuth's name. As a seasoned public speaker for a program to increase diversity in the staffs of student publications, Fuller was comfortable talking about the experience of being black in a white bread society. Chapter 15 articulates the process whereby she fit herself into the Nancy Drew stories which so engaged her imagination. She read them, as many white girls did, as adventures that held out exciting possibilities in worlds she had not yet experienced. To do so she recreated Nancy and some of her friends as black girls.

Dinah Eng is an editor and columnist for Gannett News Service who was a finalist in the Journalist in Space Program that was aborted after the *Challenger* disaster. She had written one evocative column in which she briefly described reading Nancy Drew stories to herself because her Chinese immigrant parents could not read English stories to her (Eng 1991). In another column she, like many other readers, linked her adult quests for adventure to the heroes of her childhood reading, including, of course, Nancy Drew (Eng 1989). So we invited her to participate. As she describes it in chapter 16, the transformation she engaged in while reading Nancy Drew was to imagine that she was white and inhabited the world in which Nancy was her friend.

CHAPTER TEN

"Reading" the Stories of Reading:
Nancy Drew Testimonials

Bonnie S. Sunstein

In her book *Writing a Woman's Life*, Carolyn Heilbrun writes, "I suspect that female narratives will be found where women exchange stories, where they read and talk collectively of ambitions, and possibilities, and accomplishments" (Heilbrun, 46). And what we've learned to call literature *is* our stories exchanged—written down and validated by culture. At the Nancy Drew Conference, the stories lay inside our talk. They sat in the brief biographies people mailed to us with their registrations. For us on the planning committee, the stories had flowed for over a year. For the participants, stories wrapped themselves around the edges of sessions, during meals, and on the journeys to and from the conference. These stories told about literature, but in the telling they became literature itself.

During the year, as we planned, we noticed an interesting phenomenon. Each time any of us mentioned the Nancy Drew conference to someone, we'd find a story. Sometimes it was about a shelf of dusty blue books with orange letters. Sometimes the story was about hiding a flashlight under the sheets with a sister or a best friend. Sometimes it was about a mentor: a teacher, a librarian, a mother. Sometimes it involved punishment and guilt, admonitions that "good girls" don't read trash. The tellers of these stories were mostly women: secretaries, lawyers, writers, waiters, professors, bus drivers, journalists. Some felt guilty for reading Nancy Drew under the gaze of culturally literate parents. And some felt guilty for *not* reading Nancy Drew under the gaze of gutsy friends.

But always these stories were about literacy. They told how we tied together our public and private reading lives, how we tied what we were reading at home with what we were reading at school. Always, these stories questioned where and how we developed our habits of reading; where and how we developed our habits of writing. With the texts of Nancy Drew, we adopted the language of mystery and middle class, we learned new vocabularies, and some of us tried our hands at writing the genre we were reading. Our Nancy Drew stories often disrupted what we were supposed to think about who was in charge of our literacy. They showed us that when we were in charge of our reading we took better charge of our lives.

At lunchtime in the Ballroom of the Iowa Memorial Union on the day of the conference, over two hundred readers gathered to exchange their Nancy Drew stories. Our ages defied definition and category. It was an intimate gathering of hundreds—in a very public place. We sat at long tables eating box lunches, sharing memories. Four microphones flanked the tables. Behind us, our daughters and nieces and young friends lay splayed and curled against the polished wood floor, elbows bent, hands supporting books and chins, feet askew, eyes quietly reading the Nancy Drews which were the topic of our conference.

Although we had labeled this session a "testimonial," we didn't like the term. This was not a meeting for testimony. No one needed to be convinced of anything. There was not much argument. We had not intended to speak in tongues, to sprinkle magic powders, or to swear allegiance upon an old Nancy Drew volume. The language and magic were already present in the literacies we had in common. We knew that the participants at this conference needed a forum to share their own stories; we wanted to offer a large room and a chunk of time for gathering our stories.

What follows is my slightly edited version of that session. I want to offer a bit of background commentary on the thoughts that directed the flow forward, but mostly I want to share the exchange. It was sixty powerful minutes of mostly women—talking collectively of reading, in Heilbrun's words, of "ambitions, and possibilities, and accomplishments."

As the leader of the testimonial, it was my intention to allow the stories to flow naturally. This session, as folklorists say, was "an induced natural context" (Goldstein). It was my job to "read" the spoken stories, as I heard them, and to allow them to flow from a large number of people into a very large space. We had arranged the room, provided an indoor picnic, and allowed an hour for informal talk. I knew, though, that microphones could be intimidating, that age differences and professional differences might disrupt people's comfort. Spoken stories don't follow predictable patterns, but I knew there would be patterns (Allen). And I knew, too, that since the subject was reading and writing, it would be fine to read what others had written. I came to the session ready to read stories we had received from people who did not attend the conference.

I had organized the written stories into themes which I hoped would trigger others. And so the stories flowed naturally with nudges from my predetermined categories. The talk layered itself with our ambitions followed and our ambitions failed, possibilities realized and possibilities clouded, accomplishments attained and accomplishments squelched. But what all the stories shared was the common thread of personal literacy: the hunger for reading, creating more reading through writing, problem-finding and problem-solving.

Hidden in Research: A Story

"In the spring of 1986, I discovered Case One of the Nancy Drew Files on the shelves of a Montreal bookstore." Marty Knepper, professor and Nancy Drew reader, opened the session. "I opened to page one and began to read":

> Hands on her hips, Nancy Drew stood in the middle of
> her bedroom and surveyed the situation. New clothes lay every-
> where—strewn across the bed, draped over the backs of chairs,
> and spilling out of shopping bags.
>
> Laughing at the mess, Nancy reached for a just-bought
> pair of designer jeans. "How do you like the new look in private
> detectives?" she said, slipping the jeans on. "Undercover and
> overdressed!"
>
> "I'd give anything to have a job like yours." Bess Marvin
> studied the label on an oversized green sweater that would
> be perfect with Nancy's reddish-blonde hair. "Not only did you
> get to buy a whole closetful of clothes for it, but you'll probably
> be asked out by every good-looking boy at Bedford High."

. . . Nancy studied herself in the mirror. She liked what she saw. The tight jeans looked great on her long, slim legs and the green sweater complemented her strawberry-blonde hair. Her eyes flashed with the excitement of a new case. She was counting on solving the little mystery fairly easily. In fact, Nancy thought it would probably be fun! "Right now," she said to her two friends, "the hardest part of this case is deciding what to wear." (*Secrets Can Kill* [1986], 1–3)

"As I read the opening of this first book in the new Nancy Drew series, my heart, to quote Carolyn Keene, 'flew into my mouth.' I was enraged. How could Simon & Schuster turn Nancy Drew into a 1980s materialist, a narcissist, a yuppie?" Knepper had conducted a survey of young readers and reported it in a research paper which she presented to our audience. But her research survey had begun with her own story, which she shared with us first:

Nancy Drew was one of my earliest and most satisfying fictional heroines. A shy, bookish child growing up in a 1950s family with lots of rules and little money, I longed to be Nancy, with her confidence, wealth, independence, loving friends, and indulgent parents. I admired Nancy, who seemed to me to be "perfect": altruistic and yet assertive, brainy and yet attractive, a big eater and yet thin, supercompetent and single-minded and yet loved by everyone. All the contradictions seemed reconciled in Nancy.

In the suburbs of Des Moines in the 1950s, most of our mothers were full-time homemakers who were sublimating their own heroic dreams by baking cookies, sewing our clothes, and serving as Girl Scout leaders. I recall sitting on the front steps in the summer time with a neighbor girl, each of us racing through those blue Nancy Drew books. I suspect we dreamed of lives other than our mothers'. In the case of the two of us, as it turned out, I got a Ph.D. and my neighbor became a nun. Perhaps Nancy suggested another way to be a woman in the world: a smart, independent, talented, autonomous woman who solved problems, helped others, and was respected.

Given my personal history, I was outraged at this first exposure to the new Nancy Drew. My instinctive reaction was that the new Nancy could not possibly be a positive role model for young girls as the older Nancy was for me. I decided, however, to study the old Grosset & Dunlap Nancy from 1930 through the 1950s (was she so perfect a role model?) and the new Nancy in the Simon & Schuster Nancy Drew Files series (is she a self-centered yuppie?), and find out how the new Nancy evolved as she did. I also decided to interview some children from Sioux City, Iowa, to see how they felt about the old and new Nancy Drew. I wanted to see whether my views of the old Nancy's perfections were pure nostalgia for my own childhood fantasies, as I suspected was the case, and whether my reaction to the new Nancys was merely a sign of aging crankiness about malls, designer clothes, high-tech toys, and trendy teen lifestyles.

Rereading Nancy in the late 1980s, after several decades of feminist scholarship, I was forced to acknowledge that the original Nancy was certainly a defender of a faded Victorian American aristocracy, and was in many ways classist, racist, and sexist. But I could still feel her attractiveness as a fantasy hero for young girls. But these days I'd rather read about the adventures of some of the adult female detectives who have emerged in the past twenty years. My own reactions to Nancy some thirty years later did not surprise me much, but the readers' responses from the children did shock me a bit. . . .

My reassessment of my own reading and my hour-long interviews with each of the children have led me to realize that each generation of women has its own complex psychic needs, which various forms of popular storytelling allow us to satisfy in various ways. We always revere the heroes of our childhood, I suspect, because they allow us to work out our own rebellions and accomplish our own goals. For me one of those heroes was Nancy Drew.

Decoding Reading Memories

For many of us lunching in the ballroom, as we listened to Marty conclude with her thoughts of Nancy as a role model, we knew we had read Nancy the same way. Tiffany Holmes remembered that a secret code, based on her childhood Nancy Drew reading, strengthened her early adulthood. She spoke into one of the microphones:

When I had my first apartment, where I lived alone, I said
to myself, "Who is in more need of rescuing, who takes more risks
than a young single woman about to embark on a series of blind
dates?" Now I was fortunate in that my overhead neighbor was
at the same stage in life. So I said, "How about having a secret
code?" When one of us has a blind date, the other will call. If
you're having a good time, speak French. It doesn't matter if it's
only a word or two. If you're not thrilled, try Spanish. The situation is under control but I am not enchanted. Spanish. If, however, you want immediate help, for the other to call in the cavalry,
send a telegram. Your grandmother is ill: speak Russian. Red
alert. I offer this to you to adapt to whatever situations you find
yourselves in. It's given us peace of mind.

Holmes's feeling of security echoed in the stories that followed.
Young readers quietly turned pages of Nancy Drews as they lay on
the floor behind our tables. Phil Zuckerman, publisher of Applewood
Books, which reprinted the first of three original Nancy Drews in
1991, offered a few letters. Here is one:

Dear Applewood Books, This brief message to thank you
for publishing the reprints of the Nancy Drew mystery stories,
to bless you for allowing us to go home again. In the space of
three books I returned to a world I thought long lost; an innocent, enchanted place where I've never felt so secure again. My
question, of course: Will there be any more reprints? Hopefully,
W. T. Bagley, Richboro, PA.

When Zuckerman finished, I added a letter from Ann Pearson
in Alabama, who offered a humorous note about how Nancy Drew
connected her language development to her sociocultural and geo-
graphical knowledge:

I did learn vocabulary, especially from Nancy. Until I read
her I never heard of a "roadster." And I remember being bowled
over when she asked friends over for "luncheon." In my juvenile
mind I thought those were only for brides until my mother informed me that is what Northerners eat in the middle of the
day. I myself ate "dunnar" at noon and supper at night. So Nancy

has been of invaluable help to me in dealing with the Yankees.
(Pearson)

Pearson's letter triggered another sociocultural response, one
which held some tension and resistance:

> My name is JoAnn Castagna. That's an Italian name, the
> kind of name you don't find in Nancy Drew books. When I was a
> kid reading Nancy Drew I think I only went through about three
> of them before I gave up because Nancy Drew was everything I
> *couldn't* be, *not* everything I *could* be. She ended up representing
> for me the kind of WASP ideal, the kind of kid who had a father
> with lots of money instead of a father who had never gone to col-
> lege, whose mother—although she had died, was clearly not my
> mother—who had a foreign accent. So I guess for me, I'm not
> here to celebrate Nancy Drew, but I'm real interested to hear you
> folks who enjoyed her.

The room became silent. "That's an interesting theme," I noted,
hoping that others would add their resistance and talk a bit about
what Nancy Drew *couldn't* be as well as what she could. "I think a
lot of us may have a little bit of that submerged." I wondered what
these memoirs might turn up. I knew that a little tension and disso-
nance would unearth stories.

> "I'm Jean Wagner," came a voice from the microphone:
> Nancy was a great inspiration to me growing up. My father
> *was* an attorney and they always referred to Carson Drew as a
> criminal lawyer when in fact he *never* did anything except put
> criminals away. My father did some criminal work so he was more
> like Carson. I was always kind of timid, and at one point in my
> life, I guess in my early thirties, I joined the police department
> and everyone said "*You?*" Nancy could do it, and I felt Nancy with
> me in my police work when I was involved in certain cases and in
> investigations. There was a triple murder in an adjoining commu-
> nity and I drove down there, and of course all the police lines
> were up and no one could go in. But I, Nancy, was escorted in be-
> cause it was a crime scene and, as the sergeant said, "You should
> see this because you might not get to see another one." So I got

behind the police lines, which Nancy certainly would have done. In fact, she would have blocked the police out if she could.

Jean's connection to her father and her police work emphasized the nature of searching. At this point, Karen Cyson added another dimension:

> I'm not going to talk about what the books actually did for me but what the *search* for the books did for me. I grew up in Roseville, Minnesota, and went to the Ramsey County Library, and every time I went in I walked right up to the front desk and said, "Where are your Nancy Drew books?" And the librarian would look at me with disgust and say, "We don't have *those* here." But I did it every time I walked in there. Meanwhile, in order to get them I had to exchange books with my cousins and with my best friend and with other girls in the neighborhood so that we could all read all the stories. What that taught me was if you don't like the system you have to keep picking at it and picking at it and picking at it until you get what you want. And while you're working at it you have to network outside the system to help yourself.

Clues to Readers' Support

"Librarians were a lot more important than we ever acknowledge consciously," I responded. "The librarian as gatekeeper—or mentor—is a really important theme." Karen's librarian's negative attitude had sparked her own ingenuity. She discovered other ways to find the books she wanted, and she learned how to navigate a system. Her story linked directly to one I wanted to read, an opposite view of a librarian, written by Annette Meyers, a mystery writer in New York:

> The 1940s war years were bleak and colorless for a girl growing up on a farm in what was then rural New Jersey. It was the school library that gave my life color. I loved the library and the librarian, Bessie McLean, who always seemed to know what I liked to read, and I read everything. One day she literally slipped me a book and said, "I think you will like this." It was *The Clue of the Tapping Heels* (1939). I had never read anything like it. I

quickly devoured every other Nancy Drew book, eagerly waiting for each new edition. Dear Bessie McLean, now in her eighties, reminded me recently that at the time the Nancy Drew books were not considered proper reading for young girls and she was not supposed to buy them for the library, let alone recommend them. How fortunate for me that she did! I probably would not be a writer of mysteries today if I hadn't seen the world of possibilities that the Nancy Drew books opened up for me.

And this brought a librarian to the microphone:

The negative aspect of the librarian inspired me to be a book buyer today, although I am also a librarian. My father was a naval aviator stationed at Pensacola Naval Air Station during the Korean War. The base library, of course, didn't stock anything like Nancy Drew. If I wanted to keep reading Nancy, I had to save my money and get my mother to drive me downtown to the bookstore and buy Nancy. There was a lot of rain in southwest Florida in the winter, and each time I saved enough, the windshield wipers used to say, "The Pass-word-to-Lark-spur Lane" or "The Mys-ter-y-of-the-Brass-Bound-Trunk" as we were driving downtown. My experience with Nancy in those Florida winter rains really inspired me. Mysteries are for rainy days inside. There's nothing better.

The suggestion of such support in childhood brought Barbara to the microphone:

My best friend when I was a child was Janey. When we were in third grade we discovered Nancy Drew and we loved her with all our hearts and we also loved Carolyn Keene. When we were in fifth grade we were worried that Carolyn Keene was maybe getting old and we felt like we wanted to take over writing Nancy Drew. So we wrote a letter, an impassioned letter, telling of our great love for Nancy Drew, that we would be willing to offer our services as writers when we grew up. And the letter I have in return is from Alice Thorn, who is chief editor of juvenile books. It says, "Dear Barbara, thank you for your interest in our authors. It is not the policy of this firm to disclose their home addresses.

However, if you will write directly to the author you have in mind c/o Grosset & Dunlap, we shall be glad to forward your letter." So actually, maybe we didn't even get the letter sent, maybe we wrote this letter asking for an address, and somehow this intimidated us that it would never get to her.

But in my adult life, around 1980, I was involved in a terrible marriage. On one winter night before I got out of my marriage, I went to my parents' house and I got all my Nancy Drew books. I reread every single one and it helped me feel like a person again, not like the crazed woman I had become. And my friend Janey now has a Ph.D. in counseling and she's a therapist. She's still not feeling satisfied in her life. We're in our forties now. She tries to supplement her life as a therapist by pretending to be Nancy Drew, a detective, as she's sitting listening to people's problems in her work.

As children, these women understood that their loyalty to Nancy Drew was the result of loyalty to a writer. They wanted to take control of Nancy Drew by becoming Carolyn Keene. Instead, they took control, as we all do in adult life, gradually, with Nancy's strength as a guide. Katy Koch wrote about her obsession with Carolyn Keene, and it was at this juncture that I decided to read her letter:

What? There is no Carolyn Keene? Ned, hurry, let's get on that right away. I'm a Nancy Drew addict. Count me among the countless thousands of blooming adolescents who claimed her as their personal heroine but also among those whose personal bonding with Carolyn Keene prompted a pursuit of writing which led to a career in journalism. I can't tell you how many Saturdays I spent at age twelve at my dad's Olivetti, hammering out the humble beginnings of my own girl detective stories. I can't even remember my sleuth's name now, but my admiration for Carolyn Keene held fast as type on a newspaper flat. She was, I fancied, an adventurous woman, middle-aged with hair in a bun, someone who would be equally at home crawling in khakis on the floor of an ancient ruin as in a business suit addressing a male-dominated boardroom on the finer points of detective work. Carolyn

Keene was, in my mind, a grown-up Nancy Drew. She was also as close to an idol as I've had in my life.

Mildred Wirt Benson's presence that day offered many of us, like Katy, who think of ourselves as writers, an opportunity to meet another version of Carolyn Keene, still adventurous, still a writer, still a woman with the strong spirit that offered us inspiration.

"I had a few Nancy Drews in my small home town that were given to me by an aunt. I read them and reread them." Chris Maltby from Tacoma, Washington, spoke into the microphone. She had spent her morning listening to the winners of the Nancy Drew essay contest for children. Her fascination with writing and writers linked her own past history with the kids she'd just observed.

And I didn't read much Nancy Drew again until I became aware of the Stratemeyer Syndicate and the fact that revisions had occurred. When I was in library school I wrote one paper comparing two books, a Hardy Boys and a Nancy Drew. My professor said, "I think you have a master's paper here." So I spent a good two years reading and comparing revisions, going on to do research and getting a very different perspective. Most of us out there know that there are kids that still have a passion.

I just came from hearing the contest winners. I wanted to hear what the kids said. I asked them a question: "If you've read the early ones, which do you prefer?" And a lot of kids preferred the earlier versions. These are very literate kids who don't stumble over words like "roadster." My daughter started reading them as a second grader and that was the same age as a girl in the session today. My daughter read a Nancy Drew a day, every day, until she finished everything I had, to and fro on the school bus. She was an avid reader. My youngest boy got involved in the Hardy Boys. My middle son picked up a few Hardy Boys, read them, and said, "Mom, they're all the same." And they were, all right. I made a close acquaintance with a friend's daughter. She's thirteen now, an avid Nancy Drew fan. It doesn't matter which edition; there's something in there that really clinches for certain people.

If I were to do research again, this time it would be on what it is that draws an individual reader to a certain type of book.

I love fantasy. I don't care for science fiction. Feminism aside, there is something in you that locks in you and you hold onto that throughout your life. There's some interesting feminist psycho-therapy that says go back to the girl you were when you were ten years old. And I think that's what Nancy Drew is for a lot of us.

In one short sweep, Chris had described her own formal and informal academic pursuits: from her aunt who was an early reading mentor to her professor who encouraged her own fascination with the history of Nancy Drew editions, from her own children to those she had just seen at the workshop.

A Case of Generational Links

Chris began a line of thought about people and their reading habits. The group was quiet again. I was thinking about the children and young adults we'd seen all day. Many were lying on the floor, reading as we spoke into the microphones. A few sat at the tables with their mothers, aunts, and friends. Others, I knew, were at the computer lab writing mystery stories. They were living reminders of our own histories, our young obsessions. They were mostly girls. I had been moved by their presence all day. The age span of participants at this conference was remarkable. I wanted to include them.

"What about the kids? Let's hear from some of the kids. Anybody read any good mysteries this morning? Or write them? Want to tell us?" The kids who were reading in the rear of the ballroom continued to read. They weren't ready to share; they were too busy having the experiences we were remembering. Adult readers. Child readers. What are the differences? What happens when an adult rereads a book she's read as a child? These are questions that have intrigued me as a professional. I believe that the act of reading is a transaction between reader and writer, based on who that reader is at a given time in her life (Rosenblatt). The power of this notion found its place at this conference, and I wanted to harness it. But instead, I stopped trying to interrupt the kids.

Another woman echoed my thoughts in her next story, an observation about revisiting a book as an adult:

I just want to say that when I first read these books I was growing up in Oregon. I didn't pay much attention to the details of geography, for example. But as an adult, I reread them after I'd been living here in Iowa for about ten years. And I said to my husband, "This woman who wrote these must have grown up in the Midwest." I think the storm scene in *The Bungalow Mystery* (1930) was so unique to the Midwest that when I found out about this conference, I said, "See, it is true, she was from the Midwest." And that's what I am enjoying more. To reread these books as an adult is to enjoy the details, things I missed as a child. My friend's mother had saved a pile of books. We talk about our mothers of the fifties not doing the things Nancy was doing, but what linked us to them as girls were the Nancy Drew books. I think that's the link we'll have for future generations of girls and boys.

The generational links, thoughts of our reading histories, continued. Another woman spoke of her aunt's book collection and her connection to the physical qualities of the books: "Let's hear it for the aunts," she cheered. "I've heard aunts mentioned about twenty-five times already." She explained that she had written a piece about her memories. She read:

During the fifties, I inherited a bookcase of blue clothbound first editions of Nancy Drew from my aunt. A slender silhouette of a girl detective was embossed in orange on the spines of the sturdy books. I loved to gaze at the lineup of Nancys marching across my bedroom shelves, all slightly bending from the waist, looking-glass in hand, examining a piece of some sort of evidence, invisible to me. The leading department store had the newer versions of the series, but whenever I perused the latest installments I was pleased to have the originals. My grandparents had purchased them in the same downtown store during the Depression and I liked the legacy of having the books handed down. The original volumes were thicker and more substantial than most of the ones I saw later. They were stitched, not glued. They had pages that would lie flat. I liked the dated illustrations.

As she continued, she began to analyze the reading itself:

> They were stories set in an era I wanted to know more
> about. Like my students today who want to know more about the
> sixties, I found the pre–World War II period intriguing. The nar-
> rative imagery seemed so terribly elegant. Phrases like "stopping
> at a roadside inn to have cinnamon toast points and cocoa." The
> language was so quaint: the "plucky sleuth donning a gingham
> frock and dashing off in a roadster with chums." Where did they
> get those words? I used to amuse my college classmates and jour-
> nalism colleagues by quoting verbatim passages etched in my
> memory.
>
> I loved the Russell Tandy illustrations inside of the books
> as well as the covers. I was fortunate enough that my aunt had
> saved all the dust jackets and pasted them into a book so that
> I could look at Nancy across time as I read. She was seen in
> semiperilous situations. I could see how she changed from
> those cloche hats and slender skirts of the 1930s to a sort of
> Andrews sister during the forties and finally a modified Sandra
> Dee style, which was when I stopped reading. I had very little
> interest in boys back then and reading about Ned Nickerson
> did not reinforce any enthusiasm for dippy men. He seemed
> to be a handy dance partner, someone Nancy could rescue once
> in a while. I was particularly intrigued at a bound and gagged
> Nancy, encumbered with high heels that I never imagined I
> would master. She managed to tap out a code and be saved.
> Her deductive reasoning powers were something I wanted to
> emulate.
>
> When I started buying paperback books, the first one I pur-
> chased was called *The Art of Thinking*. My parents were im-
> pressed that I hadn't squandered my allowance on candy or
> Archie comics. I think that I began reading Nancy Drew when I
> was about eight. I started them one summer and I read about
> one a day, just like vitamins. I read in the back seat of the car,
> on the porch, in my lap, under the dining table, and in bed. By
> the third grade, I was the only child in my class sporting catseye-
> shaped bifocals. No longer able to see the blackboard from my
> vantage point as a quiet little girl in the back of the room, I

moved forward and tried to learn a little bit about boldness from Nancy.

This woman's lessons from Nancy climaxed with a final reflection, a memory of the grandmother who had purchased those books and the aunt who'd read them during the Depression:

> One summer my grandmother was hospitalized. My family lived a few hours away, and we went to visit her every weekend. I was not allowed to go upstairs to see her; the hospital had a strict rule prohibiting any child under the age of twelve from visiting patients. So every Saturday and Sunday I would sit in the lobby, in the quietest corner I could find with the best light, and read the latest Nancy Drews. One afternoon my mother said that my grandmother had been asking to see me, her only grandchild. It would be okay to bend the rules just this once. I quietly closed my Nancy Drew and I slipped into a crowd of people much as I knew Nancy was capable of doing. I waited for the elevator. As we rode up to the floor where my grandmother was, my aunt suggested that I run ahead to her room and surprise her. As I entered, a doctor was stuffing a stethoscope back into his pocket and a nurse was pulling a sheet over my grandmother's head. I was too late to say good-bye. I stopped reading Nancy Drews then and there, and I grew up a little more that summer. Four decades later, I look in the mirror and I see my grandmother reflected. And while I don't consciously think of Nancy Drew very often, she was an early role model who showed me it was okay for women to be independent and brave.

Again, the ballroom was quiet. An aunt spoke:

> My name is Susan Birrell and I live in Iowa City. I'm forty-seven years old and about four years ago I got very nostalgic for my Nancy Drew collection. While I was visiting my family at Christmas, I asked my oldest niece to give me back all my Nancy Drews, at least temporarily. And when I opened the books, what I discovered inside were the names of a number of childhood friends: Babs Sharp, Diana Veasey, Ginny Wind, Sally Smith.

We had all read these books and had passed them on to one another. Today I bought a conference T-shirt to send each one of those women. And that's what I like about Nancy Drew.

Women, reading, sharing, talk, collectivity, and connectedness. Susan's memory folded into the story of the grandmother's death. Susan was chair of the Woman's Studies Program at the University of Iowa. For me, it was poignant and powerful. I tried to capture the moment with a piece I'd been saving to read. I spoke: "I think when we talk about 'connected knowing' in women's studies there isn't a better illustration than our book-friends. Thinking about who they are, who they were, and how they've shaped us as readers and thinkers" (Belenky et al.).

Adolescence, childhood, reading and writing the mysteries of their lives. "I'll read you something about Nancy Drew under the sheets," I joked. "This is from Barbara Bedway in Ohio. Many of us have talked today about our real families and our reading families." Barbara wrote:

We needed a mystery, my sister and I, so we went looking for one. That year we discovered the Nancy Drew series and the remarkable word "sleuth" entered our vocabulary. We read the books after school and during recess. Though we weren't allowed to read during meals, we took the books to the dinner table and read until every glass of milk had been poured and poured again, every conceivable condiment requested, and simple good manners dictated that the meal must begin. We read them under the covers at night with a flashlight passed back and forth between our beds. There were fifty-six books in the series and we had to finish them all. Every book ended with a mention of another mystery that would challenge the young sleuth next. And here we were, two reasonably good elementary school students in Ohio aged seven and nine, utterly obsessed with and available for detective work. And no mysteries presented themselves the way they seemed to seek out Nancy Drew. With the school year ending we had only one goal: to find a mystery and solve it before summer's end.

Barbara's story continues to describe the mystery they solved. "I won't read you what happened," I teased the conference participants as I noted the time to myself. The group was beginning to feel to me like a book club, a gathering of reading "chums" itself. "I'll give you the reference instead. It's from *Ohio Magazine*, November 1989 [Bedway]. If you want to know what happened, you'll have to read it."

Another participant noted her reading family, the influence of yet another aunt, and a lifelong vision:

> I first discovered Nancy Drew through an aunt. I was eleven years old, kind of older than other girls were when they started reading the books. Nancy Drew had a profound effect on me for reasons that had to do with my background. When Nancy used to speed away from River Heights in her blue coupe, I sat in the passenger seat. Only I was speeding away from my small northern Minnesota town where women's destinies were to be good wives and mothers. I had other ideas. Nancy gave me a sense that a girl could be more than a housewife and that her skills could be more than cooking and doing the dishes. I wanted to be a teacher. And while I read Nancy later on, I was also reading *Jane Eyre* and *Wuthering Heights*. I like to think that Nancy gave me courage to pursue my dream despite obstacles. I'm older, I'm a university professor. I've achieved one of my lifetime goals. And I study Nancy Drew now from the point of view of one who looks at the books from a historical longshot. And I'm aware that in reality I did not see my life reflected in the books. As a woman, for what I wanted to accomplish, it was probably best that I didn't.

She summarized Nancy Drew's power to move so many men—so gently, quietly on the page. Many of the people in the lroom had sat in the passenger seat of Nancy's roadster, speeding ay from something, sleuthing their way toward solving the mys- ies of their own literacy, social positions, and professional goals. I ᵤ₋ₓed the participants to show me their ages: How many over fifty? Forty? Thirty? Twenty? Ten?

"If you've been looking around as I've been looking, and think- ing about what's happened here in the last hour," I said, "you're go- ing to be thinking about how words connect us, and how stories when they are exchanged—and when they are written—become our literature. They are ways that we have to join us to one another—chums to chums, sisters to aunts, mothers to daughters, teachers to students, librarians to hungry readers. They are ways we have to talk to other generations, to share thoughts and experiences with relatives. Stories *are* our living literature. And thank you for contributing your stories to the literature of Nancy Drew."

CHAPTER 11

Children's Series Books and the Rhetoric of Guidance: A Historical Overview

Nancy Tillman Romalov

Whether children's reading of mass-marketed series books should be encouraged or discouraged is the subject of a long-raging debate. This essay will provide a bit of historical background to the debate. For to fully understand the controversy we need to consider the broader cultural contexts which have nourished it. In particular we need to recognize this campaign against series books and other mass-produced fiction as part of the history of popular culture in America, of the ongoing discourse over "high" and "low" culture, of larger debates about literary value and about who gets to do the valuing. Uncovering the specifics of the debate reveals our attitudes and policies regarding reading and readers and the role of educators and librarians in determining certain cultural standards.

I will begin by returning to the emergence of the public library movement in the late nineteenth century and specifically to the rise of children's services in the public library, since this development coincided with the rise of the popular series books published by Stratemeyer and others. The public library movement was part of larger reform efforts of the Progressive Era that sought to shape public behavior. In the course of enacting their mission public librarians generated a rhetoric of guidance that created and has helped maintain a dichotomy between different types of fiction and reading, between what has variably been labeled popular (i.e., low, subliterary, escapist, trashy) and elite (i.e., edifying, uplifting, artful) literature.

The public library movement in the United States was established in the mid-nineteenth century on the principles of Americanizing foreigners, controlling social and urban problems, and uplifting readers. According to recent library histories, the public library was originally subsidized by capitalists and political leaders who saw it as a way of extending genteel culture to workers and their children (Garrison, Geller).

When the American Library Association was established in 1876, the right of children to public library service had not yet been recognized. Most libraries set the age at which children should be admitted to library privileges at between twelve and fourteen. It was, in great part, the recognition that youth were reading dime novels and other so-called sensational literature and the horror with which this literature was viewed by many adults that led to early library work with children. If they were not allowed full library privileges, librarians argued, children would be limited to reading dime novels and similar "immoral literature" which they felt incited readers to disrespect authority and created a taste for the sensational, the ugly, or the merely mediocre. Their mission was to get children into the library, where their reading could be carefully guided.

It was a persuasive argument, and by the end of the century age limits had all but been abolished. Once the matter of whether to admit children into public libraries was settled, the focus of the debate centered on what kind of fiction should be available to them. The first children's librarians had been trained to view the library as a "moral force" and felt that it was their duty to make certain that children read nothing but "wholesome" literature: a vague term, to be sure, but one around which librarians could rally. All sides agreed that dime novels—those distant cousins of the Stratemeyer series books—story papers, and cheap books had no place in the library's collection and devised ingenious plans to reform readers found smuggling such literature into the library. But they were less unified when debating the popular new adventure novels of Horatio Alger, Oliver Optic, or later the adventure series of the Stratemeyer Syndicate.

Often the debate was drawn along class lines. One librarian explained that children "who are born and bred in the habitation of labor . . . cannot and will not read what, as a rule, I am willing to recommend" (Johnson 1990, 21). For them Alger and other popular authors were permissible. They might not be desirable for every library, another librarian argued, but were appropriate in libraries located at or near factories, where children of workers could enjoy them and perhaps graduate to better things. In arguing for including in the children's library books which might not be considered of high literary quality, one librarian promoted a double standard by suggesting that any book which "showed a child from the poorer class of laborers how well-born people acted and spoke" was of value even if it was neither a classic nor likely to endure (Carrier, 231).

With the advent of the mass-marketed series novels, librarians and educators faced a slightly different foe, and their responses varied. Dime novels were visibly unsavory; the boys' adventure stories, while admittedly sensational and often preposterous, seemed a lesser evil. But the series book offered a surface respectability. They *looked* wholesome. Book covers showed groups of young boys and girls engaged in healthy outdoor activities; blurbs on the jackets and in ads promoted them as stories which upheld American values: "These are clean, wholesome stories that will be of great interest to all girls of high school age," reads an ad for a Marjorie Dean story. The Girl Scout Series was promoted as being "absolutely free from cheap sensationalism, yet legitimately absorbing, genuinely modern . . . the characters are modeled from . . . the highest ideals of girlhood."

Nevertheless librarians fought these books too, employing some of the same arguments they had used against dime novels and adventure tales, but constructing a more subtle discourse which focused on questions of aesthetics—that is, on the quality of prose and nature of the books' production. Much of this early antiseries rhetoric is characterized by vague generalizations, name calling, dire warning, and subtle pressure tactics. If they could no longer confidently label these books "bad," they would at least campaign against mediocrity. The worst thing about the series books, librarians argued, was that they "steal the child's time and leave nothing in return" (Thompson, 427), that they cause "mental laziness," induce a "fatal sluggishness" and "intellectual torpor" ("Platitudes," 130). An editorial in *Library Journal* in 1905 asked: "Shall the libraries resist the flood [of series books] and stand for a better, purer literature and art for children, or shall they 'meet the demands of the people' by gratifying a low and lowering taste?" (*Library Journal*, 916). The answer seemed clear: they should take charge.

Some who were opposed to series books recognized their potential subversiveness. Time and again librarians protested that series book heroes were too adultlike; they were not *real children*. Real children didn't rescue the family fortunes, were not self-sufficient or independent. Librarians worried that reading about omnipotent children was dangerous because it could lead to feelings of discontent, causing children to dream, perchance to act upon the dreams, or worse, to behave disrespectfully toward adults. In justifying the exclusion of all series books from a standard text used to train teachers and children's librarians, the authors argued that the series book "all too often throws into attractive relief characters who have broken the traditions and conventions which society has found essential to its highest goal" (Gardner and Ramsey, 15).

It is also interesting to note the ways in which this discourse was affected by notions of reading as a gendered behavior. Some professionals worried about the effects of girls reading boys' series books. G. Stanley Hall, the recognized authority on adolescent psychology throughout most of the twentieth century, warned against girls' attraction to the boys' adventure stories. In an address before the National Education Association in 1905 Hall argued:

> The danger is very great that the modern schoolgirl will
> early in life acquire false views of it, will make excessive and im-
> possible demands on it, which will cloud her life with discontent
> in the future. (Hall, 868)

He argued that girls needed to read books calculated to fit them for domestic life and womanly vocations.

Between 1910 and 1920 a number of institutions became involved in the campaign to limit children's reading of series books. With the professionalization of children's literature and children's library services throughout the Progressive Era, the attacks on children's "unregulated" reading took on a more organized, institutional character. As librarians' role in guiding young people's reading became more clearly defined, their attack on popular mass-marketed fiction became more organized, and hence more effective. Efforts at standardizing the selection of children's books for libraries and schools increased with the establishment of librarian training schools and the growth of children's book reviewing. In addition to the American Library Association, other organizations joined in the effort to oversee children's reading. The NEA (National Education Association), NCTE (National Council of Teachers of English), and the PTA (Parent Teacher Association) also began publishing reading guides, all directed toward getting children to read the "classics."

The attacks on series books escalated when the chief librarian for the Boy Scouts of America, Franklin K. Mathiews, became involved. The Boy Scouts were also in the business of publishing boys' books under Mathiews's supervision, but, as Mathiews found out, the boys preferred reading Stratemeyer's syndicated books to the sanitized adventure stories offered by the Boy Scout organization. When Mathiews discovered that Stratemeyer controlled nearly 80 percent of all the books that came into the hands of American youth, he began his own campaign. In addition to publishing new inexpensive editions of "clean adventure stories," which he hoped would outsell Stratemeyer, he lobbied parents and educators through his extensive writing. His most viperous article was entitled "Blowing Out the Boy's Brains," in which he likened Stratemeyer's literature to alcohol in its habit-forming and ruinous effects: "The chief trouble with these books is their gross exaggeration, which works on a boy's mind in as deadly a fashion as liquor will attack a man's brain" (Mathiews, 653). Series books were unreal, suggestive, overstimulating, Mathiews argued. He was also annoyed at the way in which the books were produced: "Not written but manufactured"—that is, they were not "art" but "commodity." This particular objection has remained constant throughout the history of the series books controversy. If a book is mass-produced, or ghostwritten, it is not bona fide literature, and consequently reading such books is an unworthy activity.

The effect of Mathiews's attack on the sales of series books was negligible. Librarians became frustrated, for it was clear that perhaps for the first time in the history of children's book publishing they were not in a position to guide children's responses, since readers controlled, to a great extent, the reading process as well as the purchase of series books. The undermining of librarians' authority and loss of control over children's leisure activities no doubt contributed to their opposition.

By 1920 the professionalization of children's literature was in full swing and campaigns against series books entered a new phase.

The ALA had taken an official stance against series in 1921 in an article entitled "Why the ALA Does Not Endorse Serials for Boys and Girls" (Bowman). Their reasoning sounded many familiar notes: the books are poorly written, sensational, and a waste of time and libraries' money. By 1925 a number of professional periodicals which reviewed children's books had been founded: *Booklist*, *Elementary English*, the *Horn Book*, the *Three Owls*. In 1922 the prestigious Newberry award was established. All this activity resulted in more attention being paid to children's reading, but also in more standardization and concentration of the field in the hands of the professionals. Educators and librarians now attempted to quantify the nature of the problem; they conducted research studies, polls, and random samples to try to answer the question of what children were reading and why. Underlying their efforts ran the basic question: why, contrary to our best advice, do children insist on reading series books?

Typical of such studies was Arthur M. Jordon's *Children's Interest in Reading* (1921) from Columbia University, in which he recognized the popularity of series books, attributing their appeal to the rather obvious fact that they speak to interests of boys and girls. A 1922 study from Johns Hopkins University concluded that a book's external appearance was a significant factor in book selection. The physical dimensions and appearance of the books most likely to be read fit the description of series books exactly: attractive covers and illustrations, short chapters, large print, wide margins, and much dialogue (Bamberger).

A study most often cited in the years to follow was issued by the ALA in 1926. *The Winnetka Graded Book List* and its supplement were based on a reading survey of over 36,000 children across the country. According to Deidre Johnson, this study continues to be statistically misinterpreted (Johnson 1990, 44–45). Nevertheless, what educators read from the survey was the disturbing fact that the reading habits of fifth, sixth, and seventh graders were dominated by Stratemeyer's books—the Bobbsey Twins, Tom Swift, Honey Bunch, and others. Those books which were "unanimously rated trashy" by librarians received near-perfect interest scores from the respondents. In effect, the *Book List* had exposed the undeniable popularity of the series books.

The debate over series books culminated in 1929 with a series of articles published in *Wilson Bulletin*. Mary Root, a prominent library figure in America, had compiled a list of "Books in series not circulated by standardized libraries," which was published in the *Bulletin*, along with responses to the list. Whereas earlier attacks on the series had been vague and general, this one was specific; it listed titles and authors of many of the most popular series books: the Khaki Girls, the Girl Aviators, the Automobile Girls, the Rover Boys. Although intended to help librarians weed their collections, the list was in effect a blacklisting of series titles. Root's article sparked a lively debate in the pages of the *Bulletin*, but the response from librarians was overwhelmingly in favor of her stance.

The publication of Root's list marked the climax of a half-century-long campaign on the part of librarians to suppress dime novels and series books. It was indisputably successful, since series books would stay out of most libraries until the late sixties and early seventies.

From 1931 to the 1960s all was relatively quiet on the series book front. Radio, comic books and pulp magazines, motion pictures, and the rise of television competed with the series book for readers' leisure time and diverted professionals' attention toward these new foes.

By the mid-sixties the climate had begun to change. Circulation of children's books in libraries across the country had dropped, and national attention to the problem of "why Dick and Jane can't read" forced libraries to begin to reevaluate their exclusion policy and to allow selected series to circulate. A 1966 paper entitled "In Defense of Trash" called for a revision of the criteria by which librarians measure literary quality and argued that libraries were in effect "censoring" public taste by not stocking series. That charge is a particularly sensitive one to librarians who have become ardent about upholding the Library Bill of Rights (American Library Association Council). At the same time, and in reaction to this new acceptance of series books, criticism which specifically addressed issues of racism and sexism in the series books was being articulated. In general, though, by the 1970s librarians and educators were taking a stance that defended children's freedom to read broadly and freely. It was clear that reading was no longer a favored activity among children, and librarians sought to redress that situation. Anything that could get them to read, and away from the television, was worth championing.

Yet the debate goes on. In the summer of 1991 it flared up in Boulder, Colorado, when the children's librarian at the Boulder Public Library was asked to justify her policy of not buying Nancy Drew, the Hardy Boys, and other older series. She defended the library's position on the grounds that the books were "sexist, racist and poorly written" and that "library money is better spent on other books" (Hoover, May 26, 1991). Cries of censorship ensued. An editorial in the Boulder paper denounced the library's policy, arguing that popularity of books was reason enough to stock them ("Mystery"). Other libraries in the area were quick to disassociate themselves from the Boulder library policy: "We carry them because they are classics," a librarian at a different institution said. "We want kids to come in and read. We can't be telling them what to read" (Hoover, May 26, 1991). In the end, the Boulder library was forced by public outcry—and what the children's librarian called the "nostalgia factor"—to reconsider. Nancy Drew and friends would be stocked but kept in a special collection; they would be in the library but not cataloged (Hoover, July 11, 1991).

What this recent controversy makes clear is the degree to which the debate has shifted its focus over the years. The stance "We can't be telling them what to read" would have been unthinkable to a librarian fifty years ago. Yet this position appears to be the prevailing one in our time. Reading itself has become the goal, and anything that helps promote it will have the support of the majority of children's librarians in this country. The content and quality of children's reading have become secondary, at least in the arena of public discussion. The original reason for the exclusion of the older series books from the Boulder library—that they were racist and sexist— was never examined in any depth, for example. It is also worth noting that the books that were called "trash" not so many years ago are today being hailed as "classics," a reversal which should at the very least make us leery of either label.

CHAPTER 12

Using Series as Bait
in the Public Library

Barbara Black

As a librarian I am charged with the selection of high-quality materials. This mandate presents a problem for librarians faced with the decision whether or not to purchase mass-marketed series books. For some professionals the decision is clear-cut. Series books, the consensus seems to be, are not quality. Developed from a strict formula, filled with clichés, they move from climax to climax with little effort at description, characterization, motivation, or explanation. It is argued that they do not open children and young adults to new interests or ideas. Moreover, such formulaic fiction cannot help but perpetuate stereotypes or create new ones. Series rely on the creation of familiar characters who appear in each book in new situations. With this predictability stereotypes inevitably follow. The reader needn't think about how characters will respond because they will certainly respond in the predictable way that readers have come to expect from others in the series.

A good book surprises. It draws readers in with characters that an author has taken time to develop, characters who are rich in background and motivation and with whom the author has—and the reader can develop—a relationship. Those opposed to series books in the public library have mustered some compelling arguments. Children's literature is a bridge to adult reading, and it is important that the bridge lead to works of substance and not merely to the same rung on the adult ladder.

I work in an institution that believes strongly that the most important part of the selection equation for a public library is the readers—their interests and tastes, what they choose for themselves to read. I think that it's a value that we as librarians must all have. While I personally consider some of the series books to be schlock I think it's presumptuous of me to think someone shouldn't read what I would choose not to. Even the series that I think are not particularly well written I regard as bait. I think they give me credibility with kids, particularly with reluctant readers. If I choose to exclude these from my collection, they would look at what I do select as "the other." To exclude the popular series books in a sense excludes these readers from my library.

I. don't spend a large percentage of my budget on series. The thing I fear most about series fiction is that it can quickly eat up a never-adequate budget. Even if we're up to no. 80 of a series, we still have to have no. 1 for the kid who is just beginning. Replacement also has an impact on the budget: the books fall apart quickly because they're read so much. One solution is to buy multiple copies of the books and bind one, so there's usually one that will hold up a great deal longer. I would have real difficulty *not* buying these popular books for our young adult collection, just as I would assume that an adult fiction selector would have difficulty justifying excluding popular adult fiction not considered "quality" by some arbiters of taste.

I don't promote series books such as Nancy Drew, Sweet Valley High, or the R. L. Stine books because I don't have to. These are books that sell themselves, and kids come to them naturally. I acknowledge that they exist and often use them to draw a kid to another series such as the Tillerman series by Cynthia Voigt or the Anastasia books by Lois Lowry. I think that position is perhaps unique to public libraries, which have become a bit more populist since the days when ruling capitalists used the library to pass on their gentility. As a public librarian I have the unique position of being able to emphasize the pleasure of reading and I always try to remain grounded in that.

As a librarian I believe my responsibilities go beyond the mere selection of books. My role involves promotion of books as well. I do have a responsibility to guide kids through what they're reading.

I think it's important that we see that as a part of what we do. And given that, series books do have a place. A lot of what kids like about series is the familiarity of the characters, and I think other series, like the Cynthia Voigt books, take that familiarity of character and expand upon it with great depth of characterization and situation.

CHAPTER 13

Series Books and Competing Mandates
in the School Library

Joel Shoemaker

Ever since I received the invitation to participate in the Nancy
Drew Conference every piece of paper and every journal that
crossed my desk seemed to relate in some way to this topic. One
article that came my way talked about the library as passport to the
universe. This quote particularly struck me: "I read voraciously
and indiscriminately: Nancy Drew, biographies from everyone from
Amelia Earhart to Herbert Hoover, histories and junk. I also read
over and over fairy tales. 'The Ugly Duckling' was comfort that someday I too might be graceful as a swan. 'The Emperor's New Clothes'
confirmed my hunch that adults were not all-knowing and all powerful despite what some of them said" (O'Toole, 78).

Just a mention of Nancy Drew, in passing; but in what company? With fairy tales that carried subversive messages, and "histories and junk"! The reader acknowledges, in retrospect, that the
quality of the books she read varied tremendously, but recognizes
that the process of reading voraciously empowered her to find her
own place in the world. How critically important (and commonly experienced) this developmental stage remains today.

Peter Dickinson, a well-known author, suggests that while kids
shouldn't be encouraged to read rubbish it's better to read something than nothing. He quotes Dr. Samuel Johnson: "I'd like a child
to read first any book that happens to engage his attention. Because
you have done him a great deal when you have brought him enter-

tainment from a book. He'll get to better things afterwards" (Dickinson, 7). In a book called *Genreflecting*, Dr. Johnson is again quoted to Boswell: "Sir, I would put a child into a library and let him read at his choice" (Rosenberg and Herald, xv).

In an article entitled "Secret in the Trash Bin: On the Perennial Popularity of Juvenile Series Books" Anne Scott MacLeod analyzes the appeal of books such as Nancy Drew: "These books offer reassurance. They are predictable and familiar, they present relationships that are very stable" (127). And Nancy was so capable and accomplished:

> There is literally nothing that Nancy cannot do. She solves mysteries, of course, that's her forte. But in the course of each mystery adventure she demonstrates competence in dozens of other things as well. She drives "speedily down the road" and maneuvers her car expertly into parking spaces. She arranges and plans, advises lawyers and bankers, takes part in plays and emergency operations at a moment's notice (always credibly); repairs a damaged painting so that an expert can barely detect it. She rides, plays golf and tennis and swims well enough to be an Olympic champion. She is equal to any situation, keeping her head when all about her are losing theirs, and, in contrast to her chums who have more typical feminine reactions: "George and Bess were doing the best they could but were frightened and unable to work calmly," Nancy is always able to work calmly. And when she has succeeded—as she always does—no one is jealous. Nancy is simply admired and respected more for her accomplishment. (MacLeod, 137)

MacLeod goes on to state that the real secret of Nancy's success, in her opinion, is that she shows a model of equality, respect, and power. Those three things taken together, and in particular, she suggests, for young female readers, add up to their real appeal. I like the fact that there is something subversive about Nancy Drew. She does things that the adults around her can't do and that empowers kids to go beyond expectations, too.

There are critics on the other side of this issue who, when read with a certain voice, seem positively snooty. Mary Louise Lake is a librarian from Florida who entered the fray in 1970 with an article called "What's Wrong with Series Books?": "It's unrealistic to expect people who have not had a wide experience with good literature to be able to recognize a superior style out of hand. One can learn the signatures of literature as listed in a book but only wide reading and comparison will enable one to evaluate merit" (1109).

Indeed, well-respected authors have taken a similar stance. Here's James Thurber to E. B. White: "The United States does not read the right books in large numbers, which may be what is the matter with the United States and what is right about the books" (Heines, 255). To me, this smacks of intellectual snobbery and elitism.

The critics of Nancy Drew and other series books are not themselves above stereotyping when they call the authors of these books "hired hacks." Mildred Wirt Benson and some others who are gifted and prolific authors who chose, for whatever reasons, to write under pseudonyms are not deserving of that reference.

I would be willing to capitulate on one point of criticism of series books, however, and that has to do with the matter of racism in many of the pre-1960s books. There is no morally correct rationalization for promoting racist attitudes in books today. Yet, like the Holocaust, our racist history can't be denied; instead, our kids have to learn about our past and learn from it. If one of the ways they can learn about it is by reading fiction in which changing racial attitudes are shown, I think that might be a valuable experience. It should be mentioned that our kids don't come to us as a blank slate—*tabula rasa*—they come with a lifetime of experiences. And they are remarkably adept at sorting out what is real and current from what is not applicable to them in their lives.

Who decides what books to read, the librarian or the reader? I would firmly come down on the side of the reader making that choice. I must trust the readers to make their decisions about what to do with the information they get from the book and trust to their own good sense to put it into context with the rest of their life.

Having said that, I must acknowledge that my everyday working-world reality poses some limitations to this philosophy. If the highest demand in a library is for a particular type of literature, why shouldn't that be the librarian's highest priority? The answer to that is contained in two documents that I am obliged to keep in mind as I make selection decisions for my junior high school library: the Library Bill of Rights and my district's selection policy.

The first three paragraphs of the Library Bill of Rights read:

1. Books and other library resources should be provided for the interest, information and enlightenment of all people in the community the library serves. Materials shall not be excluded because of the origin or background of those contributing to their creation.

2. Libraries should provide materials and information providing all points of view on current or historical issues. Materials should not be proscribed or removed because of partisan or doctrinal disapproval.

3. Libraries should challenge censorship in the fulfillment of their responsibilities, provide information and enlightenment. (American Library Association Council)

In the first paragraph the Bill of Rights addresses the issue of request and student demand. The second paragraph speaks to the issue of political correctness and social attitudes. And the third section charges us as professionals to fight censorship in whatever form it might take.

Now consider some key points of my school district's selection policy: "The responsibility for selection of materials . . . is delegated to the certificated staff employed by the school district . . . to implement, support and enrich the curriculum," it states in paragraph one. This says that my first priority is to serve the curriculum, not to serve popular demand.

The criteria to be used in the selection of materials: "Materials should support and be consistent with the educational goals and objectives of the district. Materials shall meet high standards of quality in factual content and presentation. Materials shall be appropriate for the subject area and for the age, ability level, emotional and social development of the students for whom the materials are selected. Materials shall have aesthetic, literary or social value."

You can see some areas of potential conflict here. The next paragraph is a fairly recent addition: "Materials shall be chosen where appropriate to help students gain an awareness of and to foster respect for diversity. Materials shall be designated to motivate students and staff to examine their own attitudes and behaviors and to comprehend their duties, responsibilities, rights and privileges as participating citizens in a pluralistic, nonsexist, democratic society." That's quite a complex charge.

And the next paragraph presents a loophole you can drive a Mack truck through: "Materials shall be selected for their strengths rather than rejected for their weaknesses."

The policy also states: "Biased or slanted materials may be provided to meet specific curriculum or objectives." If the issue is racism, you can choose materials which are racist in order to teach that subject or about ethnic groups or about history. For instance, there are revisionists who say the Holocaust never happened. Doesn't this policy suggest that we need to have materials in the library that show their point of view?

We've got conflicting demands here. Now, in fact, in my school library I have about five Nancy Drew books. Two old ones and three of the newer Nancy Drew Files. I teach seventh and eighth graders right now and they are not reading these books in my collection. I have had no requests for these books for the two years I've been in this library. Part of the reason for this may be that there is a very extensive collection at the Public Library downtown. If I had a lot of demand for those books I think I could justify them within this selection policy. But I don't have the demand, so I'm not buying them.

The problems I face are typical of school librarians everywhere: limited budget and highly varied and very demanding patrons including faculty, staff, administrators, students, and parents. The budget issue is a serious one, and it affects decisions I make on a daily basis. I also think, however, that librarians sometimes hide behind that issue to justify the decision not to purchase certain materials which, in fact, they reject on other, perhaps unspecified, bases. It's a challenging mandate that is put before us librarians as we strive to find the best balance between demands of these often competing policies and philosophies.

CHAPTER 14

Nancy Drew and
the Myth of White Supremacy

Donnarae MacCann

y intention in this essay is to examine the Nancy Drew books within the historical context of the myth of white supremacy in the period leading up to the 1930 publication of the first books in the Nancy Drew series. As a prefatory note, I would add that since the subject here is literature we should be considering artistic form as a necessary part of our discussion. As a guiding principle, the white supremacy myth is never a necessity of form. In short, books do not have to be racist for any reason whatsoever and certainly not to achieve artistic form.

The main subject is the social and political setting surrounding the first Nancy Drew publications. At the time when Nancy first appeared on the scene, a consensus about the character of African Americans had been established in mainstream America. In 1971 the historian George Fredrickson summarized the elements of that consensus as it existed in the late eighteenth and early nineteenth centuries in his work *The Black Image in the White Mind: The Debate on Afro-American Character and Destiny, 1817–1914*. Idus Newby, in *Jim Crow's Defense: Anti-Negro Thought in America, 1900–1930*, has also traced this consensus and has found that the elements had not changed substantially in 1930, the year that *The Secret of the Old Clock* and two other Nancy Drew mysteries were first published (Newby, xi). There are several ingredients in this consensus. These are not new ideas, but they are important.

First, the white population generally agreed that blacks were different from whites intellectually and temperamentally as well as physically. Second, they believed that blacks were inferior to whites in fundamental ways, especially with respect to intelligence. Third, they believed that the gap between blacks and whites was permanent or subject to change only after a very long evolutionary process. Fourth, they believed that intermarriage was to be condemned because to cross such so-called diverse types would be damaging to civilization—that is, white people believed that the qualities that produced progress would be weakened by racial mixing. Fifth, they believed that, given black inferiority, prejudice against blacks was natural whenever blacks aspired to legal, political, or economic equality. Therefore equal status was not possible in the foreseeable future.

These various dimensions of the white supremacy myth had support from groups at various points on the political spectrum. White extremists joined in this consensus and the so-called moderates and reformers were also believers in the assumption that blacks were permanently inferior. They differed only on matters of policy (Newby, x). Reformers believed that the so-called inferior group would be less troublesome if people had better opportunities. The moderates believed that tolerance and forbearance was the proper response to so-called black limitations. The extremists believed that harsh forms of repression were sad but necessary. Some extremists recommended deportation; some, sterilization. And one congressman from Georgia, James Griggs, even suggested extermination. According to Congressman Griggs, "The utter extermination of a race of people is inexplicably sad, yet if its existence endangers the welfare of mankind it is fitting that it should be swept away" (Newby, 189). Griggs was referring to African Americans as the group that he would "sweep away."

It is astonishing to hear a representative of the government suggesting genocide, but racism was being promoted in academic and artistic circles as well as in the government and the discourse was often extremist in nature. The much celebrated novelist William Faulkner, for example, stated in 1931: "Negroes would be better off under the conditions of slavery than they are today." "Negroes," he said, "would be better off because they would have someone to look after them" (Newby, 70). Faulkner does not say that *he* would be better off if enslaved. His premise is that blacks require a unique social system because they cannot function as ordinary humans.

One would think that religious leaders would take a different view. But they also attempted to explain that blacks were less than human. One excerpt shows how religionists sometimes argued the case. In a book called *The Negro: What Is His Ethnological Status?* the Reverend Buchner H. Payne had this to say: "As Adam was the *Son of God*, and as Adam was light [white] and in Him is no darkness [black] *at all*, how could God then be the Father of the negro, as like produces like. And if God could not be the *Father* of the blacks because he was white, how could our Savior . . . carry such a *damned color* into heaven where all were white?" (Payne, 87–88).

Some writers of religious books insisted that they were on the side of science when they argued that black people were really beasts rather than humans. They were using the same rationale as the so-called scientists who placed African Americans on an evolutionary scale making them closer to apes than to people. Members of the scientific community used Darwin's treatment of the "survival of the fittest" theory to predict that blacks could not survive in the face of superior Europeans. Similarly, historians used this argument and insisted that social betterment programs would only interfere with this cosmic plan that elevated some groups and sent others into decline.

Ideas like these from historians, scientists, and theologians influenced professional educators as well as the general public. The various campaigns against African American education included the argument that blacks would become unfit for the type of work that white society demanded of them. A series of quotations gives the feel of what this argument was like. One southern writer complained at the turn of the century that "the higher culture of 'coloured universities' . . . merely spoils a plough-hand or housemaid" (Newby, 177). With amazing candor the chairman of the board of education in one North Carolina county said: "Compulsory education may be fatal to the cotton crop" (Anderson 1988, 96). The chairman of the faculty of the University of Virginia said: "Whites should cease to support free schools for the blacks because the schools tended to make some Negroes able to compete with whites" (Anderson, 96). An editorial writer for the *Richmond Dispatch* stated in all seriousness: "Many families distinctly prefer nurses and cooks who cannot read and write" (Anderson, 97).

We can see in these quotes that the white supremacy myth and the institutions that support it are self-serving inventions on the part of the white establishment. And so determined was the white mainstream in its insistence in holding blacks in menial jobs that white educators associated a liberal education for blacks with criminality. Here is a quote from a 1910 article in the *Columbia University Studies in History, Economics and Public Law* that makes this link: "The young educated negroes are not a force for good in the community but for evil. . . . They condone the vices which are increasing in the race . . . their moral natures are miserably perverted" (Odum, 41–42). And in even blunter terms, politicians claimed that increased black criminality and decreasing illiteracy were "linked like Siamese Twins" (Newby, 178).

It is not surprising that children's books tended to reinforce the myth of inferiority and even criminality. And both themes are present in *The Secret of the Old Clock* (1930) and *The Hidden Staircase* (1930). When Nancy Drew meets the African American caretaker of a cottage that she is investigating in *The Secret of the Old Clock*, the reader meets a set of familiar stereotypes about black character. The essence of the whole characterization is that this black American is incapable of moderation. And although the intent was probably to create humor, what we see is humor in the form of contempt. The author presents him as a drunkard, a liar, a person who has constant run-ins with the police, an unreliable employee, and a fool. As you watch the details of the character emerge in just a few pages of text, you feel as if you have been transported to a black-face minstrel show and are watching a skit in which actors blackened their faces and drew huge white mouths as a way to ridicule the African American.

Like a character in black-face, Jeff Tucker, the African American in this story, behaves nonsensically in every scene, even when he is being useful to Nancy as a witness to the robbery she is describing to the police. His so-called comic nature works as a demarcation line between two cultural worlds, one of which is irrevocably inferior. Specifically, this is what happens: Jeff comes up to the cottage he's supposed to be taking care of and finds that the furniture has disappeared. He is still somewhat drunk and, after he releases Nancy from the closet where she is a captive, his imagination runs away with him. He exclaims, "Suppose you had o' starv'd ta death in dah, or da house had burned down or you was scared into fits?" (141).

Nancy calms him down as one would calm down an excited child. When she questions him about why he was not guarding the cottage as he was paid to do, he replies: "I was just all fed up bein' a caih-taker. It ain't such an excitin' life, Miss, and while I's done sowing all mah wild oats, I still sows a little rye now an then." "Yes Jeff," says Nancy, "I can smell that on your breath right now" (141). At this point Jeff describes what has recently happened to him: after being lured into a fancy car by a white man who later offers him a drink, Jeff ultimately ends up lying in a hotel completely plastered. Here the writer adds a scene that ridicules African American religion. Jeff says: "Aftah while I didn't feel like I was ridin' in no automobeel at all. I thought that de chariot had done gone and swung low an' I was a' bein' wafted off to some place in the genreel direction o' heaven" (142). The reference here, of course, is to an African American spiritual.

Finally we are given a picture of Jeff's police record. He tells Nancy that the police have run him in more than once, just because he was enjoying himself. And Nancy says, "I suppose you can tell me where the jail is?" "'Deed I can," says Jeff. "Fact is, dis is my *favorite* jail" (148). The police are given an account of what has happened and then Jeff lies about his part in the adventure, saying that he was kidnapped and given a sleeping powder which knocked him unconscious. The story continues with Jeff rolling his eyes and trying to sober up, referring to himself disparagingly as a "black boy," although he is a father of seven children. Every detail in the scenes with Jeff points to blacks as unruly, untrustworthy, dissipated, and mentally deficient.

It is worth noting that in the revised edition of *The Secret of the Old Clock* (1959) Jeff, the African American, has been turned into a white man, and it would be hard to find a more respectful, affectionate, and intelligent portrait of a working-class person. The white Jeff Tucker uses a little down-home slang from time to time, as when he says, "I was plain hornswoggled" (117), but he comes off as a hero: Nancy promises to intercede on his behalf so he will not lose his job over the robbery. He was certainly not on a drunken binge when the thieves entered the house, but he had been lured to a place supposedly to ward off trespassers and had been captured and locked in a closet.

The black character in the second book in the series, *The Hid-*

den Staircase, also has been removed, and white characters have been substituted in later editions, probably because the black woman in that book is an accomplice to the crimes committed. A couple of quotations illustrate the point. Nancy's friend refers to this African American woman by saying she looks as though she were an ogre and Nancy says, "I never saw a more surly looking creature. She looks positively vicious" (132). She is the villain of the piece, in part, so this is not an illogical statement, given the setting and characterization, but throughout this woman is described as fat and slovenly and she speaks in the usual dialect—really a kind of mock-dialect since the emphasis is not on the oral qualities but on suggesting a lack of intelligence.

Commenting in 1989 about the new editions of these books, Paul Deane (who wrote a dissertation at Harvard in 1966 on series books) says that African American characters were usually removed altogether, as in this case. In short, the series book literature has become largely an all-white literature. Deane asks the question: "How can healthy ideas be developed about persons who never appear?" (Deane 1989, 160). Children are not even allowed vicarious contact through literature. He is, I think, rightly appalled and baffled by the continuing invisibility of blacks in series books.

When Edward Stratemeyer began the Old Glory series in 1898 with a book called *Under Dewey at Manila, or, The War Fortunes of a Castaway*, he had the captain of the ship speak these lines: "Give me a white man for stevedore work, every time. The wust of 'em are worth three niggers!" Here he is referring to the Kanakas, the indigenous people of the Hawaiian Islands. But he calls them "niggers." African Americans, it seems, provide Stratemeyer's point of reference when he casts aspersions upon people of color. And members of the press who reviewed his books did not object. A Boston newspaper columnist described Stratemeyer as having acquired a wonderfully successful knack for writing an interesting, educational story that would appeal to young people. The Nancy Drew stories evolved within this same ethnocentric intellectual world that applauded Stratemeyer's early publishing ventures.

But what is it in our present society that compels publishers to erase African Americans completely rather than include them as fully human individuals? What do children of color feel when they see themselves excluded from such an important cultural phenomenon as literature? What do they feel when they see their language and culture reduced to inferiority? What happens when the so-called mainstream white child sees black characters as incapable, insignificant, or unattractive? And what happens when young people who are white see racism receiving approval in children's literature? What kind of society is it that entertains one group of children at the expense of another? These are questions we must continue to address. I close with the United Nations Declaration on the Rights of the Child. Principle number 10 reads: "The child shall be protected from any practice which may foster racial, religious or any other forms of discrimination."

CHAPTER 15

Fixing Nancy Drew:
African American Strategies for Reading

Njeri Fuller

I began reading Nancy Drew books when I was in third grade
because I was tired of reading picture books and wanted to read
chapter books. The first Nancy Drew book I read was *The Secret of
the Old Clock* (1959). I read the revised editions from which most
minorities were eliminated. I read Nancy Drew from third grade
until I was a senior in high school. I would check out three or four or
five at a time; it was nothing for me to check out at least ten books
and read them all in two weeks.

I loved that Nancy was so smart. She could do amazing things.
She had this freedom, her father was proud of her, her friends all respected her—and she had a car. I loved the mystery plots; I would
try to figure out what happened before the mystery ended, try to put
together all the pieces before she did, try to think like Nancy Drew.
But each time I would come away questioning the descriptions of the
characters. There are very specific descriptions in each Nancy Drew
book; you remember that Bess is slightly short, plump, and has
blond hair. You know that George is tall, thin, and athletic and has
short cropped hair. Nancy Drew had blond hair in a cute kind of bob.
And of course there were descriptions of Ned. Of all the people she
encountered, though, none were people of color unless they were the
bad guys.

A book I specifically remember is *The Mystery of the 99 Steps*
(1966), in which Nancy goes to France. The criminal in that book is

Monsieur Neuf, Mr. Nine. He was described as having a swarthy complexion. I had to look up "swarthy" in the dictionary because I didn't know what it meant. And when I found out it meant a person of dark complexion I began to wonder what nationality this man was. Well, it said he was French, but he had dark skin. This made no sense to me as a third grader because the idea of minority groups in foreign countries was unreal to me.

What I found myself doing was trying to take myself away from the descriptions in the books by making Nancy a black girl like me. In reading about Nancy Drew, I began imagining that I *was* Nancy Drew. I would also make some of her friends black. I couldn't get past the description of Bess, though; she was *too* blond. But George seemed the closest in description to African American friends I might have. She was described as being athletic, and that's usually one of the terms you hear associated with African Americans. If nothing else, we can do sports, or so says the stereotype.

I wonder now whether any of my friends, if they read Nancy Drew, felt the same way I did and how many of them were able to "fix" Nancy the way I did by making her into themselves, by making Nancy's life their life. Her world certainly wasn't our world. Although I grew up in a suburban middle-class neighborhood, I didn't have a housekeeper who had taken care of me since the "tender age of two" (that's a phrase from the books that I will never forget; I have never thought of the age of two as particularly tender). My friends and I didn't have prominent attorneys as fathers; we didn't have the freedom to just pick up and go to all parts of the world. Our world wasn't all white. And I wonder what kind of hurt these books have caused some people. Here was a heroine whom we wanted to admire, who was our age, who had so much intellectual ability and so much fun. But her world didn't include any of us.

When we talk about Nancy and her blond friend Bess and her athletic friend George and Ned and all the crew, we have to question from whose point of view we are writing or speaking and ask what the reader is going to take away from the work.

Some of the questions raised by Donnarae MacCann are really good questions, particularly as we look at the new Nancy Drew books that have come out recently. I was very excited when I learned that they were updating the Nancy Drew books. I expected that she was going to be more in line with what I imagined a nineties woman would be. But I was disappointed to find the same formulas. There are no African Americans, there are no Asians, no Latinos in the new books, unless they happen to have a small part, like working in a restaurant, or they happen to witness the crime. Nancy solves the crime; Bess and George still help her.

I can no longer read Nancy Drew as I did when I was younger and had no other frame of reference. I've tried to read her just as I used to, nonstop and fully absorbed. But I just cannot do that. I see all the flaws, all the problems. I can no longer accept that Nancy Drew world. Now I am a grown woman who thinks that people have the right to be depicted as they really are.

Why is it, when you look at literature, television, newspapers, and other media, that minority groups are disproportionately shown as criminals, welfare recipients, and uneducated individuals? I am an African American woman who graduated at the top of my class. And I'm not the only one. Reading Nancy Drew would have you believe that a person like me is an anomaly, a special case. That's why I question these books today. It's sad to me that the newest books of the Nancy Drew series still consist of an all-white world where other people who look like me are still on the fringes of society.

There are a lot of things about Nancy that I really like and admire. But what bothers me most now is that I really can't see how making someone invisible can be considered a good thing. I believe that there have to be books where everyone is included, because a lot of children don't live where they can come in contact with someone of another race or religious belief. But in books you're able to meet all different kinds of people from wizards to dragons. So why not someone who's African American, or Asian American, or Jewish?

It is puzzling to me why it isn't more economically viable for books to be written about minorities. In the television industry that market has been recognized. The Nielsen ratings have shown that there is a black audience and that African Americans watch television more hours than European Americans. But I think part of the problem has to do with the perception that the majority of minorities in this country are poor and can't afford these things and wouldn't read them anyway, and so the products are not meant for them.

In my hometown neighborhood, where there is a large concentration of African Americans, we have a mall where the bookstore recently closed because they said it wasn't making a profit. That caused a whole flurry of petitions by people wanting to keep that bookstore in the mall because it was the only bookstore in the area. They closed it anyway, although as a concession a satellite library was opened. But that library has only a few books that are Afrocentric in nature and it just doesn't offer the choices that you have with a large chain bookstore. I think it's asking a little much for people to get on the bus and ride for thirty minutes or an hour to go in search of better reading material.

The Nancy Drew books didn't destroy me. But I have to ask: when will there ever be books we can call classics in which I am represented in a wonderful way? And when will such books become as accessible in libraries and bookstores as are their mainstream white counterparts?

CHAPTER 16

Befriending Nancy Drew
across Cultural Boundaries

Dinah Eng

I used to love reading Nancy Drew books. I'm one of those readers who has a vague impression in the back of her mind that Nancy was great, but I can't tell you a thing that happened in any of these books. I just remember that she was so wonderful and that I couldn't wait to read the next book.

My parents came to America from China and my first spoken language was Chinese. I was about three or four years old when I learned to speak English. The person who taught me how to speak English was a Baptist missionary. She used to give me all kinds of books to read, so by the time I got to kindergarten I was already starting to read little books. I was in the third grade when I started reading Nancy Drew. My parents tried to get me to look at math and other things in school and not spend so much time reading. Even my teachers at school said to me, "Well, don't you think Nancy Drew is a little advanced for you? Why don't you go back to the Bobbsey Twins?" But I remember thinking, I don't care what other people say, I really enjoy reading the mysteries in these books. I like it that this girl character gets to do all kinds of things. So I kept reading them.

At the time, we were living in New Jersey; when I was nine years old my family moved to San Francisco, which was very traumatic for me because I had to leave all my friends behind. I lived in a New Jersey town where we were the only Chinese family at the time and all my friends were white. Then we moved to San Francisco and we lived in Chinatown, where suddenly we were surrounded by all these people who looked like our family. But there was nobody around who looked like any of my friends. So I took Nancy Drew as my friend. After school I would go to used bookstores to try to find other volumes I could trade and read. My parents wanted to push me into going to Chinese school after regular school so I could learn more about writing and speaking Chinese as they did at home. I didn't want to do that; I wanted to go read Nancy Drew books. So I just kept reading these mystery stories. When I think of what Nancy Drew meant to me as a child I see her as a friend I could spend time with, because I was very lonely at that point.

As Njeri Fuller says, in the media there aren't many images of minorities. When we don't see ourselves on television, in the newspaper, or in other media, it's as though we don't exist. As a child I think that translated into the feeling that I wasn't really Asian. I could look in the mirror; I could see that my face was different from everybody else's, but inside I felt that I was white. I felt like I was Nancy Drew at times. Being Chinese American, I had to deal with a culture in which my parents said to me, "You're Chinese, you must believe this and this." At school, people said, "You're American so you must believe this and this." So I had constant cultural conflicts to resolve.

When I think about what I got out of reading Nancy Drew, there are a lot of things I'm grateful for, even though there were few, if any, Asian characters in those books. There was Nancy's intuition. I think that we women are often more in tune with ourselves and with things that go on in the world around us than men are, and I believe we all need to listen to ourselves and what we are feeling inside. Nancy Drew is a very curious person who seeks out adventure, and I think one of the things she teaches is that there are many things in life around us that we don't understand, and it's good to be open to possibilities.

Today I don't read mystery stories in the classic sense. Most of the books I tend to read are religion, philosophy, even science fiction or fantasy. These speak to me of the mystery of life, rather than just a whodunit or a crime. For me, the mystery of life is the one we all face and want to solve in many ways. And I suppose the answers are going to be very different for all of us. But one of the answers for me is that I truly believe we are alive to love each other. That's one of the things that Nancy Drew also teaches, I think, in that she is a very caring, compassionate character who always seems to reach out to people who are in trouble and in need. That's something I learned from her as well.

Nancy seemed to be somebody who was not shy. She could reach out to strangers and talk to them, no matter who they were. I considered myself a very shy person in that I tended not to speak to anyone unless spoken to first. Culturally, as an Asian American, I was taught to be on the quiet side, not to be assertive and not to question authority. So when I read the antithesis to these attributes in a fictional character I thought, well, that sounds better than what I'm taught at home. I think I probably assimilated some of her independence as well.

As an Asian American, I look at children's literature and other books and see that with very few exceptions there really aren't very many books that have minority characters. I've begun to respond personally to this lack by writing my first novel, which deals with Asian American women. While it's not in the format of a mystery, part of the reason I wrote it is to talk about being Asian American, being female, and to look at the mystery of life and who we are.

When I go back and look at some of the Nancy Drew books now, I don't see many references to Asians and the ones I do see tend to be supporting characters who didn't have very much to do or say. But because of the joy of sharing an imaginary adventure with Nancy, I like to think I've gone on to spark that same joy in others who read what I write.

PART III

Collecting and Studying Nancy Drew

If I were to choose a book character to come alive to make this a better world, it would be Nancy. But Nancy is not a real person and never will be. Her books can make a difference though. She influences many young girls growing up in a cruel world. I think a book character, by displaying honesty, courage, persistence, generosity and by valuing good friends can make a difference. If all characters in books and movies were like Nancy, the world might be a better place to live.

—CLAIRE VICTORIA FOLKINS,

AGE 11, GRADE 5,

PENN ELEMENTARY SCHOOL,

NORTH LIBERTY, IOWA

ost of the factual information that we have about Nancy Drew's history, like other aspects of popular culture, has been painstakingly unearthed by the tireless digging of ardent fans and collectors of series books. Because these mass-produced products have been disparaged by book people ranging from librarians to teachers and fine booksellers, the books that have been sold by the millions would be lost for future study if not for the collectors.

Inspired mostly by the nostalgia reflected in the stories told throughout this book, collectors have devoted their leisure time and disposable income to finding, accumulating, and getting to know everything they can about the books. They have formed organizations of like-minded collectors of old series books, developed newsletters and fanzines, and held conventions and informal meetings to buy, sell, and trade books and to exchange information about them.

Although there are organizations, newsletters, and conventions of collectors and fans of other less popular series, such as the Judy Bolton and Betsy Tacy books, no institutions have formed around Nancy Drew in particular. Her collectors and fans have dispersed themselves among the more general groups of collectors and gleaned information from the study of other series. At least part of the explanation is that information about the Stratemeyer Syndicate and its books has been closely held and shrouded in mystery. First Harriet Stratemeyer Adams and the staff of the syndicate perpetuated the secrecy surrounding the ghostwriting process that made its books so popular. More recently, the Stratemeyer business has been engulfed in a large entertainment conglomerate which had shipped the company files off to exile in a warehouse in New Jersey.

The collectors have pieced together the chronology of the hundreds of editions of Nancy Drew that now number more than two hundred, using every skill in the detective's tool kit. They have dissected, cataloged, and committed to memory the developing characters, the plots, and even the dialogue particularly of the original editions. Like Christian fundamentalists in full command of the text of the Bible, some collectors can cite chapter and verse in response to virtually any question on the details of the stories. In fact, we have called on their store of knowledge quite often when readers and journalists have posed questions we could not answer.

As they have accumulated books and gathered information

about the books as material products, the collectors have by necessity probed the conditions of production, the arrangements with the
writers, and, as Geoffrey Lapin reports in chapter 5, the identity of
Carolyn Keene. To explore this closely guarded information, collectors have treasured every note and memo and ancillary document
they could find, both as material objects having sentimental and economic value and as useful information to help answer questions.

Like the collectors, many of the academic students of Nancy
Drew were led to the study of series books by rediscovering fond
memories of their childhoods, although some approached the subject
retrospectively through the controversies among librarians, educators, and cultural critics. Even in the field of popular culture, and
certainly in those disciplines that have officially discredited the
books, the study of children's series fiction, especially girls' fiction,
has not been central or highly valued. The sort of passion that drives
collectors is suspect in scholars, so scholars have, with some exceptions, done their work without using or acknowledging the work of
the collectors.

As the study of kids' series books has not been quite respect-
able, researchers have for the most part approached these books
quite conservatively. They have encountered the books and their history through the theories and systematic methods of the humanist
and the social scientist, which often distill the life and charm out of
the books. Their studies have been rather narrow. Suffering from the
same limited access to relevant information that the collectors have
encountered, they have contributed what collectors regard as relatively little so far to the store of factual knowledge about Nancy
Drew books that the collectors had already accumulated. And since
they overlook the work of collectors, they often get the facts wrong.

On the other hand, scholars have begun to move the study of
these books toward questions about their cultural significance and
the personal engagement of readers with them. In the process, they
are beginning to confer academic respectability on the interest in
these books that the collectors have long maintained. And they have
joined the collectors in their search for material to inform their interests. Together they have made the collection of children's series
books and manuscripts in libraries and archives newly important.

Despite the convergence of interests of collectors of Nancy

Drew and scholars and the fact that a few scholars are also collectors, their motives, methods, and world views on the value of the books and their respective stores of knowledge about them have kept them apart and in general quite suspicious or even contemptuous of each other. They remain at odds, for example, over what should be done with the most valuable of series book resources and memorabilia. While collectors see them as rare commodities with commercial value, as trophies to be individually owned and hoarded, scholars seek the assembly of documents into open but carefully guarded and well-cataloged library and archival collections for all to use.

As rediscoverers of Nancy Drew we came to the subject through an interest in throwing the whole subject open to exploration in a very public way. The object was to permit those who were merely faithful and devoted readers to learn about the objects of their affection from anyone who had insight and information to offer. In planning the conference, we drew on the work and experiences of both collectors and scholars, though navigating between them was sometimes tricky. Since we learned invaluable lessons from each group, we hoped the conference would bridge the chasm that divided them. Recognizing that might not happen, we planned a separate program for scholars on the day following the public conference, but opened it to anyone who wanted to attend. And a group of collectors, expecting they might feel out of place at a conference planned by academics, organized their own informal gathering at a local motel to buy, sell, and trade books and hold rump sessions.

One of the high points of the collectors' gathering was attracting Nancy Axelrad, one of the partners in the Stratemeyer Syndicate for many years. Having seen Mildred Benson on ABC News the first night of the conference, Axelrad decided to drive six hours the next day to attend. Finding the collectors' gathering, she agreed for the first time to respond to collectors' questions late into the night, filling in many gaps in their knowledge. As one of the scholars presented a paper the following day and speculated about the authorship of one of the books, Axelrad sat near the back of the auditorium, surrounded by enthralled collectors as she wrote out a list from memory of the writers and revisers of the books. And they learned that she had given that information and some syndicate records to the library at Yale University.

In the chapters that follow, collectors and librarians explicate their part in the Nancy Drew phenomenon from firsthand experience. As the accumulators and disseminators of information for the use of others with an interest in Nancy Drew, each of the people represented here discusses or makes evident the particular significance of the types of information he or she collects and makes public. At the same time, they convey the different values that ground their work and govern their approaches to the study of Nancy Drew. For the reader and new student of Nancy Drew, these pieces offer valuable information about where and how to begin or to expand their collections or research.

David Farah, who publishes *Farah's Guide* to Nancy Drew books, has probably accumulated more factual information about the many editions of the Nancy Drew books and their characteristics and value in the book collectors' market than any other person. He has produced ten editions of the *Guide*, gathering the information during his free time while he studied first optometry, then medicine, and most recently law, and earned degrees and licenses in each. Because he is regarded as *the* authority among many collectors of Nancy Drew, we considered his participation essential to planning a program credible to collectors. He is the person others seek out to ask detailed and specific questions, from how to determine the value of a particular edition of a book to which book features a plot with bluebirds in it (a question we once referred to him).

In a session on collecting Nancy Drew, Farah made an annotated presentation about the books and newsletters useful to those interested in learning more about collecting Nancy Drew and series books.[1] When he finished there was plenty of time for questions. The unedited transcript of the session resembled an interview or press conference with Farah. So that is the form in which we have presented his contribution in chapter 17. While it has the bumpy quality of its form, the interview also reveals a good deal about the process of collecting and the nature of research Farah has done to become the authority he is.

Gil O'Gara publishes the *Yellowback Library*, one of the series book newsletters, which frequently includes material on the Nancy Drew books and is an invaluable resource for devotees.[2] His story in chapter 18 about how he came to collect series books and publish the newsletter echoes stories many others could tell about their attraction to collecting Nancy Drew. As he describes the focus of the newsletter and its editorial policies, he highlights many issues of particular importance to collectors.

As several other essays in this book indicate, doing research on Nancy Drew and Stratemeyer series books has been difficult because the most valuable resources—the papers of the Stratemeyer Syndicate, which conducted its book packaging business in secret—have been unavailable for general use. A few researchers have gained access to a few of the papers here and there, as Geoffrey Lapin reports in chapter 5 that he did in exchange for lending Grosset & Dunlap first editions of the books Mildred Benson wrote. Nevertheless, the library and the archive remain important resources and hold materials of considerable value if one knows how to use them. And within a few years the Stratemeyer Syndicate papers will be available for researchers at the New York Public Library after they have been processed and cataloged.

Chapters 19 to 22 address what might otherwise be rather arcane issues, how archives and libraries acquire and process their collections and make information in them useful to researchers. But, like everything else that is part of the Nancy Drew phenomenon, these subjects open up new mysteries that have challenged professionals in both fields. In wide-ranging essays here, Esther Green Bierbaum in chapter 19 and Karen M. Mason in chapter 20 present the task of doing research on Mildred Wirt Benson's career and contribution to the Nancy Drew series as bibliographic mysteries.

Bierbaum, a library school professor who teaches cataloging among other subjects, focuses behind the scenes on the librarian's tools for finding and documenting authorship on the one hand and a writer's body of work on the other. In the process, she explicates how the derogation of series books among professional librarians over the years has affected collection and cataloging practices and makes doing research very difficult.

One of Karen Mason's first tasks on becoming the first director of the Iowa Women's Archives was to learn about the Mildred Wirt Benson papers and the Nancy Drew books she had never read so she could participate in the Nancy Drew Conference. The task took her to Toledo to meet Mildred Benson and discuss her work and the papers she had given to the Iowa archives and to computer databases and on-line catalogs of manuscript collections in other institutions.

Mason's essay in chapter 20 reflects these two activities. She begins by describing the materials in the Mildred Wirt Benson collection and illustrates how they provide insight into the process Benson followed in writing books other than Nancy Drew. The examples, like those given by Deidre Johnson in chapter 2, offer hints about what one might look for when the Stratemeyer materials become available.

In the second part of her essay, Mason picks up the research mystery Bierbaum introduced: how to find information about Mildred Benson and children's series books. While Bierbaum explores conventional research and public library resources, Mason pursues the mystery in guides to archive collections throughout the country. She, too, finds that the official disdain librarians have had for children's series books has made the search very difficult.

Following Mason, Robert A. McCown, who heads the Special Collections Department of the University of Iowa Libraries, in chapter 21 introduces us to the value to researchers and collectors of the university's unique collection of books by Iowa authors, including the works of Mildred Wirt Benson. Although the Nancy Drew books are in the Library of Congress, where their copyrights were registered, and other collections may have more complete runs of Nancy Drew, the Iowa collection offers the special quality of featuring virtually all of Mildred Benson's work. Therefore one can read the Nancy Drews in the context of the books, such as Penny Parker, which Benson regarded as her better work or all thirteen books she wrote under several pseudonyms in her busiest year (1939).

To say that it is difficult to do research on children's literature is not to say it is impossible, as the other writers in this section point out. In chapter 22 Karen Nelson Hoyle, curator of one of the largest and most important archival collection on children's literature, explains just where and how this work can be done and what one can find in the most important collections in the United States. Particularly interesting in her essay is her account of how those who have published work on the history of children's series books have done their research. She concludes by describing the strengths and emphases of the major collections.

NOTES

1. *Farah's Guide* includes information on series book periodicals and reference works. It is available from David Farah, 401 E. California Boulevard, #106, Pasadena, CA 91106. The 10th printing of about 500 pages costs $60.

2. Published by Yellowback Press, P.O. Box 36172, Des Moines, IA 50315. Subscriptions cost $30 a year.

CHAPTER 17

An Interview with David Farah

Could you explain how you started collecting Nancy Drews?
FARAH: I got my early Nancy Drews from my brother, who had
bought them at a garage sale. He had the early Mildred Wirt Benson
copies, so, although I was born in the 1950s, the Nancy Drews that I
read were actually editions from the 1940s. I grew up having fond
memories of those books. The Hardy Boys and the Tom Swift books
didn't really interest me that much; I forgot them quickly after reading them.

I was collecting paper memorabilia in general in the 1970s. You
may remember from school the *Classics Illustrated* magazines which
were printing serially. The way you could tell an earlier from a later
edition of the same number was from the list of magazines already
published in the advertisements. I was buying Nancy Drews at the
same time and they used a similar system in their advertisements;
as more books were published they changed their ads. This is how I
learned to date the books. So I would go into dealers' stores to buy the
books and would be told that all these books were first editions. It was
obviously untrue, but I didn't have much success when I tried to point
out to a dealer that it couldn't be a first edition published in 1930
when the ad in the back of the book lists books published in 1960.

So in 1975 I started writing down in a notebook what I knew
existed and what I could figure out from it. I was reading *Boys'
Book Buff*, the only magazine of its kind in the late 1970s, and began

corresponding with other collectors. When Gil O'Gara's magazine, *Yellowback Library*, came out in 1981 I sent in an article on one of the Book Club type editions of Nancy Drews, which eventually led to a column in Gil's magazine on collecting aspects of the Drew books.[1] All the while I was working on my guide. When the series for Gil was done in 1985, I published the first printing of *Farah's Guide*.[2] The main reason I published the guide was so I could go into a store, carry a book, and say, "It's black and white, it's not a first edition, it's not worth $6,000, it was published last year, that's why it lists books published last year."

The problem with collecting series books is that, unlike most books, series books have only one copyright date, the date when they were first published. They kept the same copyright date in all subsequent printings until the books were revised. So a copy of an original Nancy Drew will have a 1930 copyright date for twenty-nine years, until the book is revised in 1959.

The *Guide* has a couple of aspects. If you own a book you want to sell, but are afraid of underselling it, the *Guide* can help you establish a price. In this age of baseball cards and all, most people are afraid they're going to sell something that would have paid their house mortgage. I get calls all the time from people who want to retire on their Nancy Drews. My basic line is this: if you own it it's probably not rare. The hardbacks were saved by the millions; they were like *National Geographics*—practically everybody saved their hardback books. And unless you happened to be alive and reading them around 1930 or 1931, the odds are that what you have is relatively common and not worth much. That's the bottom line in collecting Drews—there are millions of them out there. The really rare and valuable series books are the ones that weren't popular.

How does someone tell which Nancy Drews are less common?
FARAH: Some information about the number of copies published has been revealed by Grosset & Dunlap. This information correlates pretty well with the experience that collectors have finding the books. At any time when a set of books were on the shelves, people bought the newest title and they bought the first and second title. So at any time the most common books are the first and second—which is why everybody has a copy of *The Secret of the Old Clock* (no. 1, 1930)—

and the last title, which was often a first edition. The rare books, the scarce books, are the middle numbers, or those books that were un-attractive and people didn't buy them, like *The Clue of the Broken Locket* (no. 11, 1934), which had an awful cover. For example, when there are thirty volumes, volumes 10 through 15 would be the scar-cest, whereas volumes 1 through 8 would be fairly common. As the series keeps expanding, then, those middle numbers move up.

The things that are particularly sought after in the Drews in-clude first printings of the book, first printings of the revised covers and revised texts, and certain unusual books; for instance volumes 22 (*The Clue in the Crumbling Wall*, 1945) and 30 (*The Clue of the Velvet Mask*, 1953) were printed in very odd formats in their first printing and they're considerably more valuable than anything around them. *The Clue in the Crumbling Wall* has a unique dust jacket and must not have been widely distributed. It's a hard dust jacket to get; there have only been about ten or fifteen copies ever advertised for sale publicly. *The Clue of the Velvet Mask* came out at the time they were changing the end papers from the blue silhouette endpapers to the man digging. They must have printed a small num-ber of volume 30 with the old blue silhouette papers, which consti-tutes the first printing. It turns out that the first volume of no. 30 is worth much more than the first printing of no. 29 (*The Mystery at the Ski Jump*, 1952) or no. 31 (*The Ringmaster's Secret*, 1953).

The first printing of the first three books are the most sought-after. *The Secret of the Old Clock* (1930), *The Hidden Staircase* (1930), and *The Bungalow Mystery* (1930), to the best of my knowl-edge, have never been auctioned or sold. Recorded sales exist only for volumes 4 and up.

How do I know if what I read as a child was written by Mildred Wirt Benson or was a revised edition of those early books?
FARAH: The first revised editions were *The Secret of the Old Clock* and *The Hidden Staircase* in 1959. If you read anything before 1958 or 1959, you read the originals. Of the thirty-six books out at that time, twenty-three are Benson texts. Volumes 8, 9, and 10—*Nancy's Mysterious Letter* (1932), *The Sign of the Twisted Candles* (1933), and *The Password to Larkspur Lane* (1933)—were written by Wal-ter Karig, when Mildred briefly broke her association with the Strate-meyer Syndicate over a fee dispute. Of the other volumes, we know of

several authors. George Walker, Jr., wrote the original manuscript for *The Clue of the Leaning Chimney* (no. 26, 1949). Margaret Scherzo, a prolific writer of adult mysteries, wrote *The Secret of the Wooden Lady* (no. 27, 1950). *The Clue of the Black Keys* (no. 28, 1951) was drafted by Wilhelmina Rankin, and *The Mystery at the Ski Jump* (no. 29, 1952) was written by Alma Sasse. Charles Strong wrote the manuscript for *The Scarlet Slipper Mystery* (no. 32, 1954). Harriet Adams, the eldest daughter of Edward Stratemeyer, wrote the original manuscripts for the other Grosset & Dunlap titles through volume 56, *The Thirteenth Pearl*, in 1979, and one or two of the Simon & Schuster volumes. Since Simon & Schuster's takeover of the series in 1979, there have been many authors, both male and female. There have also been many persons who did editing and revisions on the original texts.

It's been my understanding that Ms. Benson did not write the ending to The Mystery of the Ivory Charm *(no. 13, 1936). Is that correct?*
FARAH: No. There is an odd twist on that. When Benson wrote something and got it back from the publisher, she never read it again. She stuck it on a shelf and went on with her life. The plot of *Ivory Charm* was written by Edna Stratemeyer, Harriet's sister. Edna plotted only a few Nancy Drews and they're all very bizarre. In *The Ivory Charm* people die, so Edna Stratemeyer plotted a resurrection scene which Benson then wrote. But when Benson was asked years later if she wrote the resurrection scene she said, "Of course not." So that's how the rumor started. But she went back and read it and said, "Oh, yeah, that was just that terrible, strange plot I couldn't do anything about."

Do you have a favorite Nancy Drew book?
FARAH: Yes. My favorite is the original printing of *The Secret of Red Gate Farm* (no. 6, 1931). I remember the cave scene, and the demasking in particular.

Did you think that was the KKK running around in there?
FARAH: Absolutely. And my favorite line from a Nancy Drew is from that book. There's a point where Nancy is seeking the woman who sold the perfume and she's going down the street and the woman escapes her and goes into a building and Nancy stops a man and asks,

"Did you see a woman go into that building" and the man answers, "You mean Yvette Wong." And Nancy says, "She looked French-Chinese." Those who read the books know there's absolutely no humor in a Nancy Drew. Mildred Benson's Nancy Drews are identifiable by the fact that, unlike most children's series books, there are no jokes. So humor in them must be taken out of context and as an adult. That *is* my favorite line.

Is my perception correct that there is a lot of guesswork necessary in this business of collecting information about series books?
FARAH: Absolutely. There is so much not known about children's series books. Generally, the things we read as children and remember well, until recently, were not studied seriously in academia. So most of this ended up being done by collectors because there were no other sources. I think we'll all concur that *any* reference that comes out will be helpful because there is just a huge gap in information. And it hasn't been helped in the Nancy Drew and Hardy Boys series by the fact that the records that exist—which are extensive; they include practically every document that ever involved the Drews—are not public. We don't have access to them. The reason we're having to guess at all this is because the people who own the files, for their own reasons, won't give the public access to them. So, in essence, all the questions on who wrote what and who illustrated what and why and how the books were produced could be answered in about a year's worth of research on the files as they stand. But barring the possibilities that the public will get access to the files, this is the only way we can do it now—piecemeal, one reference at a time.[3]

Would you define a "series book"?
FARAH: A series book, in the collector's market, is defined as what a series book collector collects. This is why I say that: in the early 1980s a major series book collector proposed defining a series book as "any group of three or more books which contained a continuing character." This caused quite a heated discussion in the field. The problem is that it doesn't cover all the books that are routinely collected by collectors. There are whole series of books with dog characters and continuing horse characters and there were debates about whether they were covered. Then there were debates about whether a series had to be in hardcover or softcover or published in

a serial. The Wizard of Oz books are quintessential series books, but they have their own collectors' market and are completely separate from series book collectors. Horatio Alger books, which really aren't series books—they don't have continuing characters—*are* part of the series book market. Howard Garis Uncle Wiggily books and Thorton Burgess Mother West Wind series aren't part of the market because they have their own societies.[4] So generally, the series book market is defined as continuing-character books that aren't covered by other societies.

The definition probably doesn't include dime novels and softcover books that were published in the late 1800s and early 1900s because, again, they have their own collectors' organizations. The *Girls' Series Companion* (Emburg) has a definition of girls' series that doesn't include noncontinuing character books, so, for instance, Mildred Benson's mystery books for girls, which were published as a series but have noncontinuing characters, won't be found there, as well as a whole bunch of books that were produced in uniform format, advertised as a series, and collected by series book collectors. So it gets to be a sticky subject.

When did it become commonly known that Mildred Wirt Benson was the author of Nancy Drew?

FARAH: In a newspaper interview as early as 1931 Benson (then Wirt) said she wrote the Drews. And in reference works such as *Something about the Author* or Who's Who of this and that over the years,[5] she is on record as the author of the books. So anybody looking in that material would have known. The problem was that the Stratemeyer Syndicate maintained complete silence on who wrote their books until 1966. In that year Roger Garis, the son of Howard Garis, broke the silence when he wrote *My Father Was "Uncle Wiggily,"* telling about how his father wrote all the Tom Swift books for the syndicate. Apparently in response to that leak, Harriet Adams, Stratemeyer's daughter, who directed the syndicate at that time, started releasing publicity that her father had written the early Nancy Drew books and that she had written the later ones. This information was picked up by all the major newspapers and magazines. For the next fifteen years, until her death in 1982, she repeated the story in countless interviews.[6] Thus, if you search any database now, everything you find about Nancy Drew or Harriet

Adams from 1967 onward is suspect as being publicity. Every major newspaper carried her story. As recently as fall 1992 *Ms.* magazine (Vivelo) carried the inaccurate story, as did the *Smithsonian* in October 1991 (Watson). Fortunately, a *New York Times* reporter covered the Nancy Drew conference and corrected the historical record (Brown, April 19, 1993).[7]

NOTES

1. The column "Basic Nancy Drew" appeared in *Yellowback Library* 6 (December 1981) through 30 (November/December 1985) (Farah).

2. See part 3, note 1, p. 151.

3. Material related to the Stratemeyer Syndicate has been donated to the New York Public Library and will eventually be made public.

4. The Horatio Alger Society is an example of a collectors' organization.

5. Benson was not identified as the writer of Nancy Drews in *Something about the Author* (Olendorf) until the 1991 edition. Harriet Stratemeyer Adams was listed as the author in the 1971 edition (Commire).

6. For example, she hosted a fiftieth birthday party for Nancy Drew in 1980 and identified herself as the writer of all the books (Bumiller).

7. See also Greenberg in the *New York Times*. There were news stories on Mildred Wirt Benson as the writer of Nancy Drew in many other media in the weeks surrounding the Nancy Drew Conference in 1993.

CHAPTER 18

Yellowback Library and the Collector

Gil O'Gara

I began reading series books in the first or second grade, even before realizing that they *were* series books. These were the approved books on the library lists in our county: Miss Pickerell's adventures, Pippi Longstockings, the Mushroom Planet books.

One day when I was nine a neighbor showed me a book she had just finished reading. It was Carolyn Keene's *The Haunted Bridge* (1937). She explained with some excitement that Nancy Drew, the main character, was a girl detective who had a great many adventures, all of them recorded in a long line of other novels. She showed me the listing on the back of the book and then loaned the story to me. It may have taken me all of one day to read it, such was my fascination for the character, the tale, and eventually the genre. I began borrowing more books from her and then discovered and became equally enamored of the Hardy Boys, Tom Swift, Jr., and others.

And that is how I became what I am today.

I was fortunate that we lived near a small Nebraska town, about twelve miles from our farm. The library was also small, built during the Depression by the Work Projects Administration (WPA). Money being tight, the library had filled its shelves with volumes of inexpensive juvenile literature—primarily fifty cent series books. It appeared as if library purchases had ceased around World War II, except, of course, for the daily newspaper. Thus it was a great place to catch up on the series books of bygone days. There I discovered that

Tom Swift, Jr., actually had a famous inventor father who had a series of his own. There I discovered the works of writers Leo Edwards, Clarence Budington Kelland, and others. It was a treasure house of imagination, adventure, and continuity.

Eventually I managed to read nearly all of the series books the library had. I began to seek books on my own, looking in thrift shops, charity shows, garage and farm sales. I was becoming a collector as well as a reader.

Years later I discovered that there were other people out there in the vast world with the same interests. One common element I encounter in nearly all of the collectors of series books is the initial feeling that they are the only ones with such an interest, the only collectors of juvenile fiction of this type in the universe. I believed it myself. Eventually, however, I was able to contact men like Bob Chenu and Harry Hudson,[1] two of the greatest figures in old time boys' book collecting, through ads they had placed in general collectors' publications not geared directly to books.

Soon I decided to begin my own publication. Bob Jenning's *Boys' Book Buff* was being published for series book collectors,[2] but it had gotten to that random frequency which signals the first stages of death. Previously Alan Dikty's *Boys' Book Collector* had prospered for about thirteen issues, but it had folded.[3] The *Dime Novel Roundup* was publishing quite a bit about series books—I had contributed some articles myself—but I thought another magazine would certainly do no harm.

At that time Fred Woodworth came out with his *Mystery and Adventure Series Review*.[4] I was cautioned that there would not be much of a market for my idea with his new magazine in progress. I subscribed to it; but in reading the magazine, I realized that my approach would be rather different and that it was unlikely that anyone could confuse my work with his.

I issued the first number of *Yellowback Library* in January 1981.[5] Issue 126 came off the presses in December 1994. It consists of from 30 to 50 percent advertising, with news, reviews, and letters from readers. However, despite its definite slant toward the acquisition or sales of juvenile series literature, I have always attempted to include a number of articles on the genre.

While *Yellowback Library* is not an academic publication, we have run many articles by recognized scholars in the field, including Deidre Johnson, J. Randolph Cox, and Kathleen Chamberlain. But the magazine draws primarily collectors. I have tried to keep the magazine on a level which appeals to those in the hobby who are most interested in completing collections by their favorite authors and gathering format, publishing, or bibliographic data or who simply enjoy reading the fiction for the sake of relaxation and entertainment.

I have also tried to "hit the field broadly." We have run series of articles, such as David Farah's "Basic Nancy Drew," which appeared regularly for 24 issues, and Sean Bourke's information on collecting series books in Europe, to give two specific examples. Because I enjoy the genre in and of itself, I publish any articles related to series books, whether they are directed at collectors of boys' or girls' series or run toward the peripheral children's books. I even include material on dime novels, not because there is a great deal of interest in these items today, but because they preceded the series book and, in many ways, were the forefather of much popular juvenile fiction. I want to educate the modern series book collector about this area of literary history. And besides, I collect dime novels and nineteenth-century literature and want to keep some interest alive in that field.

The magazine is issued every month, usually around the tenth, and I have managed to keep it pretty much on schedule. When I was late getting one particular issue out due to the pressures of work and the complications of life in general, it wasn't long before the rumor went out that I was ill or in the hospital or that I had been involved in a terrible car accident. Eventually it built into an exciting theory culminating in my death, and people were calling my wife to ask about the funeral. Some even asked if they could get their subscription money refunded.

After that incident I was determined to maintain a stricter timeline and to keep on schedule. It was, in retrospect, a nice way to see if anyone really cared about the magazine.

I have no axes to grind, and *Yellowback Library* is not the medium for material calculated to offend. My purpose is to provide a network for collectors to find those books they seek, or for dealers to reach the collectors, and, in general, to allow everyone a chance to get in touch and come to know one another. I tend to be moderate in my approach to the material. I avoid subject matter or content which could offend or hurt the feelings of others. Overall, I think I have managed to provide the sort of magazine that is acceptable to as many people as possible.

For instance, I received an ad from a dealer concerning "vintage erotica." I turned him down. The ad was inappropriate, especially for a magazine dealing in children's books. Perhaps it was the odd name of the publication, but I think he was misled regarding the purpose of *Yellowback Library*.

All in all, *Yellowback Library* offers a medium through which we can exchange series books, learn from one another, and simply find a means of getting along with each other.

NOTES

1. Hudson was compiler of *A Bibliography of Hard-Cover Boys' Books*, rev. ed. (Tampa, Fla.: Harry Hudson, 1977).

2. Out of print. Volume 1 appeared in 1977.

3. Out of print. Volume 1 appeared in 1969.

4. Out of print. Volume 1 appeared in 1980.

5. The *Yellowback Library* is available from Gil O'Gara, P.O. Box 36172, Des Moines, IA 50315. Currently $30/year for 12 issues.

CHAPTER 19

A Bibliographic Mystery: Missing Books, Missing Authors

Esther Green Bierbaum

There are two parts to this bibliographic mystery: the books that were not there in the library and the author, who was missing from the catalog. Let us look first at the Case of the Missing Books.

The Case of the (Somewhat) Missing Books

For the first forty years or so of their existence, the Nancy Drew series, along with their fellow members of the Stratemeyer stable, were nonbooks. They could be bought, all right; try Woolworth's. But as far as the librarians and their bibliographic power structure were concerned, the books were not on their shelves. Indeed, officially, the books did not exist. They were not listed in the *Children's Catalog* and other selection guides from which public and school librarians made their purchases. They were not discussed in children's literature textbooks. The H. W. Wilson Company did not print library catalog cards for them. But, in one of those strange anomalies one bumps up against in Nancy Drew bibliography, the Library of Congress did print cards, because all but three or four of the early Carolyn Keene titles appear in the *National Union Catalog Pre-1956 Imprints*. In other words, the Library of Congress was collecting Nancy Drew back in the 1930s. Moreover, the library has been microfilming the series since 1991.

My own experience with the public library bibliographical

blackout meant that, because my parents did not buy books that their taxes had already paid for in the public library, Nancy was missing from my life. Or she would have been, had it not been for my friend Anne, whose reading was not limited to the library's shelves. She solved the problem for my entire sixth grade in an entrepreneurial spirit that would have made Nancy proud: she rented out her Nancy Drews at a nickel a pop.

Not content with simply delisting Carolyn Keene's heroine, librarians included the Stratemeyer output in published lists of books *not* to be included in libraries and indulged themselves in vituperative, if not hysterical, attacks on series books in general, the Stratemeyer books in particular. In an unfortunately typical 1935 article, Lucy Kinloch called series "worthless, sordid, sensational, trashy and harmful books" and "the menace to good reading." "Under wise supervision," she concludes, "this trash will find its way to the furnace, where it belongs" (Kinloch, 74). In this recommendation, she echoed Lewis Terman himself, who had weighed in on the series books in 1926, measuring their "costs" in "wasted hours, a perverted reading taste, a false sense of reality, and a direct loss in education." He would prefer for them, he added, "cremation to segregation" (Terman and Lima, 81). In 1957 Phyllis Fenner deplored Nancy for being "saucy" and "strong-headed," while she "performs all kinds of stunts, [and] solves mysteries involving high-powered motor cars and expensive perfumes" (Fenner, 128).

The campaign against the series has recently been crumbling, aided by the scholarly study of popular culture and hastened by the realization that reading begets reading. As Rudolph Bold notes, the inclusion of formerly proscribed reading does not mean "dropping any of our literary standards," but rather "that librarians realize that for many in our community those standards are idealistic and practically unattainable" (Bold, 1138–1139). And as Eileen Goudge Zuckerman has pointed out, Nancy Drew is often the gateway for young readers to other series and to other books (Zuckerman, 74).

Yet the Battle of Nancy still goes on. Gillian McCombs, in a 1992 article on developing popular culture collections, notes that her informal telephone poll of public libraries around Albany showed that only one of the five libraries queried had Nancy Drew books. A similar poll conducted in Iowa City found quite different results: *all* the public libraries had Nancy Drew books; some actively promoted them. For the most part, they are the "new" Nancy Drew books. A Colorado contretemps sputtered on for more than a year in 1991–1992. It pitted the Boulder children's librarian, who declared Nancy Drew to be "junk food," against indignant parents with fond memories, while librarians in nearby communities rather self-righteously defended their inclusion of the books. The ultimate resolution seems to have been to put gifts of Nancy Drew titles on the shelves, but not in the computer catalog, thus making Nancy bibliographically invisible and squaring the librarian's conscience with the edicts of the selection gurus (Hudson). This, I discovered, many years after my Nancy mania had subsided, was also the solution in my Nancyless library. Silly child, that I should have relied upon the card catalog for bibliographic information!

There are indications that the antiseries movement did, indeed, have a somewhat chilling effect on library shelves. On the other hand, the series books were never entirely banished. The evidence for both observations comes from the files of OCLC, the online bibliographic utility that serves as an electronic union catalog for approximately 5,000 participating (i.e., cataloging) libraries. These files furnish data about the number of libraries holding a particular title and edition; and these holdings data show that the Stratemeyer and other proscribed series are not found in libraries in the same numbers as the "safe" and approved series listed in the standard collection guide, *Children's Catalog*, or the Rosenberg and Rosenberg (1972) checklist. Table 1 shows holdings data for titles published between 1925 and 1935, the decade of the birth of Nancy Drew. Proscribed and "marginal" series such as the Bobbsey Twins and Perkins's Twins books have been collected less extensively than approved series such as Ransome's Swallows and Amazons and Lattimore's Little Pear. Among the proscribed, however, Nancy was less chilled than any of her fellow series except for the Hardy Boys, and she trumped the opening publication of Mary Poppins and the Little House books.

And so our first bibliographic mystery, that of the missing books that were never as completely missing as their opponents might have wished, is being resolved with changing times and less punitive and prescriptive attitudes toward the library patron's reading choices. But the second mystery, that of the missing author, is a long way from solution.

Table 1. Libraries Holding Various Titles (OCLC Data)

Author	Title / Year	No. of Libraries Holding Title
Lattimore, E.	Little Pear (1931)	592
Brooks, W. R.	Freddy the Detective (1932)	488
Ransome, A.	Swallows and Amazons (1931)	368
Montgomery, L. M.	Anne of Green Gables (1935)	274
*Dixon, F.	(Hardy Boys) The Great Airport Mystery (1930)	109
*Keene, C.	The Bungalow Mystery (1930)	79
	The Mystery of Lilac Inn (1930)	76
	The Hidden Staircase (1930)	75
Pease, H.	Shanghai Passage (1929)	68
Hope, L.	Bobbsey Twins & Their Schoolmates (1928)	64
*Keene, C.	The Secret of the Old Clock (1930)	64
*Sidney, M.	Five Little Peppers (1930)	58
*Perkins, L. F.	The Norwegian Twins (1933)	57
	The Spanish Twins (1934)	56
Wilder, L.	Little House in the Big Woods (1932)	26
Travers, P. L.	Mary Poppins (1934)	6

*Authors described by Rosenberg and Rosenberg as producing series of "consistently low quality" or as "marginal" in other lists (Rosenberg and Rosenberg, 1).

The Case of the (Really) Missing Author

Consider what a bibliographic record (the equivalent of a catalog card) from OCLC, the Library of Congress electronic union catalog, had told us about *The Hidden Staircase* until 1995:[1]

8	100	1	Keene, Carolyn w cn
9	245	14	The hidden staircase / c by Carolyn Keene.
10	260		New York: b Grosset & Dunlap, c *c1930*.
11	300		iv, 206 p., [1] leaf of plates: b ill.
12	400	11	Her Nancy Drew mystery stories v [2]
13	500		Illustrated lining-papers.
14	650	0	Detective and mystery stories.

Quite correctly—in bibliographic terms—the author is listed as "Carolyn Keene." According to the bibliographic rule, an author better known by a pseudonym is listed under the pseudonym, a provision which results in Mark Twain appearing in the catalog. But most library catalogs also have an interesting item of information: in some way or other they tell us that, for example, even though the author's "real" name was Samuel Clemens, we should look for his books under Twain, and, conversely, that Samuel Clemens used the pseudonym of Mark Twain. The Library of Congress makes this distinction official in what is called a personal name authority record. It has done such a service for Carolyn Heilbrun, who has a literary identity as Amanda Cross as well.

However, if one looked up Carolyn Keene in the name authority file, the Stratemeyer/Adams misinformation was perpetuated; there was no hint of Mildred Wirt Benson:

4	100	10	Keene, Carolyn. [AACR2]
5	400	10	Quine, Caroline
6	400	10	Keene, Carolyn, c pseud. [OLD CATALOG HEADING]
7	500	10	Stratemeyer, Edward, d 1862–1930
8	500	10	McFarlane, Leslie, d 1902–
9	663		Joint pseudonym of Edward Stratemeyer, Leslie McFarlane, and others. For works of these authors written under their own names, search also under: b Stratemeyer, Edward, 1862–1930; b McFarlane, Leslie, 1902–

Indeed, with nearly perfect consistency, standard biographical dictionaries and handbooks of pseudonyms, lists of Stratemeyer books, and various writers, reviewers, and commentators all name Edward Stratemeyer as the author of the first three Nancy Drew books, published in 1930, and his daughter, Harriet S. Adams, as the author of the subsequent members of the series.[2] Thanks to Geoffrey S. Lapin, Mildred Wirt Benson herself (both of them writing in *Books at Iowa*), and a writer for the *Zanesville (Ohio) Times*, some people know better. This persistent misinformation regarding authorship has completely obscured the identity of Benson writing also as Carolyn Keene—or as Ann Wirt, Don Palmer, Dorothy West, Joan Clark, Frances K. Judd, or Frank Bell.

According to the best bibliographic practice, links should be made *in the public catalog* from any one name to the others, so that a reader acquainted with one aspect of the author's output is also able to seek works written under other names, whether real or pseudonymous. Because of this lack of linkage, Benson scholarship is considerably handicapped. Other "Carolyn Keenes" did not suffer this identity blackout. Leslie McFarlane, for example, has the proper Library of Congress notice—as does Stratemeyer himself.

Mildred Benson also wrote under her own names, Mildred Benson, Mildred A. Wirt, and a variant, Ann Wirt. There were no authority records for any of these names, although books written under these names have been in the OCLC database.

In addition, Mildred Benson wrote under her own, non-Stratemeyer, pseudonyms of Don Palmer, Dorothy West, Joan Clark, Alice B. Emerson, and Frank Bell. None of these names had authority records, although the titles of the books she wrote under those names were also in the OCLC database. She herself stated that "few of my books ever rated display on librarians' shelves" (Benson 1973, 27).[3]

Yet the Library of Congress has provided name authority and name links for authors of books held by fewer libraries than many of hers—for example, Laura Lee Hope of the Bobbsey Twins.

When it comes to the Benson name authority, the catalog of the University of Iowa Libraries is a model of what should have been. Thanks to the work of local catalogers and the scholarship of the staff in Special Collections, not only do we have the correct identities of Mildred Wirt Benson, but the reader can look up any one of Benson's name variants or her numerous pseudonyms and find out the other names and the titles associated with them:

KEENE CAROLYN	BENSON MILDRED
*Search Also Under:	*Search
BENSON MILDRED	BELL FRANK
GORMAN CAROL[4]	CLARK JOAN
	DUNCAN JULIA K
	EMERSON ALICE B
	JUDD FRANCES K
	KEENE CAROLYN

BENSON MILDRED (*continued*)
*Search
PALMER DON
THORNDYKE HELEN LOUISE
WEST DOROTHY
WIRT ANN

Unfortunately, this information was unavailable to patrons of 5,000 OCLC libraries or to patrons of the libraries of RLIN (Research Libraries Information Network), because Iowa does not ordinarily contribute its name authority work.

We can go to the library these days and find Danielle Steel and Madonna on the adult shelves, and such pedestrian efforts as the Berenstain Bears and a Disneyized version of Christopher Robin in the children's section. It is hard to believe that public libraries were once so devoted to saving us from ourselves that they set out to make nonbooks of the enormously popular Nancy Drew series. It is also difficult to understand how such a popular and prolific author as Mildred Augustine Wirt Benson—whose books have remained on home and library shelves for over sixty years—should have been relegated to bibliographic obscurity. That is indeed the mystery of the missing author—and, indeed, a travesty as well.

NOTES

Reprinted in revised form from Esther Green Bierbaum, "Bad Books in Series: Nancy Drew in the Public Library," *Lion and the Unicorn* 18:1 (June 1994): 92–102.

1. The University of Iowa Libraries submitted its name authority records for Mildred Wirt Benson to the Library of Congress in January 1995, and they were accepted. The OCLC records were to be changed.

2. For example, see Fred Atkinson, W. J. Burke and Will D. Howe, Rosenberg and Rosenberg, and Deidre Johnson (1982).

3. Of the books published under the name of Mildred Benson, *Dangerous Deadline* (1957) shows 44 holding libraries and *Quarry Ghost* (1959) 27, while *Pirate Brig* (1950), a more ambitious novel published under the name of Mildred A. Wirt, has a holdings count of 27.

4. Carol Gorman, another Iowa author, is listed in the University of Iowa Libraries catalog as writer under the Carolyn Keene pseudonym.

CHAPTER 20

The Case of the Missing Manuscripts:
Doing Archival Research on
Children's Series Authors

Karen M. Mason

*Kristie rolled a sheet of copy paper from the
typewriter and, with a quick intake of breath, raised
startled eyes to the shadowy doorway. Across the street
from the deserted college journalism office, the chimes
of Old Trinity carilloned the hour of seven.*

*Not the clear cadence of the striking chapel bells, but
another sound had caught the girl's attention. Footfalls,
soft and steady, whispered on the freshly-scrubbed
hallway, padded closer and now hung suspended at the
entranceway to the student newspaper workroom.*

*Aware that she sat alone in a slowly darkening room,
Kristie snapped on the overhead, swinging electric bulb.*

*Framed in the doorway stood a tall man of angular
features, whose well-cut tweeds and gold-rimmed
spectacles suggested that he might be a faculty member.
Kristie, however, was quite certain she had never seen
him on the campus. (Benson,* Quarry, *1)*

So begins *Quarry Ghost*, the last novel written by Mildred Wirt
Benson. The book was published in 1959 by Dodd, Mead, and
Co., although it almost didn't make it into print. A letter written by
Benson to her publisher reads in part:

Dear Miss Bryan:

I have an idea which may salvage QUARRY GHOST. The entire book will have to be rewritten, but all swim scenes and characters could be saved, pretty much the same chapter arrangement kept and same interchange between characters which I would need for any successful re-write. . . .

Following your suggestion, dead body would be eliminated, the mentally deranged G.I. skin-diver, and the international intrigue. . . .

Other changes: Kane Bradshaw, in new version becomes the villain. (Benson to Dorothy Bryan, March 18, 1958, Benson papers, Box 1, *Quarry Ghost* materials)

The letter, along with two drafts of *Quarry Ghost*, are part of the Mildred Augustine Wirt Benson papers, which Benson donated to the Iowa Women's Archives at the University of Iowa in 1992.

Although quite a small collection, measuring only about eight and one-half linear inches, the Benson papers are useful sources for historical research from a number of angles.

This is not a Nancy Drew collection. It does not include any manuscripts or correspondence concerning the Nancy Drew books, and it only includes a letter or two of correspondence with the Stratemeyer Syndicate. The only material relating to Benson's authorship of Nancy Drew is correspondence between Mildred Benson and members of the University of Iowa Libraries staff, who were attempting to compile a list of all the books she wrote.

The Mildred Wirt Benson Papers contain valuable bibliographical and biographical information and are useful for studying her early short fiction as well as some of the novels she wrote. The papers also shed light on her career as a journalist and on her avocations, which are reflected in the feature writing she did on aviation and archaeology. There is little in the papers relating to her childhood, other than a photograph of Mildred Augustine in front of her childhood home in Ladora and a copy of her first publication. But her college years at the University of Iowa are documented by the memory book she kept while a student at the University of Iowa. This scrapbook contains newspaper clippings, photographs, programs, and memorabilia chronicling her involvement in athletics (she swam and played basketball and soccer) and music (she performed frequently on the xylophone). She also wrote for the *Daily Iowan*, was on the yearbook staff, and was a member of the Cosmopolitan Club.

The University Archives in the Special Collections Department at the University of Iowa also holds relevant material, including University of Iowa yearbooks dating from the time Mildred Augustine was a student here. In addition, the University Archives has her master's thesis, a study of newspaper illustration in metropolitan and small city daily newspapers and country weeklies (Augustine 1927).

Also in the collection are newspaper articles and columns written at various times during her career, from the 1920s through the 1990s. Benson has been a journalist all her life; she stopped writing fiction in 1959. The Iowa Women's Archives holds the papers of several women journalists and will eventually receive more news clippings and related material from Benson documenting her half century as a court reporter, feature writer, and columnist for Toledo newspapers.

The University of Iowa material pertaining to Benson is interesting not only for the samples of newspaper writing it contains, but also because settings in Iowa and scenes at the university often provided the backdrop for her novels, even though they were not identified as such. For example, *Quarry Ghost* takes place at a school called Hagers College, whose president happens to be named Hancher (the name of the president of the University of Iowa in the 1950s). The story concerns Kristie Coleman, a journalism student and swimmer who becomes involved in a controversy between a professor, the college president, and various other characters over a dinosaur egg acquired by her college. While the plot was Mildred Benson's invention, the setting and characterization of *Quarry Ghost* echo her experiences at the University of Iowa.

Like Kristie, Mildred Augustine wrote for the student newspaper while attending college. She was also a swimmer and belonged to the Seals Club, a women's swimming club that sponsored swim meets for girls as well as various aquatic events such as the annual Eel-Seal Revue and the Iowater Regatta. Thus, it's particularly fitting that we have this manuscript.

The *Quarry Ghost* manuscripts and accompanying material are also useful in providing insight into the process that went into writing, rewriting, and resubmitting a book for publication. There are two drafts of the manuscript, many pages containing Benson's penciled changes. When preparing her papers to send to the Iowa Women's Archives, Benson annotated or attached notes explaining many of the documents that illuminate the process. About the *Quarry Ghost* manuscripts, she wrote:

> The book as submitted was rewritten. . . . So far as I know, these are the only [manuscript] sheets available on any of my published books. Series books never were rewritten but were based on plots accepted by [the] publisher in advance. On a few individual books on which plots were not submitted—including Quarry Ghost—rewrites were made. With the exception of these cull sheets I know of no other [manuscripts] remaining on [my] published books. (Benson note, Benson papers, Box 1, *Quarry Ghost* materials)

Thus we know that *Quarry Ghost* was written independently by Benson.

But her papers also include plot outlines for a Penny Parker mystery and a volume in the Boy Scout Explorers series. These plot outlines consist of a list of characters, a summary of each chapter, and suggested titles for the books. Benson notes that she made two copies of each plot outline, sending one to the publisher and keeping one to use as a working copy.

Mildred Wirt suggested three alternate titles for the first volume in the Penny Parker series: *Mark of the Witchdoll, Clue of the Witchdoll*, and *Spell of the Witchdoll*. In the end it was published as *Tale of the Witchdoll*. Among the characters were Penny Parker, whose father owned the *Riverview Star*, a crusading newspaper; Louise Sidell, Penny's chum; actress and dancer Helene Harmon and her brother Melvin, who runs a séance establishment and uses an assumed name; Nellie Marble, the owner of the doll shop; and, my personal favorite, Ivan Lavelle, enemy of the Harmons who assumes the disguise of a hunchback *and* that of the old woman who runs the shop. The chapter summaries, each about a paragraph in length, contain fairly detailed outlines of the action in each chapter. The plot outlines, manuscripts, and correspondence with editors provide a window onto the process of writing juvenile fiction.

I had no idea what I was getting myself into when I agreed to discuss this subject. I am not an expert in children's literature or, more specifically, juvenile series fiction, but I am an archivist; I know how to locate sources. So I assumed I'd be able to track down the papers of children's series authors with a few searches of national databases and guides. I was dimly aware that librarians and educators considered series books "bad" for children, but I didn't realize the ramifications this would have for my research. It appears that besides banishing series books from many library shelves, this attitude has had the effect of hindering research on the subject. Perhaps because the genre of series books has not been accorded much recognition in academic circles, archivists and manuscript curators have tended to overlook the papers of children's series authors in their collecting.

My perspective is that not of an expert in children's literature, or juvenile series fiction, but of an archivist. What I tried to do was track down manuscript material concerning children's series books using some standard archival reference tools. Although the result of my search was not terribly satisfying, it was instructive for what it revealed about some of the problems in trying to do this type of research.

If you're starting from scratch, the place to begin is the *Directory of Archives and Manuscript Repositories in the United States*, put out by the National Historical Publications and Records Commission (NHPRC). This guide lists approximately 4,800 archival and manuscript repositories in the United States and gives basic information about each one, such as address and phone number, collecting scope, and major holdings. Since each repository is allotted only a paragraph or two to describe its holdings, the guide necessarily paints with a broad stroke. Nonetheless, it is useful for determining which repositories hold major collections on children's literature authors. The guide is intended primarily as a directory, so its index is limited in the number of subject headings listed. Thus, "children's literature" is included in the index, but there are no more specific terms such as "juvenile series" or "serialized fiction." Only nine repositories are indexed under the heading "children's literature"; these range from the rich and sizable holdings of the University of Minnesota's Children's Literature Research Collections and the University of Southern Mississippi's deGrummond Collection to public libraries that have papers of one or two authors.

After these rather disappointing results, a guide by Lee Ash and William G. Miller is a welcome change. Entitled *Subject Collections: A Guide to Special Book Collections and Subject Emphases as Reported by University, College, Public, and Special Libraries and Museums in the United States and Canada*, this two-volume set lists more than a hundred libraries under the heading "children's literature." It even includes a subset of children's literature called "juvenile series." The rub is that most of the eleven repositories listed under "juvenile series" appear to collect only books; only a few mention manuscript holdings. But at least this guide provides a few leads.

While guides of this sort inform researchers about repositories that might contain holdings relevant to their research, published guides such as the National Union Catalog of Manuscript Collections and databases such as the Research Libraries Information Network contain descriptions of individual collections.

The National Union Catalog of Manuscript Collections, known fondly as NUCMC, contains descriptions of personal papers, organizational records, and other collections of primary sources held by archival and manuscript repositories across the United States. It is by no means an exhaustive list of holdings. It includes only those descriptions of collections submitted by individual repositories, and many repositories do not report to NUCMC. Still, for over three decades it has been the one central place to look for holdings of repositories across the country. NUCMC does have quite a few collections indexed under the subject heading "children's literature." However, there are no listings under "juvenile series," even though the term is listed in the index.

The Research Libraries Information Network, known as RLIN, is an on-line computer database that lists descriptions of repository holdings at the collection level. Thus, when the Iowa Women's Archives begins inputting records, RLIN will contain a few paragraphs and as many subject headings and added entries as I wish to use to describe and provide access to the Mildred Wirt Benson papers.

At present, around 200 institutions are entering records into RLIN. Most of these are major research institutions, particularly large universities. In addition, NUCMC is entering descriptions of holdings reported to it. The University of Iowa Libraries is a member of Research Library Group, Inc. (RLG), which operates RLIN. The Special Collections Department has been inputting records into

RLIN for several years or so and the Iowa Women's Archives will begin doing so in the near future. Then researchers will be able to learn about our collections at other member libraries.

One can search RLIN by subject phrase, personal name, or corporate heading (for organizations or institutions). I tried searching under many of variations of the phrase "children's series." The subject phrases "children's series books," "serialized fiction," "series—publications," and "serial publication of books" yielded nothing. The phrase "children's series" yielded one record: the Blanche Seale Hunt papers at the Western History Collections, University of Oklahoma in Norman. Hunt was the author of the Little Brown Koko children's stories.

Until I began my search I had no inkling of the problems that syndicates and pseudonyms could cause researchers. I thought I would try searching under the phrase "pseudonyms," since many children's series books were written under pseudonyms. I then searched under the preferred Library of Congress subject heading, "anonyms and pseudonyms." Neither yielded any results. I also tried several personal name searches, under authors' real names as well as their pseudonyms. Sadly, neither "Carolyn Keene" nor "Nancy Drew" produced any results, or even any clues. For the most part my RLIN searches were an exercise in frustration.

Why was I so unsuccessful in my searching? In a 1953 letter written to the assistant director of the University of Iowa library, Mildred Benson alluded to the bibliographic problems created by ghostwriting and pseudonyms:

> There never has been a complete listing of my books anywhere.
> The Library of Congress attempted to do it a number of years ago.
> However, the Stratemeyer Syndicate for which I did considerable
> work in such series as the Nancy Drew, Kay Tracey etc., under
> pen names copyrighted by them, objected to any listing except in
> their name, and the Library agreed to this. I wrote the books, and
> I think it might be well to have my complete list somewhere on
> record, as the Nancy Drew volumes in particular have been
> claimed by persons who had practically no connection with the
> series. (Benson to Grace Wormer, February 25, 1953, Benson papers, Box 1)

Obviously, it's hard to track down the manuscripts of children's series books when the identities of the authors have been suppressed.

But another reason for my lack of success is the way that archival collections have been cataloged. Archivists are notoriously idiosyncratic. Many find Library of Congress subject headings at best cumbersome and at worst entirely inadequate for describing their holdings. So they construct their own subject headings, thus making it difficult for researchers to determine what subject headings to search under. And different repositories may index collections at different levels, some giving each collection only two or three subject headings, others giving twenty-five. This will, not surprisingly, have some effect on access to the collection. I thought a lot about this when I considered how I would catalog the papers of Mildred Wirt Benson, who wrote under twelve names.

But such searches are also limited by the number of repositories that are members of RLIN. Most of the published guides derive their information from questionnaires and so are dependent on the good graces and compliance of repositories in filling out and returning their questionnaires. Many repositories, especially smaller ones, do not have either the financial resources or the staff time necessary to belong to RLIN or to report their holdings to any such national guide or database.

Thus, one of the main problems with trying to locate manuscript sources through published guides or automated databases is that there is no one guide or database that includes all repositories.

The low status accorded to the genre of series books has also contributed to the problem. While a few institutions, most notably the University of Minnesota, the University of Southern Mississippi, and the University of South Florida, have deliberately collected children's series books, few others have made the concerted efforts necessary to track down the papers of syndicates and writers. Given the secrecy surrounding the authorship of series books, this is often a difficult task.

I'm afraid that the case of the missing manuscripts does not have the sort of tidy ending that one finds in Nancy Drew mysteries. Tracking down the papers of children's series authors—especially those who used pseudonyms or wrote for syndicates—requires that the researcher be something of a sleuth. Like the heroines of these series books, researchers must seek clues in out-of-the-way places. As my own research illustrates, the missing manuscripts won't generally be found through traditional routes, at least not at this time. Rather, chance conversations with chums and stout-hearted collectors, bibliographies and footnotes in scholarly works and in fanzines, and consultations with archivists and librarians are all likely to yield clues as to the whereabouts of archival sources. Whatever route one takes in seeking these manuscript sources, a good deal of sleuthing will be necessary. But as the Mildred Wirt Benson papers demonstrate, the results are well worth the effort.

CHAPTER 21

Mildred Wirt Benson Books
and the Iowa Authors Collection

Robert A. McCown

In addition to the Iowa Women's Archives holdings of Mildred Wirt Benson manuscripts, the University of Iowa Special Collections Department also houses in its Iowa Authors Collection copies of the published novels written by Mildred Wirt Benson.

The Iowa Authors Collection has about thirteen thousand printed volumes as well as related manuscript materials for over two thousand Iowa authors. The collection is made up of the writing of Iowans and is not necessarily a collection *about* Iowa. It covers a wide range of subjects and forms, including fiction, poetry, drama, biography, history, science, mysteries, children's books, autobiography, cookbooks, and family histories. There is no "yardstick of quality" for admission of a book to the collection; we do not act as referees. Thus the collection is, in fact, an accurate reflection of the output of Iowa writers.

The collection was started after World War II in order to preserve the record of Iowa writers for the benefit of present and future generations of Iowans. Another hope was that such an impressive history might also stimulate students interested in writing. Most importantly, the books and manuscripts would be available for reference and research.

The collection holds not only first editions, but all subsequent editions as well, including translations, paperbacks, large print editions, and limited editions. When possible, the book jackets are left on the books.

When the library chooses to acquire materials for Special Collections, it makes a commitment to provide responsible custody for that material in the future. In other words, collections should be preserved, should be provided protective housing, appropriate environmental conditions, fire detection and suppression systems, effective security, and a staff which has been trained to properly handle and care for the collection.

Books in the collection are obtained in a variety of ways. Many books were donated by their authors, their relatives, or friends. Every month a list of known Iowa authors is checked against a record of new books published. Out-of-print books are sometimes difficult to obtain, but catalogs of antiquarian dealers are searched for hard-to-locate volumes. In addition to printed books, the collection contains manuscript material—that is, correspondence, reminiscences, diaries, journals, drafts, photographs, and similar papers. Such manuscripts customarily come as gifts from the authors or their families. In addition, for many of the authors we collect biographical information which we maintain in alphabetical file folders. Newspaper clippings on an author, for instance, can often answer a reference question.

In the mid-1960s Frank Paluka, then head of the Special Collections Department, wrote a book entitled *Iowa Authors: A Bibliography of Sixty Native Writers* (1967). This volume contains a list of books by Mildred Wirt Benson, compiled with her assistance and believed to be complete through 1963. It includes both English and translated editions. Frank Paluka set out to acquire a copy of every book on the list. Later there appeared a complete list of books by Benson in an article by Geoffrey Lapin, in *Books at Iowa* (1989). Many of the Mildred Wirt Benson volumes now in the collection were the gift of Geoffrey Lapin, and others were purchased from antiquarian booksellers.

Years ago the staff of Special Collections decided that it was important to preserve the writings of Iowa authors and set up a well-defined plan to acquire books and manuscripts by Iowans. While some of the books in our collection can be found in other libraries, this collection is unusual. I think we can fairly say that the Iowa Authors Collection not only has Iowa significance, but is of regional, national, and even international importance. If the collection did not exist, future understanding of such Iowa writers as Mildred Wirt Benson would be greatly diminished.

CHAPTER 22

Sources for Research on Nancy Drew

Karen Nelson Hoyle

I t is fitting to note that academic interest in reading Nancy Drew first drew the attention of educators at the University of Iowa. It was on the Iowa campus in 1967 that G. Robert Carlsen, then a University of Iowa professor, wrote *Books and the Teen-age Reader*.

Before that time few scholars had considered adolescent literature a field for serious study. Carlsen's book was one of the first to deal with the reading needs of young people, specifically by identifying the qualities of various kinds of writing especially suited to these interests. His book not only described the characteristics of books that appeal to teenagers, but also included suggested titles in each category for such young readers. Carlsen's work was revised and updated in 1971 and 1980. Two of Carlsen's former students, Kenneth L. Donelson and Alleen Pace Nilsen, as members of the faculty at Arizona State University, built upon Carlsen's work in a book of their own, *Literature for Today's Young Adults*. This book also has been used widely and is now in its third edition.

There is some irony in the fact that the Nancy Drew Conference was held on the campus of a major university when we consider in what low esteem books such as the Nancy Drew series were held generally by high school teachers until fairly recent times. Donelson and Nilsen observed that "whatever disagreements librarians and English teachers may have had over the years about books suitable for young adults, they ineffectively bonded together and opposed the books produced by Edward Stratemeyer and his numerous writers" (Carlsen, 509). The country's establishment of librarians and teachers of English condemned Stratemeyer and his authors, including his daughter, Harriet Adams, and Mildred Wirt Benson. Interestingly, many of the participants in the Nancy Drew Conference were among the same librarians and teachers who had opposed such literature for youth only a few decades ago.

Despite this widespread condemnation of such series as the Nancy Drew stories (and perhaps even because of it), they quickly became bestsellers, loved by thousands of girls for decades. Because librarians and teachers refused to buy such books, which they considered to be "trash" or at best "pap" with little educational or cultural merit, families, friends, and young readers themselves purchased them by the thousands, much to the joy of the publishers (and the dismay of self-styled "cultural leaders"). Today these same books are championed by some academics as significant contributions of our national popular culture and are sought by curators for preservation and future study in rare book collections.

In earlier years, when most professional educators were snubbing the series books, there were a few forward-looking individuals in the academic world who understood the importance of this maligned genre and insisted that their research libraries acquire such books.

Russell Nye at Michigan State University was a pioneer in urging recognition of boys' and girls' series books as significant contributors to the nation's popular culture. As early as 1969 a few writers saw the value of such studies. That year an article by Arthur Prager, "The Secret of Nancy Drew—Pushing Forty and Going Strong," was published in *Saturday Review*. In 1971 Selma Lanes, a reviewer for the *New York Times*, discussed series books in her work *Down the Rabbit Hole: Adventures and Misadventures in the Realm of Children's Literature*. After completing her doctoral dissertation on Vladimir Nabokov, writer Bobbie Ann Mason reread some of the girls' series books she recalled fondly from her youth and in 1975 wrote *The Girl Sleuth: A Feminist Guide*, published by the Feminist Press.[1]

In 1975 Marilyn A. Nichols wrote a paper in partial fulfillment of requirements for her M.A. degree in Library Science at Minnesota, entitled "A Study of the Nancy Drew Mystery Books Series." Its purpose was to test the hypothesis that in spite of changes in authorship Nancy Drew books had actually changed very little from their first publication over more than forty years. Another article on this series appeared in the *New York Times Book Review* in 1975 by children's poet Karla Kuskin, called "Nancy Drew and Friends."

Deidre Johnson compiled and annotated a definitive checklist, *Stratemeyer Pseudonyms and Series Books* (1982). She has since written her dissertation in American Studies at the University of Minnesota (1990) on Stratemeyer, and in 1993 Twayne Publishers issued her book *Edward Stratemeyer and the Stratemeyer Syndicate*. Mildred Wirt Benson's authorship of the early Nancy Drew books was finally brought to public attention by Geoffrey S. Lapin in a 1983 article in *Yellowback Library*, "Carolyn Keene, Pseud."

Freelance researcher Carol Billman included the chapter "Nancy Drew, Gothic Detection" in her book *The Secret of the Stratemeyer Syndicate* (1986). A collectors' group, the Society of Phantom Friends, published the *Girls' Series Companion* (Emburg), ambitiously annotating each title listed.

Among organizations concerned with such popular books for young people the annual joint national conference of the American Culture Association and Popular Culture Association designate a separate section for papers dealing with series books and dime novels.

Special Collections as Research Sources

One of the best guides to such holdings is *Special Collections in Children's Literature*, published by the American Library Association in 1982. An updated edition on relevant national and international repositories is being prepared. Twenty sites of interest to the series book researcher will be listed.

One of these is the University of South Florida in Tampa, which has the Harry K. Hudson Collection of American Juvenile Series Books, including over 4,000 titles written for boys and 1,500 for girls, some dating back to 1901. The collection has 185 Nancy Drew items, consisting of 122 hardcover and 63 softbound books, with multiple formats for many of its Nancy Drew hardcover volumes. For example, *The Secret of the Old Clock* is represented by the blue cloth edition of 1930 as well as the glossy picture cover edition of 1987. It also has a sampling of related books such as *The Nancy Drew Cook-*

book, My Nancy Drew Private Eye Diary, later spinoff paperbacks, and other "Drewiana."

The Library of Congress, as the recipient of all U.S. copyrighted publications, owns the originally submitted copies of these series books. Other notable repositories listed in *Special Collections in Children's Literature* include the Baldwin Collection at the University of Florida in Gainesville and special holdings at Indiana University and the University of Minnesota.

The deGrummond Collection, founded in 1963 at the University of Southern Mississippi, has quite a number of boys' and girls' series books, including some of the Nancy Drew titles. In addition, it has Andrew Svenson's manuscripts, galleys, illustrations, and correspondence for his Happy Hollister and Tolliver series titles. Carol Billman did much of her research for her *The Secret of the Stratemeyer Syndicate* with the deGrummond sources.

Wellesley College Archives, in its Margaret Clapp Library, has an alumna biographical file for Harriet Stratemeyer Adams, a member of the class of 1914. She was one of many authors who worked on the Nancy Drew books. Her file there contains newspaper and magazine clippings and a list of the courses she took at Wellesley. The class of 1914 collection has a folder of clippings and advertisements for Nancy Drew and Hardy Boys books (1968–1982), another folder which has Stratemeyer's "Hints on Procedure for Writing Children's Books," an outline for the Nancy Drew book *The Crooked Banister* (1971), and some correspondence. The 1914 class yearbook and record books of the class reunions are also there. Unfortunately, however, Harriet Adams's personal manuscripts and papers are not in the collection.[2]

In addition to the reference sources describing special collections, other sources for information are found in electronic databases. On-line catalogs available to libraries and researchers across the country, such as OCLC and RLIN, become increasingly valuable as special collections report their holdings. Most research libraries can handle reference questions from scholars using E-mail and FAX, as well as telephone and correspondence. However, response time depends on the frequently understaffed special collections staff. Scholars and curators form an informal network of knowledgeable people, often referred to as the "invisible university," who can exchange information at conferences and through electronic mail. Individuals can subscribe to electronic exchanges or "listservs" such as Ex-Libris in the rare book and special collections field.

The Children's Literature Research Collections

I conclude with information on holdings from the source I know best, the University of Minnesota Children's Literature Research Collections (CLRC). In the reading room at CLRC, in the Walter Library in Minneapolis, some 10,000 series books about boys, girls, families, and animals are available for study. The nucleus of these holdings consists of a massive collection of dime novels, weekly story papers, and children's series novels, generously willed to the University by the late George Hess, a Saint Paul business executive. University librarian Edward B. Stanford urged Hess to donate his collection. Here can be found a later edition of *Cousin Lucy's Conversations*, originally published in 1841. All eleven of the *Aunt Jane's Nieces* by L. Frank Baum (pseud. Edith Van Dyne) are here. Most Twins of the World by Lucy Fitch Perkins, beginning with *The Dutch Twins* (1911), are also here.

Perhaps the most notable and widely known of Minnesota's Children's Literature Research Collections is the Kerlan Collection. Begun as a personal hobby by Dr. Irvin Kerlan, a devoted alumnus, the collection which he bequeathed to the university at his death in 1963 now holds manuscripts and artists' renderings for children's book illustrations for more than 7,000 titles. Its books now number more than 55,000 volumes. Of interest to students of series novels are the manuscripts for the All-of-a-Kind Family by Sydney Taylor, Kitty and Angel series by Judy Delton, and the Julia Redfern stories by Eleanor Cameron. Most of the Nancy Drew titles are also represented here, in various editions. Regrettably, there are few truly pristine original printings in dust jackets for the first thirty in that series.

Like other curators of special collections, we would love to have the first four titles in the Nancy Drew series in their first printings published in 1930. It is important that collectors, scholars, and archivists talk to each other and share each other's finds. We depend on this community to tell us where there are good runs of Nancy Drews or manuscripts for children's series books by other authors, too.

Among the two most useful tools now available for the study of children's literature in the CLRC were both compiled and published at Minnesota. The first, a must source for work on girls' series books, is the checklist *Girls Series Books*. It was first published to cover only the years 1900 to 1975. In 1992, with financial assistance from the Saint Paul Foundation, a new and greatly expanded edition appeared under the title *Girls Series Books, 1840–1991*. It lists over one hundred titles for the basic Nancy Drew series, sixty-one for the Nancy Drew Files series, and numerous other titles for the Nancy Drew & Hardy Boys series.

The second source of information on unique materials at CLRC bears the title *The Kerlan Collection Manuscripts and Illustrations*. With its 432 pages, it offers the researcher an overview of the kinds of source materials that can be found at Minnesota. A newsletter informs researchers of new acquisitions since its publication in early 1985. For example, manuscripts have recently arrived for Joan Lowery Nixon's Hollywood Daughters and Constance Greene's Isabelle books.

The CLRC at Minnesota acquires some related materials besides books, manuscripts, and book illustrations. Gifts arrive weekly, one example being an issue of the Nancy Drew newsletter. We welcome visitors to our special collections and archives and look forward to assisting them in their sleuthing.

NOTES

1. Mason's *The Girl Sleuth* was scheduled for reissue by the University of Georgia Press in 1995.

2. The Harriet Adams personal papers are part of the Stratemeyer Syndicate papers given to the New York Public Library by Simon & Schuster in the summer of 1993. They will eventually be available to researchers.

PART IV

Transforming Nancy Drew

"Goodnight, Gretchen. Goodnight, Monica."

"Goodnight, Anna."

Anna, that's me, the biggest Nancy Drew fan ever. In every spare moment you can see me curled up somewhere, Nancy Drew in hand. Tonight Nancy Drew, The Mystery of the Brass Bound Trunk *(1940), and I were baby-sitting.*

I took one last look at the kids and tiptoed into a cozy, lighted room down the hall. I made myself comfortable on the large mass of pillows behind me. Grasping the book in my hands, I began to slip out of my world and into the town of River Heights. . . .

   —ANNA DEY,

    AGE 12, GRADE 7,

    MAHARISHI SCHOOL OF

    THE AGE OF ENLIGHTENMENT,

    FAIRFIELD, IOWA

The name and image of Nancy Drew as a plucky and persistent sleuth have had remarkable durability in the last sixty-five years despite numerous changes as the publishers attempted to make new books appeal more to contemporary audiences of children. Most obvious have been changes in her appearance as pictured on the colorful covers and book jackets of successive illustrators, the systematic revisions of the books beginning in 1959, and the introduction of a very contemporary teenage Nancy in the Nancy Drew Files series in 1986. More significant have been changes wrought to take Nancy to the movies in the 1930s and to television in the 1970s as producers acquired rights to use the name but made no commitment to make their work true to some version of the books.

Despite these changes and transformations of Nancy, the concept of Nancy Drew has entered the public domain, so her name and characteristics can be referred to in everyday conversation, the mass media, and other popular culture forms without further explanation to convey ideas about curious women or amateur detectives. And characteristics associated with her evoke her name in every imaginable setting. For example, when women, especially women named Nancy, ask a lot of questions or seem to poke their noses where they are not wanted they are often confronted with the rhetorical question: Who do you think you are—Nancy Drew? Women sleuths in contemporary mysteries often compare their own techniques to hers. Both book reviewers and other characters in the mysteries often refer to these modern women detectives as updated or grown-up Nancy Drews. And when someone is called on to solve a not-too-perplexing mystery, we find suggestions that the task is one for Nancy Drew.

In each instance Nancy Drew is transformed to meet the users' needs, and it is often difficult to determine which Nancy Drew is the referent, who is the true teenage detective as users remake her to serve their purposes. The essays in this section address the process of transformation, the extension of this popular cultural icon into new realms. They have been organized along a continuum from the most specific and concrete to the most conceptual and abstract. They begin with academic interpretations of the changes between the original and revised books and books and films and proceed to a series of firsthand accounts by writers and an artist of how they have been influenced by Nancy Drew.

In chapter 23, a joint essay by a student of popular film and a cultural historian of popular fiction, Diana Beeson and Bonnie Brennen trace the changes in the representation of the story in three versions of *The Hidden Staircase*, the second and arguably most popular of the Nancy Drew books. Focusing on one story in the original version by Mildred Wirt Benson, the rewrite published under the direction of Harriet Stratemeyer Adams, and one of four Nancy Drew films produced in the 1930s, Beeson and Brennen analyze the stories and their representation in their historical and cultural contexts, comparing them to other books and films produced at the time. Their essay goes well beyond the nostalgic lament that is common to many research papers and feature articles on changes in the books to offer an explanation that helps us understand the changes.

It has become a cliché for reviewers of first novels by new women mystery writers who feature female protagonists to compare their detectives to Nancy Drew or to ask whether the authors had been inspired by Carolyn Keene to write mysteries. Like all clichés, however, the comparisons and questions are often apt if unoriginal. Indeed, many women who write mysteries *were* among those readers who either began writing their own Nancy Drews at an early age or identified themselves with Carolyn Keene as much as with Nancy Drew as they worked their way through her body of work.

Therefore, in our examination of the impact of Nancy Drew on her readers and popular culture, it was important to include modern adult women mystery writers on the program. Adding significance to the legacy of Carolyn Keene to contemporary women mystery writers is the fact that the work of American women writers at the time of the conference had only recently come to be more popular than the books of the men who had dominated the mystery field for decades, just as Nancy Drew had outpaced the popularity of the Hardy Boys books not long after she was introduced.

After considering each of a dozen or more women sleuths we knew had "consulted" Nancy Drew in their work or writers who had publicly acknowledged a debt to Nancy Drew, we settled on Nancy Pickard, the creator of the amateur detective Jenny Cain, and Linda Barnes, whose part-time professional detective Carlotta Carlyle occasionally reflects on how differently Nancy Drew would have solved the mystery confronting her.

As president of the women mystery writers and readers organization Sisters in Crime, Pickard had written the introduction to Phil Zuckerman's reprint of the original *The Hidden Staircase*. That introductory essay, entitled "I Owe It All to Nancy Drew," specifically answered the question about Nancy's influence on modern women mystery writers and their sleuths. So we have included that essay as chapter 24 rather than a transcript of Pickard's more informal talk as a representation of her contribution. Her responses to questions and comments in the transcription of the discussion session, chapter 26, elaborate considerably more fully how she has progressed from a reader of Nancy Drew to a professional writer of detective fiction.

Linda Barnes was on the preliminary list of mystery writers who might be invited before her longtime good friend Bonnie S. Sunstein joined the conference planning committee and agreed to invite her to participate. As chapter 25 reveals, while Barnes's protagonist is aware of Nancy's legacy to all fictional women sleuths, Carlotta Carlyle departs from that heritage in nearly every respect. What Carolyn Keene and Nancy Drew did leave Barnes and Carlyle were a genre of writing and a demonstration of the appealing qualities of stories told in series.

Paralleling discussion by the editor and writer of the new Nancy Drews in chapter 9, the question and answer session involving Pickard and Barnes in chapter 26 explores the process of writing mystery series in considerable depth, revealing an audience almost as interested in writing as it was in Nancy Drew.

Long after the program was completed for the Nancy Drew Conference, a manila envelope enclosing a cover letter and a page of color slides arrived in our Iowa City office from Hawaii. Laura Ruby, the artist whose work was pictured in the slides, suggested that we might want to consider showing her work during the conference. When we held the slides up to the fluorescent light in the office, we immediately recognized the familiar silhouettes of Nancy Drew from successive editions of the books. These images marched down stairs, into a steamer trunk, and across a page of what appeared to be Chinese text. In addition to the multiple Nancys in the slides were symbols and representations from other genres of popular culture such as movie mysteries and Marx Brothers comedies.

When we were able to see the entire images clearly by projecting them on a screen and then fixing them in color photocopies we could pass around, we recognized they were works of exceptional visual and technical quality. More relevant to the Nancy Drew Project, we were drawn instinctively into the task of deciphering the clues and solving the mysteries of association they posed. As we showed them to artists and others planning the conference their responses were the same as ours: to recognize many of the elements, to regard them as puzzles to solve, and to talk about the associations with the Nancy Drew book each took as its theme.

Ruby's Nancy Drew Series of serigraphs clearly represented an original and significant transformation of Nancy Drew that was at the same time both recognizable and utterly new. Despite our full program and lack of a fixed place to display the work, we arranged to bring Ruby and her prints to the conference. They were hung on several panels of portable office walls which were moved each day as the central gathering place for the conference changed. As people congregated to register, await the start of a session, or relax, they, as we had been, were drawn to the prints. Strangers asked each other's help or confirmation as they decoded the references. Collectors and scholars, adults and children, indeed most of the participants, joined in the experience the prints afforded and shared their knowledge and understanding of Nancy Drew in these transformations to a new medium.

During the conference, Ruby conducted impromptu gallery talks for participants, clearly explaining her work for anyone who asked. She made a formal presentation about the series which is included as chapter 27, illustrated with reproductions of some of the prints. Ruby explains the concepts on which the work is based and, like the other essayists in this section, describes the process of transforming the familiar, shared experience of the Nancy Drew books to a new form.

As such a familiar figure in popular culture, Nancy Drew continues to inspire transformations, particularly in the realm of parody and satire (Chamberlain 1994). In the months following the Nancy Drew Conference, a satirical play and the first in a new series of parodies drew considerable public attention. The Stage Left Theater and the Body Politic in Chicago had to extend the run of *The Clue in the Old Birdbath* several times in the summer of 1993, so popular was the 1978 play by Kate Kasten of Iowa City and Sandra de Helen (Stefaniak). Cleis Press issued the first Nancy Clue Mystery by Mabel Maney, *The Case of the Not-So-Nice Nurse*, in 1993 and its sequel, *The Case of the Good-for-Nothing Girlfriend*, in 1994.

CHAPTER 23

Translating Nancy Drew
from Print to Film

Diana Beeson and Bonnie Brennen

Nancy Drew has the distinction of remaining a teenager over a span of more than six decades. She sprang Athena-like out of the head of Edward Stratemeyer in 1930, but her stout heart and generous mind were steeled by Mildred Wirt Benson, who wrote twenty-three of the first thirty books in the series. Nancy, however, was not the creative ideation of a single set of parents. During her sixty-five years as a teenage sleuth, a multitude of authors have assumed the pen name Carolyn Keene, writing new mysteries and revising the old ones, to maintain Nancy's status as a contemporary of her reading public.

This essay looks at the changing Nancy Drew as her character shifts over time on the pages of her books and as her characterization undergoes treatment by Hollywood. It focuses specifically on the second book in the series, *The Hidden Staircase* (1930), written by Benson. A film of the same name was released in 1939, and some twenty years later, in 1959, Simon & Schuster issued a revised and updated version of the book.

An examination of Nancy Drew in two versions of the same book and a film presumably based on the book will demonstrate that Nancy Drew, as a fictional character, is anything but static, enduring, and unchanging—although that's how most of her audience remembers her. For most readers, however avidly they read Nancy Drew mysteries, their acquaintance with her was a relatively brief interlude in their recreational reading careers. After a summer or a single year in grade school or junior high, they moved on to other mysteries or other kinds of books.

Readers who entered grade school after 1959 probably became acquainted with the "modernized" postwar Nancy Drew of the 1950s. Older readers, and younger ones who became beneficiaries of the originals from the 1930s and 1940s, became acquainted with the Nancy Drew of the Depression and World War II.

In the Nancy Drew mysteries of the 1930s, our sleuth is intelligent, honest, self-confident, kind, and courageous. As an independent young woman, she actively challenges the role of women in American society. Nancy Drew works alone and frequently acts outside generally accepted boundaries. She has an exceptional relationship with her father, who treats her as an equal partner rather than as a subordinate child.

Beginning in 1959, thirty-four of the Nancy Drew mysteries were "updated" and revised. Some of the most obvious racist and antisemitic representations were removed, along with outmoded sexual stereotypes. The language was simplified and plots were redesigned, presumably to appeal to more contemporary audiences. Yet we would suggest that in their attempts to revitalize Nancy Drew much of what makes the series so exceptional was lost.

The simplified stories exclude many of the cultural signposts and messages relevant to the 1930s. Nancy's independent character is softened and in these newer texts she relies much more heavily upon others for help and guidance. The post-1959 editions encode very different messages which reflect the mores, expectations, and experiences of postwar American society.

In the 1930 version of *The Hidden Staircase*, Nancy Drew is the resourceful and efficient only child of attorney Carson Drew. Nancy confronts dangerous situations, befriends those less fortunate, and ultimately solves an important mystery. In the opening sequence of the mystery she is home alone. Her father is at work and the housekeeper, Hannah Gruen, has the day off. Nancy is threatened by Nathan Gombet, an intruder who demands to see her father. Although she is frightened by the man's strange conduct, Nancy faces him boldly and successfully handles the situation. Throughout the original book, Nancy is depicted as cool and collected in the face of danger.

The intelligent and independent Nancy Drew mirrors the changing status of American women during the first half of the twentieth century. Like other intelligent women during her era, she challenges traditional notions regarding her role in American society. The passage of the Nineteenth Amendment in 1920 was the culmination of an eighty-year struggle for political equality. Women used their newly won vote to advance a number of social changes. They focused on child labor reform, standards for pure food and drugs, and conservation activities. By the end of the 1920s, twenty-five percent of American women were employed outside the home (Women's Bureau, 35). Many fought actively for equality in the work place and in the home. Writers of fiction during the 1920s and 1930s frequently depicted this new breed of American women as confident, self-assured, and independent.

Like other fictional women of the era, Nancy does not wish to be sheltered and protected; she strives to be self-reliant and brave and wants to be treated as an active and equal member of society. Nancy's independence is supported by her father, Carson. Nancy's mother died when she was three, and Carson has raised her as a single parent. Throughout the original books, he repeatedly encourages her talent for digging into interesting cases. Nancy and Carson interact more like friends and colleagues than father and daughter. Nancy goes to Carson for support and advice but ultimately works alone. She does not rely on the police or any other authority figures.

Reflecting a prevalent ethic of the era that those in the upper and upper middle classes had a social responsibility toward those less fortunate, Nancy regularly befriends poor but honest women who are eternally grateful for her help and guidance. Readers of *The Hidden Staircase* are reminded of Nancy's kind nature in references to women she had previously aided, such as Allie and Grace Horner. In this mystery, Nancy is asked for help by Rosemary Turnbull, one of two elderly sisters, who hears noises and sees shadows in the home she shares with her sister. Nancy agrees to try to solve the mystery and, with revolver in hand, joins the elderly and frightened women. During her stay at their mansion, Nancy also experiences unexplainable music and shadows, disappearing possessions, and strange footsteps during the night. After a few days, she becomes frustrated and feels almost humiliated that she hasn't discovered even a single clue. Of course, our very patient Nancy perseveres and, even when she learns that her father is missing, resolves not to leave the mansion until she has solved the mystery.

Discovering that Nathan Gombet owns the old stone house directly behind the mansion and threatened the Turnbull sisters after they would not sell him their mansion for an extremely low price, Nancy decides that she must investigate Gombet's house without his knowledge. She tells no one of her plans, and after observing Gombet leave in the cloak of darkness she enters his house alone through an open window. She discovers a hidden staircase that connects the two houses and proves that Gombet is the ghost responsible for frightening the Turnbull sisters and kidnapping her father. Nancy consults the police only after she has solved the mystery and needs their help in apprehending the criminal.

Nancy in the Cold War Era

In contrast, the Nancy Drew of the 1959 version of *The Hidden Staircase* is depicted as far less independent and self-confident and relies far more heavily on officials for help and guidance. For example, in the original book, Nancy does not interact with the housekeeper, Hannah Gruen, at all; however, in the updated mystery, Gruen is an active participant in the story. Readers are told: "Mrs. Gruen had lived with the Drews since Nancy was three years old. At that time Mrs. Drew had passed away and Hannah had become like a second mother to Nancy. There was a deep affection between the two, and Nancy confided all her secrets to the understanding housekeeper" (2).

Throughout the book Nancy consults with Hannah Gruen; readers understand that since she was a young girl Nancy has found solace in talking to the housekeeper, who always gives her good advice. Nancy also gets an abundance of support and assistance from the police. She frequently phones in to give them clues she has found and to report anything suspicious. The police track down suspects and help Nancy interpret her leads, and they serve in an official capacity, guarding the haunted mansion and ultimately rescuing her father and apprehending the criminals. Whereas the original Nancy Drew frequently worked outside the law, the new Nancy is a law-abiding citizen. When the updated Nancy realizes that she needs to investigate the other mansion, which happens to be for sale, her friend Helen is "horrified" that she might break in. Nancy assures her: "No Helen, I'm not going to evade the law. I'll go to the realtor who is handling the property and ask him to show me the place" (143).

When it at first becomes unlikely that they will obtain the key, seemingly quite out of character, Nancy gives up and continues to search for other clues. It is clear that this Nancy Drew would never break the law.

It is not surprising that the 1959 version of Nancy Drew has a strong regard for authority. Postwar American society, with its conservative political and economic agenda, focuses on cooperation, law, and conformity. Individuals are continually urged to obey the rules, respect the law, and find legal solutions to problems rather than to take the law into their own hands.

During this era, the Cold War is seen as a dominating world presence that for the most part cancels any hopes for peace. Even socialists who are critical of capitalist society find that because of Stalinism they must align themselves with the West against the Communist bloc. The critics who do attack contemporary American society focus on its impersonal and bureaucratic tendencies and lament the powerlessness of the people to change an increasingly inhuman system (Pells, 186). Politicians react to frustrations over the spread of communism, labor problems, race riots, and increased cost of living due to inflation by instituting a series of investigations meant to determine the patriotism and reliability of Americans. Workers are forced to sign loyalty oaths and Americans are encouraged to prove that they are law-abiding citizens.

As the middle class becomes an undeniable force, scholars such as David Riesman observe a basic change in the character of contemporary American society. Self-disciplined, self-motivated, innerdirected, independent individuals are devalued, challenged, and rejected. Instead, Americans become other-directed, and their identity is linked to group acceptance and approval. Group pressures and influences become increasingly important, and getting along with others is the goal of many individuals. During this era Americans begin to emphasize conformity and focus on issues of status and prestige (Hardt, 145).

The economic and social advances attained by women during the first part of the twentieth century were seriously jeopardized in the postwar period. During the Second World War the United States government faced a severe labor shortage and actively recruited women workers for jobs once considered men's work. Women were convinced they could handle jobs as welders, riveters, drill press operators, and foundry workers. There were campaigns for equal pay, pregnancy leaves, and day care facilities. However, as men returned from war, millions of women were fired from their jobs. Campaigns began to convince women that they were no longer needed in the work place. Women were repeatedly told that their place was now in the home and that motherhood offered the most rewarding profession (Gluck, 261; Gabin).

Unlike our sleuth in the original *Hidden Staircase*, in the updated version, Nancy is rarely alone. Hannah Gruen is with her when the villain, now called Nathan Gomber, first comes to call; her friend Helen accompanies her throughout the mystery and is with her when Nancy discovers the hidden staircase. One may speculate that perhaps it was considered "improper" for young women of this era to venture out alone. In the 1959 edition, none of the characters challenge societal norms. Readers are reassured that Nancy's friend Helen is engaged and soon to be married; the two elderly sisters living together in the mansion are replaced in this version with a more traditional mother and her recently widowed daughter. Gone are the ethnic slurs and racial stereotypes; instead of the vicious "colored" servant, in this mystery the accomplice is a man with a "crinkly" ear.

Although the revised books are cleansed of their stereotypical racial distinctions, new categories of judgment emerge which emphasize conformity and group approval. In the updated *Hidden Staircase*, even the villain Nathan Gomber is not really all that bad. Nancy judges him as "the kind of person who stays within the boundaries of the law but whose ethics are questionable" (5).

Although the newer Nancy is helpful and ultimately successful as a detective, efforts are taken to portray her as a "regular" young woman. There are no extended discussions of the unfortunate individuals she has helped. The two women she befriends are relatives of her friend Helen, rather than less fortunate members of the community. Her relationship with Carson Drew is less notable, more like a traditional father and daughter. He is reassuring and helpful, even reminding Nancy to get ready for her upcoming date. Nancy attends a play and dance with "red-haired, former high school tennis champion" Dirk Jackson. After the date she reflects on the evening and considers "how lucky she was to have Dirk for a date, and what fun it had all been" (16). In the updated mysteries, Nancy Drew is portrayed as a typical teenager who also likes to solve mysteries. She is friendly and helpful, but in no way does she threaten the social expectations and norms of postwar American society.

Transforming Nancy for Film

In both the 1930 and 1959 versions of *The Hidden Staircase*, Nancy Drew's characterization reflects and responds to societal expectations. Her character, at either juncture, would seem to lend itself naturally to film adaptation. She was young, her days were filled with mystery and excitement, she was surrounded by interesting characters, and—perhaps most attractive of all to Hollywood studios—she had a large and dedicated audience.

In 1938 Warner Brothers brought Nancy Drew to the silver screen with results that readers of any of Nancy's literary incarnations would find astonishing and disappointing. All in all, Warner Brothers produced four films. In order of production, they are *Nancy Drew, Detective*, 1938; *Nancy Drew, Reporter*, 1939; *Nancy Drew, Troubleshooter*, 1939; and *Nancy Drew and the Hidden Staircase*, 1939. The films were so bad that one was cited by Justice Arthur J. Goldberg in a 1962 Supreme Court decision disallowing a practice called block booking under which motion picture distributors required television stations to buy packages of films to get the ones they wanted. In his opinion, Justice Goldberg gave some colorful examples of what television stations had to do under block booking. "Station WTOP in Washington, in order to get such film classics as *Casablanca* and *Treasure of the Sierra Madre*, also had to buy *Nancy Drew, Troubleshooter* and *Gorilla Man*" (Lewis, 80). A review of the film *Nancy Drew and the Hidden Staircase* from the November 8, 1939, edition of the entertainment newspaper *Variety* begins: "[The] tale is ostensibly a mystery story" (*Variety Film Reviews*). The qualifying word *ostensibly* provides the first clue that the film might take great liberties with the book's characters and plot. The book, after all, is unqualifiedly a mystery. The movie is not. In fact,

there is very little resemblance between the film and the book outside of the title, the names of a few characters, and the fact that in
both there is a staircase.

Nancy Drew and the Hidden Staircase, released in November
1939, was the fourth and last in a series of Nancy Drew films produced by Warner Brothers. The films starred Bonita Granville as
Nancy Drew. Granville, the child of vaudevillians, began her show
business career at an early age and broke into films because of her
uncanny resemblance to a popular fair-haired actress of the 1930s,
Ann Harding (Maltin, 100).

Granville played a number of juvenile roles and in 1936 received an Academy Award nomination in the Best Supporting Actress category for her performance in *These Three* (Shale, 320). Granville made fifty-one films before retiring in 1956. Due to the critical
acclaim she received for her role in *These Three*, she was most often
cast as an unpleasant adolescent before graduating to ingenue roles
in a succession of little noted films produced in the 1940s. "Gosh!
Wouldn't it be awful," Granville said in an interview in 1940, "if
people always remembered me as the worst brat in the movies" (Maltin, 99). Her adeptness at such portrayals is evident in her performance as Nancy Drew. In a later review of the four Nancy Drew
films, Melanie Knight wrote: "Acting, said David Hemmings once,
isn't thinking, 'it's pretending to be.' Whoever Bonita Granville is
'pretending to be' in these movies, it isn't Nancy Drew" (Knight, 8).

In Benson's 1930 version of the book, Nancy discovers the hidden staircase in an act of cunning desperation at the end of chapter 19. After finding that she is trapped in a locked room on the top
floor of the villain's mansion, the chapter ends ominously with the
following passage:

> Curiously, Nancy stepped inside the closet and twisted the
> knob. She thought she heard a clicking noise. Was it only imagi-
> nation?
>
> Eagerly, she examined the back wall of the closet and inter-
> est quickened. In the dim light, she could make out a long crack.
> She tapped the wall with her knuckles, and it had a hollow sound.
>
> "I believe I've stumbled upon something important," Nancy
> thought excitedly.
>
> With all her might, she pushed upon the knob. Unexpect-

edly, a spring clicked and the entire side of the closet wall dropped down!

Nancy struggled to maintain her balance, but could not. She toppled forward and fell headlong down a steep flight of stone steps.

A low cry of pain escaped her, then she lay still. (149–150)

The movie treats the discovery quite differently. Instead of finding herself trapped and alone, she is with her friend *Ted* Nickerson. While Nancy Drew, in later books, had a friend named Ned Nickerson, he did not appear in *The Hidden Staircase*. And no one named Ted Nickerson ever appeared in any of the Nancy Drew books. Nevertheless, Ted is a prominent character in the film.

Nancy and Ted are characterized as foils for one another. Ted is sensible, cautious, and a reluctant participant in the exploits that pass for sleuthing in the film. In contrast to Ted, the Nancy of film is flighty and manipulative. She is not invited to help people with the unexplained occurrences in their lives as she is in the book. Rather, she has a zany inability to mind her own business, and it is this quality that gets them into what Ted describes as "a jam."

In both versions of the book, the discovery of the hidden staircase is a cliffhanger used as a device to heighten the narrative tension and create the kind of suspense that draws the reader into the next chapter. In the film, the discovery is devoid of suspense. Instead, the scene is played for laughs. Nancy tries to find the secret entrance to the hidden staircase by pushing on bricks in the mansion's basement; of course, it is Ted who figures out the entrance must open by means of a lever disguised as a coat rack. He pulls the lever as Nancy is pushing on the bricks. The door swings open and Nancy executes a pratfall into the hidden passage, accompanied on the soundtrack by an appropriate clarinet *glissando*. She is seen sitting, legs splayed, firmly planted on her backside. Ted runs to her aid, saying, "You mighta busted your neck."

Nancy delivers the punchline: "I didn't land on my neck."

The scene is played for laughs because the film is a screwball mystery, a genre that descended from the screwball comedy in which suspense is used as a comic device. In 1934 the genre of the screwball mystery was established with the box office hit *The Thin Man*. The film was based on Dashiell Hammett's book and was among the first to successfully wed detective fiction with screwball comedy. Its commercial success spawned sequels, direct imitations, and variations on similar themes. As film critic Ed Sikov wrote, "Something evidently clicked between the detective drama and the screwball comedy. The studios couldn't make enough of them" (Sikov, 199). Like the western, the musical, the hard-boiled detective drama, and the gangster film, the screwball mystery became a genre unto itself with its own formulae and conventions.

The Thin Man series, along with several other notable screwball mysteries, such as Topper and It's a Wonderful World, featured some of Hollywood's luminaries. Films such as these were on the studio's A-list, meaning they had the budgets to hire from Hollywood's stable of proven box office draws and develop productions with all the style, sophistication, and polish the genre demanded. The Nancy Drew films, however, were B movies. The films were low budget; the cast was composed of young, unproven Hollywood hopefuls and a smattering of older character actors whose stars had never risen; and due to budget constraints the films were "two-reelers," generally no longer than sixty-five minutes. The B movies of the 1930s were rarely a theater's feature presentation. More commonly, they had second billing on a double feature slate.

On the surface, it might appear that the Nancy Drew films and films such as Shadow of the Thin Man have very little in common. In fact, they are quite comparable in that these films contain the classic elements of the screwball mystery genre, including leisure time, depiction of the social "upper crust," romantic or sexual tension created by a seemingly antagonistic couple, resolution of class conflicts, and gender role confusion (Gehring; Schatz, 152, 155, 159; Sikov, 15–22, 29, 92, 106, 158, 173). The Nancy Drew films produced by Warner Brothers in 1938 and 1939 contain all of these elements, thereby transforming Nancy from a capable detective with maturity beyond her years to a screwball comedian.

Leisure time is crucial to the screwball mystery. Not only does it reinforce the depiction of the characters as members of the leisure class, but it helps to explain why they happen to be home when mysterious strangers come to the door and how they have the time to spend their days tracking down clues and pursuing villains.

While leisure time usually connotes elevated social standing, the connection had to be made abundantly clear in the screwball films of the 1930s since the Depression had reduced the social standing of large numbers of Americans and given them leisure time, not by choice but by circumstance. Screwball mysteries often took place in opulent settings and the amateur sleuths tracked clues with toys of the wealthy, such as fast cars, boats, and even airplanes. These props separated them from those with involuntary leisure time. Their membership in high society also was a plot device whereby they could use their social connections to gain access to crime scenes and privileged information. The characters were wealthy enough to treat public servants, namely the police, like servants.

Leisure time and elevated social standing are consistent with Nancy Drew's literary persona. Her father was a well-respected lawyer, the Drew family employed household help, and Nancy owned a new roadster throughout the Depression. She also had plenty of leisure time and made good use of it. Most of the tales in the books take place during her summer vacation, and if all the mysteries she solved over a sixty-year period were accomplished over the usual seventy-day summer break, she averages more than three solutions per day.

Although these elements are ostensibly consistent with the character in the books, in the film they become distorted. In the books, Nancy has a certain amount of *noblesse oblige*. She is gracious and charitable in all social encounters. In the film, as the daughter of a successful River Heights attorney, she has become slightly spoiled. Her father and her boyfriend do not encourage her sleuthing. They appear merely to tolerate it and humor her because if she gets her own way she is likely to be less of a nuisance.

In Benson's version of *The Hidden Staircase*, there is not so much as a hint of romance in Nancy's life. Outside of her father and the villain, there are no major male characters. Her boyfriend Ned Nickerson isn't introduced until later in the series. It's quite clear that Nancy is single-minded in her purpose to succeed as a detective, and at least in this early work there is no room for anything that might obscure her objective. In the film, however, Ted Nickerson is a pivotal character. He is with Nancy every step of the way. Their relationship is antagonistic on the surface. They trade verbal jabs, but throughout, as is consistent with the screwball mystery genre, the viewer knows that the teasing is all in good fun and, at some point, their attraction to each other will be revealed.

The prototype for this relationship as a comic device was established by Clark Gable and Claudette Colbert in Frank Capra's classic screwball comedy *It Happened One Night*. The device employs
characterization of a couple with differing values, backgrounds, and
temperaments. They seem never to agree, yet one always goes along
with the other's plans, reluctantly and against his or her better
judgment. The implication, of course, is that the recalcitrant character is not motivated by judgment, but rather by forces more biologi-
cal in nature. Whether or not there is closure through a proposal or
marriage, it always becomes apparent that the couple's battle of wits
will dissolve into mutual affection (Schatz, 152).

In *Nancy Drew and the Hidden Staircase*, that moment comes
as Ted and Nancy are making their way through the secret passage
that connects the Turnbull sisters' mansion with its twin, owned by
the villain. They are impeded by a puddle of water. Ted suggests
it might be a deep, water-filled hole, to which Nancy replies, "Let's
find out."

Ready on the draw with a verbal jab, Ted responds, "Find out?
You find out. You won't sink with those boats you're wearing."

Nancy braves her way across the puddle, but upon hearing a
croaking frog she screams with terror and rushes back to the safety
of Ted's waiting arms. They enjoy a brief but tender embrace before
realizing no official truce has been called in the battle of the sexes.
They self-consciously disengage and Ted fires the first salvo in the
new campaign with the taunt, "Don't tell me you're a-ascared of
frogs."

While Ted takes occasional potshots at Nancy's physical and
emotional frailties, Nancy retaliates by indicating to Ted that his social background makes him not quite worthy of her. Ted, unlike
Nancy, does not have leisure time. He has to work over the summer,
delivering ice. After Ted makes a delivery to the Drew household,
Nancy says, "I do wish you'd chosen a job for the summer that was a
little more genteel." To make her case, as well as to point out that
she and Ted normally travel in different social circles, she says,
"What do you suppose people will think when they ask, 'Who's your
friend?' and I say, 'The iceman'?"

The seemingly mismatched couple from different class backgrounds is another convention of the screwball mystery. One half of
the couple, usually the male lead, is an ordinary "working stiff" with

small-town sensibilities and traditional middle-class values, such as monogamy, democracy, egalitarianism, and rugged individualism. The female lead, on the other hand, generally is from a privileged background. At the outset, she's spoiled, impulsive, self-willed, and often eccentric. As the couple work together to solve the mystery, it becomes apparent that her manners are intentional affectations and that, fundamentally, her values are the same as his.

This message of class conflict resolution was particularly important to audiences in the 1930s, when the Depression heightened awareness of economic disparities. Films using the convention of a couple overcoming their ideological differences suggested to those audiences that they should not lose faith in the traditional American ideal of a classless utopian society (Schatz, 152).

The final convention of the screwball mystery that manifests itself in *Nancy Drew and the Hidden Staircase* is gender role confusion. In the genre, the female lead is self-assured and confident that she is on equal footing with her male counterpart. In fact, she is dominant and tends to control his every action. Occasionally, this is merely exasperating to the male lead and serves to fuel the antagonism that creates the sexual tension between the couple, but sometimes female domination takes a more extreme course and results in a complete reversal of traditional gender roles (Gehring, 15). Storylines often include several scenes in which the female lead barks out orders and commands while men scurry around, hurriedly trying to comply, as in the Howard Hawks film *His Girl Friday*. Sometimes, as if the verbal indicators of dominance and control are not enough to show role reversal, the genre employs the visual cues of cross-dressing.

In *Nancy Drew and the Hidden Staircase*, both verbal and visual cues are abundantly evident. Nancy humiliates Ted in front of the River Heights police by making him appear to be a "mama's boy." She makes him spend the night in a dank cellar. She has him procure a gun for her, she commandeers his truck, and she orders him to tamper with evidence at the murder scene, an order with which he complies even though it's a felonious act.

To ensure that the role reversal is not lost on the audience, Ted appears in the River Heights police chief's office dressed in women's clothes. Nancy and her father happen to be in the chief's office when Ted is brought in by an officer who arrested him for this transgression. Ted tells Carson Drew that somebody "swiped" his clothes while he was sleeping in the cellar at the Turnbull mansion and that the satin Victorian gown, complete with bustle, was all he could find to cover himself so that he could leave the mansion after he awoke. He does not explain why he also donned the matching hat, placing it rakishly to one side, or why he also wore the bustle. Nancy, on the other hand, frequently wears trousers. While by contemporary standards pants are acceptable attire for women, in the 1930s they were considered somewhat daring, especially when Nancy is seen wearing pants nearly as often as Ted.

It's evident that the plot and characters in Benson's version of *The Hidden Staircase* were transformed from detective fiction to screwball comedy when the book became a film. The question is why?

Genre theory views filmmaking as a business. It's an enterprise comparable to any large industry and contends with virtually the same economic imperatives faced by General Motors or AT&T. Although filmmaking is an artistic endeavor, it is a commercial art; therefore, to economize and systematize production, its creators rely on proven formulas (Schatz, 5).

This view sees commercial filmmakers in close contact with their audience, whose response to individual films has affected the gradual development of story formulas and standard production practices. Film genres, such as the screwball mystery, the western, the musical, and the gangster film, are generated by a collective production system that honors these narrative traditions and develops them into basic conventions of feature-filmmaking for consumption by a mass audience (Schatz, vii). Economizing and systematizing production are measured by a filmmaker's capacity to reinvent established storytelling conventions. In other words, new forms and innovations are risky business ventures.

There are no new stories, only different characters resolving the timeless conflicts of people against people, people against nature, or people against themselves in different places at different times. A genre gives commercial filmmakers a cultural context for the story and characters in the form of "types," such as the scarfaced gangster in the pin-striped suit with wide lapels and spats, the strong but softspoken frontier sheriff, and the batty heroine of screwball comedies. It gives them the place—familiar settings, such as the main streets of desolate towns in the Old West or the comfortable mansions of the wealthy where murders inevitably take place. And it often gives them the time, as in westerns, which take place in lawless territories prior to statehood, and screwball comedies, which are set in times contemporary to their audiences. Genres systematize commercial filmmaking on the basis that success breeds success. The genre becomes the formula for success.

In 1934 MGM produced *The Thin Man*. Seeing its vast commercial success, other studios soon combined detective fiction and screwball comedy. Universal released *Remember Last Night?* in 1935, RKO came up with *The Ex-Mrs. Bradford* in 1936, Paramount contributed *True Confession* in 1937 (Sikov, 198), and Warner Brothers joined the fray with *Nancy Drew, Detective* in 1938.

In Nancy Drew, Warner Brothers undoubtedly saw the opportunity to co-opt a large share of the matinee audience with a character that already had a devoted following. A popular character plugged into a popular genre seemed destined for success. *Variety* touted the film *Nancy Drew, Detective* as "the first of a string of bread and butter pictures for the moppets" (*Variety Film Reviews*). The string ended at only four.

What went wrong with the formula? Nothing. It always worked when filmmakers followed it; the problem was that Warner Brothers didn't follow it. The success of *The Thin Man*, and others like it, came because the characters and plots were written expressly for the genre. In contrast, Nancy Drew underwent a metamorphosis in an attempt to mold her into the genre. Unfortunately, filmmakers at Warner Brothers failed to realize that Nancy Drew's appeal to the moppets, and others familiar with her through her books, was as a detective and not as a screwball comedian.

NOTE

Reprinted in revised form from Diana Beeson, "Translating Nancy Drew from Fiction to Film," *Lion and the Unicorn* 18:1 (June 1994): 37–47.

CHAPTER 24

I Owe It All to Nancy Drew

Nancy Pickard

When I was ten years old, I wrote: "I will be happy if I can have horses, solve mysteries, help people, and be happily married." In that order. For thirty years after that, I forgot on any conscious level about that wish list. When I finally came across it again, I was forty years old, married to a cowboy, doing volunteer work, and writing murder mysteries.

The child was, indeed, the mother to this woman.

It's easy enough to figure out why I wanted to "have horses"—doesn't almost every adolescent girl dream of riding Black Beauty? Growing up in the fifties made it *de rigueur* for me to want to "be happily married," and being a college student in the sixties made it nearly obligatory for me to want to "help people." But whence the desire to "solve mysteries"?

That's easy, isn't it?

I read Nancy Drew. Didn't you?

Sometimes I think I owe it all to her—my career, my amateur sleuth heroine, most of whatever finer qualities I may possess, even my blond hair, blue eyes, and my name. Nancy Drew was (almost) everything I wanted to be when I grew up: intelligent, self-confident, incredibly courageous, honest, straightforward, kind, courteous, energetic, successful, and independent. I confess that I also wished I were well-to-do and beautiful, just like Nancy. Granted, it's possible that she could have used more of a sense of fun and humor, and it cannot be denied that in her language and attitudes she reflected the white, middle-class, Christian prejudices of her day, but I'd rather blame those failings on her creators. I like to think that had Nancy but known, she never would have thought, spoken, or behaved in those ways.

Recently, for the first time since I was a girl I read the original version of *The Hidden Staircase*. First published in 1930, it may be the most famous and the most fondly remembered of any of the Nancy Drew mysteries. In 1959 the story was republished in a rewritten edition that drastically altered both the plot and the characters. If I had a daughter, the original version is the one I'd want to pass on to her. It is the edition I will give to my son.

I think it is not overstating the case to maintain that the original Nancy Drew is a mythic character in the psyches of the American women who followed her adventures as they were growing up. She may have been Superman, Batman, and Green Hornet, all wrapped up in a pretty girl in a blue convertible.

The original *Hidden Staircase* is a rich and nutritious feast of psychological archetypes, so that it assumes the quality of fairy tale and myth. Nancy herself, in the original version, is quite a heroic figure, one that in our culture we're more accustomed to seeing portrayed as a boy than as a girl: she's incorruptibly honest, steadfast, and courageous, a veritable Sir Lancelot of a girl, off on a quest to rescue the fair maiden, who is in this case her father, and to recapture the holy grail, which is in this case a silver spoon, a pocketbook, a diamond pin, and a couple of black silk dresses.

We'd have to go back to ancient goddess mythology to find an equivalent female of such heroic stature, back to a figure such as Inanna, who was the chief Sumerian deity, a woman who went to hell and back on a rescue mission. Such journeys into the "underground" are viewed in psychological terms as descents into one's unconscious; it is believed that a person must bring the contents of the unconscious into the light of consciousness in order to fully integrate one's psyche. In *The Hidden Staircase*, Nancy symbolically does just that, by tumbling like Alice down a black hole and then by journeying deeper and deeper into a really quite frightening tunnel where she perseveres with remarkable courage until she finds a way to ascend once more into the light. In so doing, she solves all mysteries and reunites everyone and everything that have been wrongfully separated. This is, at heart, no "mere" adventure story; this is myth.

In the original story, Nancy works alone, facing every terror on her own, although with the support, encouragement, and appreciation of the grown-ups. It reminds me of mythic initiation rites, where the young person is challenged, with the full backing of the adults, to prove herself. Nancy's father, in the original version, is an ideally archetypal figure who approves of everything his daughter does and praises her unstintingly. He's so proud of her he could bust, as proud as fathers are said to be when their sons make the winning touchdown in a football game, as proud as Zeus was of Athena. In the original version, Nancy is a marvel of decisiveness and resolution, and she gets to experience a full personal triumph.

Do you remember how you felt when you read the story?

I remember exactly how it was for me . . .

I was scared and had gooseflesh, and my stomach clenched, and the hair on my arms stood on end, and I tucked my feet beneath me so the boogieman under the bed couldn't grab them, and when Nancy was in the tunnel I could hardly bear to turn the page for fear of what might happen next, and yet I couldn't help turning the page to see what happened next. Oh, it was wonderful! It was delicious. It was spooky and mysterious and creepy, and I was there falling down those stairs with her, praying the flashlight wouldn't go out, feeling my way along the dark, damp walls of the tunnel, almost plunging through the wood where the stair was missing, breathing a sigh of vast relief when Nancy pulled the iron ring and the other door opened . . .

All of that is still there.

The faults are still there, the racism and antisemitism—and they make for painful reading now, just as they did for their victims back then. I hope they'll inspire us to examine our own "historical context" for the prejudices we don't know we have.

Do you want to know another truth? I miss her.

I miss the sheer joy of reading a Nancy Drew.

Evidently millions of other women do, too, because they're turning in record numbers to read the new breed of adult fictional women sleuths whose undeniable progenitor is Nancy Drew. It is surely no coincidence that my own detective, Jenny Cain, has a name that matched Nancy's syllable for syllable, and that she's slim, blond, and blue-eyed, too. My Jenny is as good as motherless, like Nancy, and she's smarter, braver, and more resourceful than her own father, like Nancy. More than one reviewer has referred to her as "Nancy Drew all grown up," which I take as truth and compliment.

The real Nancy Drew mystery may be the Mystery of the Appeal of Nancy Drew herself, and of her phenomenal attraction for successive generations of American girls.

I believe the solution to that mystery is this . . .

Nancy Drew, especially the Nancy of the original story, is our bright heroine, chasing down the shadows, conquering our worst fears, giving us a glimpse of our brave and better selves, proving to everybody exactly how admirable and wonderful a thing it is to be a girl.

Thank you, Nancy Drew.

NOTE

Reprinted in revised form from Nancy Pickard, "I Owe It All to Nancy Drew," introduction to *The Hidden Staircase*, facsimile edition, Applewood Books, 1991. Used with permission of Nancy Pickard.

CHAPTER 25

Nancy and Carlotta:
Lives Together, Worlds Apart

Linda Barnes

"'m afraid there's more to this than appears on the surface." That's what Nancy says in the 1948 *Ghost of Blackwood Hall* (138). And I agree with her. It goes back a long way . . .

I recall the names of my two auditorium teachers as if I'd attended grade school yesterday: Miss Irviline Bruner and Miss Coral Compeau. Both were elderly; one sported dyed blue hair, one wore a red wig. The librarian of the James Vernor Elementary School in northwest Detroit was less of a presence, with sober brown hair and the requisite eyeglasses. Though I can see her face clearly, I cannot recall her name.

I know that I read quickly, voraciously, and that she fed me a steady diet of books. After the bell rang, ending library hours, she would tap me on the shoulder, often frightening me. I never heard the bell when I was reading.

She recommended the inevitable biographies of Madame Curie and Eleanor Roosevelt, but mainly she provided teenage romances by authors whose names have faded from my memory. The stories, alas, have not. Typical plotline: girl at college, or about to begin her Broadway career, falls in love with a young man. They have difficulties, patch things up, and the girl gives up all dreams of education or stardom to grab that brass wedding band.

My librarian gave me nothing but "happily ever after" books. I know that she was a Miss Someone, a maiden lady. I wonder about her life, and why she steered me, avowedly her best student, her most avid reader, toward a stream of dead-end books.

Thank God for the series novel. I've never met anyone who read and loved the Maida books who didn't become an instant friend of mine. Then came Cherry Ames, who was a bit of a selfless drudge, Penny Parrish, and Nancy Drew.

And what I learned from those books was simple.

There is life after the last page. Life goes on. Books do not end at the happily-ever-after-orange-blossom part. Indeed, there is infinite possibility before us.

In Dorothy Sayers's *Gaudy Night*, Lord Peter Wimsey declares that "a desire to have all the fun is nine-tenths of the law of chivalry" (302). Nancy already knew that; I'm grateful to her for keeping the fun for herself.

I can't say that Nancy was anywhere in my conscious thoughts when I created Carlotta Carlyle. In many ways my early life could be titled "The Case of the Missing Childhood," so little do I recall of it. My love of mysteries comes from several sources. First, a hidden conservative streak. I hate the "C" word, but I need to use it here, although not in a truly political context. Books become very real to me, often more real than the events of my life. And the peril of immersing myself in a nonseries novel is formidable. I'm afraid to get involved with characters because they might die gruesome deaths. I wept through far too many books as a child. I don't have the psychic strength to keep reading Jayne Anne Phillips. I do read her, I read Jane Smiley and Alice Hoffman and many others who threaten my happiness, but I come back to those who write series books because I know the main character *will not die* and that is very important to me.

When I was a child, my family lived next door to a policeman, and one night that policeman shot a teenager to death on my front lawn. I don't remember hearing the shot, but I remember the commotion of sirens and my parents ordering me not to look out the window. Of course I looked. I didn't dream it. The next morning there were bloodstains in the grass.

I never understood that death, although I tried to puzzle out the articles in the newspaper, to question my parents as closely as I could. Shortly afterward, the policeman and his family moved away.

When I was twenty-three, a very dear friend killed himself. I'd spoken to him within the week. We'd gone to the movies, seen *American Graffiti*, laughed hysterically when the police car flew off its axle. And then he drove to Leominster State Park and attached a vacuum cleaner hose to the exhaust pipe of his car, and I never saw him again. There was a memorial service, but he was cremated and his ashes were scattered somewhere near his family's home in New York, October 28, 1973.

Years later, when I wrote my first mystery, I tried to solve the death.

Making sense out of death, that's what crime writers try to do. Often we end up asking more questions than we've answered. When I do that, I'm satisfied, for the moment at least, that I've written something worth reading.

Carlotta Carlyle is not a grown-up version of Nancy Drew simply because neither Detroit, where I grew up, nor Boston, where Carlotta roams, is remotely like River Heights. Carlotta's cop father and union-organizing mother, divorced when she was ten, are far removed from the all-knowing all-forgiving Carson and dear, gentle Hannah, the housekeeper.

Carlotta is a professional private investigator, not an amateur sleuth. He or she may succeed in England, where there's a tradition of *noblesse oblige* and a plethora of dukes' second sons lurking about with nothing to do but interfere in other people's business, but here in the United States the slogan "Don't butt in" ought to be printed on the currency.

I know this from experience. I began with an amateur detective and the only way I could make him work was to kill off all his friends and relations, which made him so depressed he could no longer detect and made me so depressed I could no longer write about him.

Carlotta takes care of herself and those who rely on her, from her various clients to her little sister, Paolina. She would resent a Carson or a Ned, or anyone who felt obliged to come to her aid. She's not dumb. She calls in the police when she's in over her head. She never goes to abandoned warehouses at midnight. But she is, because of her circumstances, because of the reality of her world, self-reliant.

Still, if I wore one, I'd take my hat off to Nancy Drew. Interfering without a license for over sixty years! Bless her and the roadster she drove in on—for she brought us all together to honor her.

CHAPTER 26

Adult Mystery Writers:
Questions and Answers

Linda Barnes and Nancy Pickard

Is there something you like about writing mysteries that you don't get in other novel genres?

PICKARD: Yes. I wouldn't get a paycheck if I wrote other types of novels.

BARNES: Here's to that. Sometimes I truly think that you don't choose what you write, what you write chooses you. It never occurred to me *not* to write about crime. Possibly this is a result of growing up in Detroit.

Do you find it restrictive to work within the same genre all the time?

BARNES: I always have a play in the back of my mind. It's a safety valve and I have a strong feeling that I'm never going to write it. But it's there. No, I don't find the form restrictive. I think that there are people who can work within form. I don't think that people who write sonnets say, "Oh my God, only fourteen lines, what can I squeeze in here?" There is something about the form that attracts me, a boundary within which I can do anything. I can use that form to say whatever I want to say. When the form becomes restrictive, I can break it. And that's a lot of fun, too. So thus far I have not found the mystery form to be anything other than a fascinating journey. If I do find it restrictive, then there's always the play.

PICKARD: I love the form. It's a great form for writers who want a little structure and a lot of freedom. One of the good things about the way the mystery has evolved in the past couple of years is that it has opened up possibilities that are nearly infinite as to what you can do. All sorts of things are acceptable that were not when Linda and I started writing. Regional mysteries are popular, for instance; that's just one small example. Women detectives are popular; that's another rather large example. You can develop a mystery with a totally emotional tone, if you want to, or you can have any sort of atmosphere. You can play around with plot variations. You can do practically anything you want to. Having said that, however, I will say that I get real tired of the necessity to have a dead body! That is a problem. I do get a little restless sometimes with the same form that I also love, but that's part of my nature. I have a feeling that if I wrote sonnets eventually I'd be saying, "I wonder if I can put that final couplet up front?"

BARNES: Every once in a while, Carlotta finds herself needing to search a room. And I'll realize that I have searched this room before. How many ways can you search a room? And then I'll know that I have to take that scene out of the book, because I don't want to keep writing the same book over again. That's not my plan. There are the set pieces of a mystery: the discovery of the body, the search of the victim's room, but I need to find another way to do it.

PICKARD: The one that really bugs me is the interrogation of suspects where the detective goes slogging around and has to ask everybody questions about where they were and all that sort of stuff. You know, I have moments where I just want to write a scene where Jenny goes in and asks, "Did you do it?" and they say, "Nope," and she says, "Okay, next." Short book.

Writers usually have to suffer a lot of rejection before they become successful. How do you endure it?

PICKARD: My period of rejection was compressed to a year and a half because I had been a professional writer ever since I got out of journalism school and that made a great deal of difference. I know published mystery writers now who wrote eight or nine novels which were all rejected before they got published. I don't know whether I would have had the courage to do that, frankly. But even the year and a half was tough. My first short story was accepted for publication and I thought, boy, I've got this thing knocked. Then it was a year and a half of rejection and rejection and rejection.

BARNES: It's a hard question to answer because there's rejection and then there's rejection. My first attempt at writing was playwriting and someone at a play festival came up to me and said, "Can I publish that?" And I thought, well, this is nice, I'll write a novel and someone will come up to me and say, "Can I publish that?" And imagine my surprise. And then the whole publishing process was—and to some extent remains to me—like one of those vast complex Avalon-Hill war games that you're given without directions and told to play in a dark closet. And you have no clue as to how to proceed. There you have a book and you think, well, I have a book and there are people who publish books, therefore I should send my book to a publisher. Wrong. No, you spend a while doing that and then you discover that it can take you six months to a year to receive a rejection notice and meanwhile they don't want you to submit your book to more than one publisher at a time. And after a while it takes on a tedious aspect, as though you'd signed up for a life of rejection.

I joined the local chapter of Mystery Writers of America after I had written my first mystery because I wanted to meet people who had beaten the system. A colleague in the group told me I needed to find an agent. He said, "Listen, it's not quite as hard as finding a spouse." And I said, "How do you find an agent?" And he said, "Well, the traditional answer is that you have to be published." And I said, "Well, you know I am a published playwright." And he said, "That counts for nothing, Linda."

But he gave me some very good advice and this was after I had had several agents. I had the only agent in Whitefish Bay, Wisconsin, for a period of time. I also had an agent in Boston for a while who was up on fraud charges in Superior Court. It was not smooth sailing; I did it all wrong.

Finally my friend said, "Linda, call the Society of Authors' Representatives in New York. Agents live in New York and they have lunch with editors—that's their function. The Society of Authors' Representatives will send you a list of agents who are not up on fraud charges anywhere. Take that list—it's a long list—select any ten names and write a one page letter; make it a good one. In that one page tell them about yourself and your book. Send that letter to ten agents and someone will want to read your book." And that's what I did, finally. And after I had cracked the agent game, four agents were willing to read the book and one agent sold it within three months. And that is how it began. If I had known then what I know now, I would not have started.

Do you read other people's works?

PICKARD: Yes, I read other people's works; I read all sorts of other works. I actually took a sabbatical last year from reading mysteries. I'd reached a point where I was getting sick of reading them. Unfortunately what happens is you begin to see technique that you don't want to see. It takes some of the pleasure out of it. It's harder to get lost in what John Gardner called "the fictive dream." So I stopped reading mysteries and it was wonderful. Only recently have I started in again. And it worked; the first couple of mysteries that I've read I've thought were wonderful. So I've realized that I may have to do that now and then. But I also make a point to read lots of things besides mysteries, including a lot of nonfiction.

Does it bother you that Carlotta has become a role model for many women?

BARNES: In some ways, it terrifies me. Carlotta is far more violent than I am. I've always been fascinated by violence, but I work it out through Carlotta. I would hate to think that people are working things out in a more active way than words, using her as a role model. Most of the time I don't think about her as a role model. Some of the time I do. Some of the time I'm very conscious, particularly when she's with Paolina, her "little sister," that there are certain things that are beyond the pale, there are certain places that I cannot take her because she must be there for Paolina and that helps me to keep Carlotta in line. You never know when you write what people may read into it. Often I'm surprised at reactions to what I've written.

PICKARD: I, too, am very aware that people use fictional characters as role models, having done that myself, but I don't think about it because I think that sort of self-consciousness is crippling to the writing process. But I'm sometimes just astonished at the responses I get. Not because I think they're the wrong responses but because they're so personal. I wrote a book called *Bum Steer* (1990) about a character who had a flirtation with a man who was not her husband and a friend of mine called and said she had received a call from another friend who'd said, "I just read *Bum Steer* and I'm so worried about Jenny and Geoff. Do you think they're going to get a divorce?" I go to signings and people say, "Is Jenny ever going to have children?" Well, the real answer to this is "I don't know, she hasn't told me yet. She doesn't even know." But this response is what makes it so wonderful and what has taught me the lesson that the mystery is beside the point. The point is the reader's identification with the character.

Ms. Barnes, you've created Sam as Carlotta's lover, but do you think he is good for her?

BARNES: I don't know, I haven't thought about it. Carlotta does things that are very difficult to do, but she makes a lot of dumb choices about men. And I think this reflects a lot of people I know who have made some dumb choices about men. I've given Carlotta a good lover and a bad lover. I've given her Mooney and I've given her Sam and I like the tension that that creates in the books. I've been very tempted lately to do away with Sam. But every time I mention it to an audience they protest. It's a problem that I have to deal with in every one of the books because Carlotta is connected to many people. And it's gotten to the point that before I start writing I need to make a list: Where is everyone? Where is Roz? Where's Sam? Where's Mooney? What's going on in everyone's life and how can I work it into this book or do I have to send them all away or do I just have an entire house explode and kill them all so that I can get a fresh group of people to work with? These are the problems that we deal with daily.

PICKARD: See, it was easier with your other sleuth when all the people got killed off.

BARNES: There's always that little touch of romance that I like to put into the books, yet, as Dorothy Sayers always said, it interferes with the mystery. And so it's peripheral to her life and Sam doesn't like being peripheral to Carlotta's life and that is one of the reasons he may write himself out of the series. We'll see what happens in the book I'm working on right now.

Where and when do you do your writing?

PICKARD: I do have an office at home but I've recently bought a laptop and now I write sitting up in bed, on my screened-in porch;

I write anyplace I want to. That's wonderful. As to that question about a schedule, I think it's a really good idea for beginning writers to have a schedule. What I've learned about my own creative process, I'll try to say briefly, is that I can no more write five pages a day seven days a week than I could go into Western Auto, where I once worked, five days a week for eight hours a day for the rest of my life. I'm not constituted to do that. I was late to every 8:40 class I ever had. I was always ten minutes late to my last real job. I have to wait until whatever wants to be written is ready to be written. And I've learned to relax with that. And when it's really good I can write fifteen pages a day—five pages, get up and take a walk; five pages, walk, come back and write five pages. And it may be ten o'clock or midnight by the time I'm finished. And I feel rested, I feel great. But if I try to write five pages on a day that it's not there, I'm exhausted and it's a miserable experience. I stopped fighting that a couple of years ago and am enjoying my work more as a consequence. Don't follow my advice!

BARNES: I try and fail to maintain a schedule. This is partially due to having a three-year-old. I used to be a morning writer, and I also used to be an erratic writer so that I would go in spurts and I would just stay up three nights. Like Carlotta, I'm an insomniac and I love to write in the middle of the night. But I don't anymore because I can't explain to my kid that I've been up all night and he's not going to get breakfast. I've tried but it doesn't sink in. So I'm trying to maintain a schedule now. And it's hell on earth. I'm really having trouble with it. I think it can be done. I don't work weekends. I take weekends off. I still get up in the middle of the night and I'll do five days of work in one night. Then I'll take the next day off and stare out the window. I try to confront my computer every day but I never measure by pages; I never even print out the pages because that would be counting.

When you start a book do you wonder who wrote those other books that have your name on them?

BARNES: It gives me a sense of confidence to know that I've done it before. But I will often get to a point in a book where I think I'm dead in the water and that's when I start calling people in the middle of the night. Fortunately I call people in California when they're not sleeping. And they say, "Linda, you've gotten out of this before and you will do it again." And those are the most comforting words I know.

Would you feel more comfortable if you were writing under another name in addition to your own so you could be anonymous?
BARNES: I really don't write under my own name. I write under my married name because my maiden name is Appelblatt and when I started writing my first agent said, "No, that's too long and funny, stick to Barnes." And Barnes has no history; it's my husband's father's stage name. So it's not a name that has any meaning to me; I feel like it's not a real name. And yet that is who I am known as. Now I'm starting to worry. The Carlotta book *Snapshot* (1993) has a lot to do with privacy. I'm starting to think that I need another name because I'm getting strange mail. I'm getting mail from people who are confined to penal institutions; I'm getting hand-crafted pick-locks in the mail. I've figured out how to work them and they're really good. But I don't want to continue the correspondence and I'm concerned that people are writing to me at my home address rather than via my publisher. So I'm starting to think that I ought to disappear and that is making me feel a little strange. There are people in my life who need to find me. I don't want them to lose sight of me. But in some ways I do want to disappear.

What early women mystery writers influenced you and in what way?
PICKARD: Well, I had a real mixed bag of influences. Mildred Wirt Benson has to be number one up there, but it wasn't only women mystery writers. Those I count as influences are as diverse a group as Mildred Wirt Benson, Agatha Christie, James M. Cain, John D. MacDonald, Raymond Chandler, Margaret Millar, and also during a period of time Daphne du Maurier, Mary Stewart—I went through a romantic suspense phase. And then at some point my own contemporaries have influenced me. For instance, I remember the first time I read a Sue Grafton novel was when I was starting my third novel and I was so impressed with Sue's ability to give the detail of scenes. I learned from her writing and it changed my writing at that point. I became more conscious of detail. And so I continue to learn from writers.

BARNES: My first real memory of a mystery was of reading *The Speckled Band* (Doyle) in school and I remember it well because there was a little ventilator shaft near my bed and I didn't sleep for nights, listening for that low whistle. So *The Speckled Band* has always been a turning point for me. And after that I didn't read mysteries for a long time and then I went to the British, to Dorothy Sayers and Josephine Tey particularly. Those were the books that I loved growing up and I did not meet the modern American male sleuth until I was in my late twenties. I began writing mysteries because I wanted to create someone I could identify with as a hero. The British dilettantes really didn't have anything to do with my life and the American guys didn't have a lot to recommend them. The women would sleep with them and die; that seemed to be a key factor in the plotline. And so my first detective, Michael Spraggue—I often call him the Mid-Atlantic detective because he really was plunked in the middle of the ocean—was born British not American. I created his dear aunt Mary, who was the first female character I really wrote and she kept threatening to take over the books. And I realized I had made a dreadful mistake and that I should have written a woman and I immediately started to, as soon as the first Spraggue book was accepted. I informed my editor that the next book was going to be about a female detective and he said, "It won't sell." And my agent didn't think it would sell either. You don't write mysteries for posthumous glory so it took me some time to make the decision to convert to Carlotta. I did not start her off in a novel because I was not willing to give a year of my life to something that would not sell. I auditioned her in a short piece, the only short story I've ever written. And the response was so good that I was able to confidently go with her and that's why Michael is no longer a functioning detective. I haven't killed him, but I don't know whether I'll write about him anymore.

Do you think it was a matter of the right timing?
BARNES: That short story, "Lucky Penny" (Barnes 1986), was written in 1983 but it didn't get published until 1986, although it kept getting sold. It was the kiss-of-death short story. Every time it sold the magazine folded before the story was actually published. And I gave up on it. I thought the editors and agents were right. And when I changed agents over an entirely different matter, I sent "Lucky

Penny" along as an afterthought and said, "Here's a giggle, this one kills magazines." And she sold it within four days to *New Black Mask*, which no longer exists. But it was published and it was nominated for every major mystery award. And then I knew that I would go with Carlotta. But it took three years for that story to see the light of day. In order to succeed in this business I think you have to be ten of the most determined people you know.

Do you have contact with British female mystery writers?
PICKARD: Yes, we speak. Although the emphasis here has been on American female writers, I do want to say that before the Lindas existed in the world, I devoured the British women writers: Josephine Tey and Dorothy Sayers and Catherine Aird and Agatha Christie and all the ones you can name, I loved. I owe them a great debt.
BARNES: I had the privilege and honor of introducing the Baroness P. D. James in Boston. I love her work. But I find that when I'm writing I cannot read it because my sentences get longer and longer and I have to control myself. The British are amused by us. They've always had women writing mysteries and they don't know why we're so backward. We think that it's a phenomenon.

Nancy, what was it like to take on someone else's work?
PICKARD: This question refers to the fact that I finished a novel, *The Twenty-seven Ingredient Chili Con Carne Murders* (1993), that was started by the late Virginia Rich, who had written three culinary mysteries, starting with *The Cooking School Murders* (1982). It was hell. It was real hard. But ever since I got it finished, it's just been a real kick. I've had the best time and the response has been such fun. But it was real tough to get into somebody else's voice, particularly since it was third person—my novels are first person. And the protagonist was a much older woman. Ten years had intervened since I first read the novels and what I liked in mysteries had changed, to some extent, and my own mysteries had changed a great deal, so I had to do a fair amount of hard work to get into the mood to do that book.

How much was written when you took it over?
PICKARD: I got a big box of notes that included about sixty typewritten pages of basically the same couple of scenes rewritten several

times. She had a complete plot outline and I wrote that book. But it turned out that book didn't work. I actually wrote two books, because I had to go through what she had started to find out that it wasn't going to work. And I think that she would have come to the same conclusion. For instance, the original plot had drug smuggling in it and these days nobody wants to read about drug smuggling. But I had to go through the exercise of honoring her original desires and trying to keep as many of her phrases or sentences as I could. And there were certain major plot things I kept, like the introduction of an old love of Mrs. Potter's. That came straight from Mrs. Rich; it had even been alluded to in another book. So I finally figured out that I needed to be accurate about the main character. If I got her so that the fans of that series would recognize her, then the rest of it would fall into place. That's eventually what I aimed for. I would think that doing it a second time might not be as difficult.

I'll tell you why I'm tempted to do it again. I got an unexpected response from women—particularly women who are older than I am—who wrote to me saying, "We're really glad to see this sleuth back and it's really wonderful to see an older vigorous woman who even has a love interest, because there aren't enough of those protagonists out there." That struck a chord with me and I thought, "Why did I start writing mysteries about a youngish woman?" Because I couldn't find them out there in the mystery world. And I was touched by these responses. I got a letter from one woman who said, "I'm writing to you at three o'clock in the morning. I just finished this book and I just wanted you to know how wonderful it is to have Mrs. Potter back and please don't let Mrs. Potter die." Well, it's real hard not to respond to something like that. So there will be more.

Who are the people you thank in the beginning of the book and what is their influence on the writing of them?
BARNES: I have the Committee. The Committee varies. These are people who have come into my life at various times and have been available to read my work. I have to backtrack a little. I spent some time as a theatrical director. And there is a point in every production at which you can no longer see it. You just are not aware; you're looking at the blocking or you're looking at the scenery. You cannot see what is going on. And I find that the same thing happens to me with a book. Long before I want an editor or agent to see my book I want

to bring in the play doctor. I want to bring in somebody who can read it and say, "You're on track or you're off track." My husband is an extremely valuable reader because he will say things like, "You have her drive off in a green car and return in a brown car, which is not good." He's the continuity man. A constant in my life has always been the writer James Morrow. Jim and I have been together since we both taught high school. Our work could not be more different, but for some reason we can rip each other's books apart and remain friends and help each other's books in ways that no one else can. And I have other members of the Committee, each of whom contributes something. So the Committee is always thanked.

PICKARD: I thank the same sorts of people. I do my research just by living, I think, not a whole lot of reading. I did a book that had to do with the funeral industry and I had a great deal of fun doing some library research on that, although I had also done some freelance writing for funeral homes for years, so that was a great help. You never know what's going to be material. For instance, I wrote a book called *Dead Crazy* (1988) that had to do with establishing a recreational hall for former mental patients. I had a friend who did that. So I went to a recreational hall and I did volunteer work there for about three weeks and I just worked in the kitchen peeling potatoes with former mental patients. That's how I did the research for that book. That was kind of fun. I had a book on domestic violence, but I never went into a home for battered women. I talked to the directors. Years before that I had been chairman of the board of a halfway house for teenage girls. I had a feeling that if you've been in one halfway house, to some extent you've been in all of them, particularly if there were a group of women. And I thought, you know, I'm a writer and I'm going to take from that experience and extrapolate from what the directors of these homes are telling me and I'm going to create this and see if I get it right. I've had responses from women who have been in battered women's shelters, or directors of them, and they say that I did.

CHAPTER 27

Drawing on a Sleuth:
The Case of the Nancy Drew Series

Laura Ruby

M y Nancy Drew Series of artworks is concerned with the nature of detection, with the ways we see and the ways in which we solve puzzles. Also, this series is concerned with the nature of art-making, how we depict the world, how we create shorthand visual notation systems to understand and to organize the world, and how we "read" or investigate an artwork.

The series incorporates a range of art-making conventions and codes from diverse historical times and cultures, as situated in the context of late twentieth century American popular culture.

The imagery of my Nancy Drew Series is visual and encourages visual as well as mental reflection. Though other senses are engaged in the Nancy Drew books and other detective fiction, the world of the film detective—of Sam Spade and Philip Marlowe and Jessica Fletcher of *Murder, She Wrote*—is visually dominant.

Light informs our visible world. Our eyes "look" and relay perceptual signals to our "seeing" brains. This interpretive brain activity is investigative—clues are gathered, particulars recorded, patterns tried and discarded, and new patterns formed and conclusions reached. In the highest order of brain decoding we recognize faces. Most of the time we recognize friends on the street, after adding up all the visible particulars of a face. But occasionally we might see a three-quarter view or less of a face, jump to conclusions, and embarrassingly misidentify a stranger. There has been a misinterpretation

The Sign of the Twisted Candles

of the clues, or possibly a deception (as when a person in hat and coat walks out a front door under surveillance, while the real target goes out the back door).

Those raw bits of "fact" or evidence are out there for us to discover; we can identify them as signs of something else, something

The Quest of the Missing Map

more complex, or we might pass by them unaware. Detection is about heightening awareness, that sense of discovery and that capacity to solve puzzles. We may pick up clues without any purpose and only after the fact discover that those clues lead somewhere. In Michelangelo Antonioni's film *Blowup*, for example, a still photographer is completely unaware that he has captured a murder on film until the murderers try to steal his negatives.

Nancy Drew and other detectives, like the photographer in *Blowup*, after getting a lead pursue many avenues to solve a mystery. Like their counterparts, researchers engaging in scientific inquiry, detectives are excited when exploring new territory; they resolutely test established knowledge and hope to find order.

In my Nancy Drew Series I often depict detective tools. These devices are employed as extensions of the senses—in particular the visual sense. Nancy Drew turns a flashlight onto the dark mysteries of the world and uses a magnifying glass, binoculars, and telescope among other visual enhancers—just as scientists may employ more sophisticated tools such as the electron microscope, spectrometer, or infrared telescope. These are the tools of the inquisitive empiricist, and they represent active engagement in the physical world on the part of the detective or scientist or artist.

My Nancy Drew Series is situated in the popular culture of the late twentieth century. This particular context draws on the cultural artifacts and conventions of earlier popular culture of this century. Just as idiomatic speech is made up of constituent elements, the meaning of which cannot be derived literally, my visual artworks are a pastiche or admixture of constituent elements that are made up of visual and verbal languages, dialects and styles particular to American cultural life. An example of an American popular idiom used for private coding would be American World War II POWs who spoke in baseball slang to confound their captors.

As I create artworks I continue to explore the correspondences between involved detection and committed art-making. I owe a great deal to the books themselves. Nancy Drew represents a sense of con-

The Bungalow Mystery

fident independence, active engagement with the world around her, curiosity and desire to put ideas together and to draw conclusions.

The books are well researched. My individual artworks grow from an appreciation for the historical research into such areas as Chinese ceramics, eighteenth- and nineteenth-century American ship figureheads, and Civil War lore, for example.

Furthermore, in my series the name Drew is ripe for word-play. It is an action word—the past, completed action of art-making. In my series Nancy, always drawing on her own resources, draws everywhere; she makes marks on the ground, crosshatches a wall, inscribes chalk circles, pens illustrations, paints light, and draws bridges. Incorporating additional puns, there are drawing room doors, shades drawn, curtains drawn back, drawers opened, water drawn, magnets drawn out, and Mah-Jongg tiles drawn.

In my series I also employ the immediately recognized Nancy Drew silhouette and lettering style on the blue clothbound covers in addition to frontispieces and endpapers. I draw upon the convention of twentieth-century book illustration so finely demonstrated by Russell H. Tandy in the 1930s and 1940s frontispieces. The depiction of action within the text is dynamic and engaging. The Nancy Drew images, as I use them, connect the act of rapt detection with the act of engrossed art-making.

I draw upon the various notational systems used currently or in the past in our culture. Morse code and semaphore were once crucial means for conveying shorthand information. The touch typing schema gave me the means to write this essay quickly. And map conventions and music notations have been widely conveyed.

I also use verbal language—often the exclamatory captions from the frontispieces of the original blue-hardcover books, with their characteristic type style; sometimes I use other written languages, such as Chinese and Italian. Incidentally, the translation for many of these coded messages is "Help!" Besides signaling danger within the artwork, "Help!" is also an indirect appeal from the artist to the viewers, soliciting their collaboration in completing the experience of art-making and art-viewing.

Like the notation systems in American popular culture, art notation systems have certain conventions, styles, and forms. Information is conveyed by the thorough understanding of an art depiction system and its application or intentional misapplication. Nancy, as

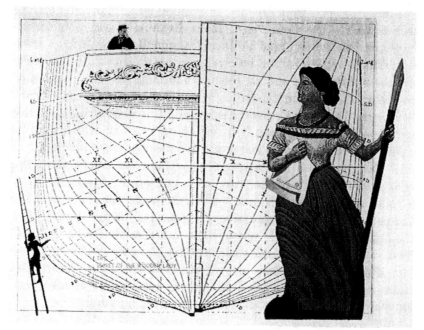

The Secret of the Wooden Lady

detective and art-maker, is found within the worlds of brush and pen calligraphy, painting, drawing, blueprint schemas of plan and elevation drawings, stereoscope photography, cartography, and the geometric system of linear perspective, which gives the illusion of apparent three-dimensional reality on a two-dimensional picture plane.

The nature of reading an artwork parallels the viewing of the world around us. We give a general glance to the scene and then with our keener foveal vision select and move from one sharper image to another. We investigate an artwork with the same chance order, reassembling the images and making our own cohesive/coherent meaning—or at least amassing clues leading to puzzle-solving.

I'd like to explain some of these themes of art-making and mystery-solving with an installation sculpture of mine, based on Nancy Drew investigations. My installation sculpture (a temporary three-dimensional artwork created for a period of time and then dismantled) is entitled *Mise Unseen*, and it acknowledges and credits the viewer as an involved participant in the detection of an artwork.

The sculpture is "about" the acts of creation by an artist and the detective work of the viewer/participant discovering and understanding clues. Its form is based on theatrical and film sets. *Mise en scène* refers to the setting for the action of a drama (in this sculpture's case the act of detection) and all the surroundings, scenery, and props necessary to the dramatic action. *Mise Unseen* is a play on words—the drama is of the viewer's participation in discovering evidence and clues; the particulars both visual and verbal, which may be come upon by chance/random order, and also by later reflection.

The particular reference of this stage set comes from the artistry of German expressionist black and white films in the early decades of the twentieth century—for example, the *Cabinet of Dr. Caligari*, in which the expressive scenic design and props intensified the dramatic action. The use of light and shadow comes from the dark, mysterious midcentury world of the *film noir*.

This installation was located in the University of Hawaii Art Gallery and was intended to evoke the art notation systems and verbal play used regularly in the surrounding art building.

The architectural and theatrical components in *Mise Unseen* of tunnel, stairs, ladders, closet, catwalk, suspension bridge, trap door, false column and doors, real and false shadows, and cast light, as well as visual and verbal "finds," are come upon in chance/random order. There is no fixed way to interact with the sculpture. Beside the kinesthetic act of walking around and through this installation and viewing it from many positions, it also engages the viewer/participant in a tactile way. The viewer's head and eyes range from floor level to 14-foot ceiling height. The viewer engages in the physical space by stooping and walking through the tunnel, standing within the trap door, pulling the closet drape back, and lifting the window shade. Along the way discoveries are made which suggest there may be others—and there are. The viewer/detective searches the territory in a varied random order, coming upon "overlooked clues." Do the Nancy Drew silhouettes create a narrative direction—larger at ground level to smaller at the ceiling height? Do her tools for detection help the viewer to explore meaning? The smallest Nancy silhouette is engaged in writing and drawing—and in two languages—the phrase "stroke of luck." Is the viewer exploring the possibility that the Nancy silhouettes have created this very artwork and now are in a quest for meaning in the act of creation? The visual and verbal clues are there.

"Brush with danger" suggests the art-making of painting, "The Cabinet of Dr. Calligraphy" both the notational system of brush and pen work and an allusion to film making. "Jaspers, Jaspers, Where'd You Get Those Raspers" refers to a popular twentieth century song, "Jeepers Creepers, Where'd You Get Those Peepers." Eyes are for seeing—and a sharper insight as Jasper Johns, American artist, has sharp perception and is grating to the critics. And "Draw your own conclusions" suggests the viewer's direct participation in the created work. One major theme of this work is the acknowledging of the artist-detective as maker and the acknowledging and crediting of the viewer as involved participant in the detection.

Finally, each of the prints in my series has content originating with the book title and its many possibilities for wordplay and punning; the content also derives from the historical and cultural research within each book, and from the clues discovered in each book's mystery. Each print, then, like each book has a wealth of clues. In the books the clues lead to problems solved. But with each print, as in the sculpture *Mise Unseen*, the viewer is engaged in an interplay of component elements in an American idiomatic cultural context.

For specific illustration of how my prints employ visual resources and my visual inferences within this cultural context, I would like to highlight some of these works.

The Mystery of the Brass Bound Trunk

This print engages the viewer in a mystery aboard an ocean liner. The print plays off the title and the subject matter within the Nancy Drew book. The large trunk, drawn in an intentionally distorted style, is wedged in a cabin while a Nancy Drew silhouette, a two-dimensional flat depiction, is busy outside the porthole chalking wet footprints in the illusory space of linear perspective where the size of objects gets smaller and recedes, indicating distance. The two-dimensional silhouette in repetition, indicating dedicated pursuit of clues, investigates inside the cabin and inside the trunk. Notice the changes of clothes: these suggest the future on-board detective work to come.

The Mystery of the Brass Bound Trunk

On top of the trunk are two different light sources, a kerosene lantern and a battery-operated flashlight. They are necessary to navigation: red marks the port or left side of a ship and green marks the starboard or right side. Of course, their effectiveness is limited as they are located within the cabin rather than visible to navigating vessels.

The semaphore flags affixed to the trunk signal attention and "Help!" Those viewers able to read the code might wonder at the urgency of the situation and who is appealing to them.

Other travel stickers on the trunk refer the viewers to the end-papers and frontispieces in several editions of the Nancy Drew books. Also, the ocean liner is one of a number of *Lurlines* that plied the waters for many decades between Hawaii and the West Coast.

There is also an allusion to the famous Marx Brothers shipboard scene in *Night at the Opera*, in which Groucho asks, rather than put the trunk in the stateroom, "Wouldn't it be simpler if you put the stateroom in the trunk?"

The Clue of the Leaning Chimney

This print is a cross-cultural puzzle. It is set in an upper floor of an American balloon-frame house. However, the wallpaper comes from Chinese newspaper articles about ancient Chinese artworks, Chinese New Year's celebrations, and the poet Li Po. A simple window frames two Nancy Drew silhouettes drawing and illuminating the mark-making, while multiple investigative silhouettes sleuth around doors and window.

The large Chinese dragon's claw draws the window shade, revealing the dragon's own origins painted on the ceramic vase within the oldest frontispiece. In addition to this early frontispiece by Russell H. Tandy, the extended shade reveals another frontispiece and an endpaper illustration from the 1950s and 1960s. This is Nancy

The Clue of the Leaning Chimney

Drew's visual history and the Chinese character for "Help!" commands the viewer to make haste, to take action.

The Haunted Bridge

This print plays on the words in the title and muses on the viewers or readers bridging the gap between the events of lived experience and the imaginary world of created fiction. The bridge, though modeled

The Haunted Bridge

on a wooden bridge style common in the early part of the twentieth century, is in fact a suspension bridge. That is, a viewer or reader enters into an artwork or film or literary work in a suspension of disbelief. Nancy Drew books are the piers of the bridge—all access to the visual imagery is conveyed by them. The span of the bridge is measured by hand spans.

The two-dimensional Nancy Drew silhouettes are pursuing evidence; one, near the far pier of the bridge, investigates her very source, and the other in the woods shines light on possible gnarly clues. The third silhouette is drawing—not the bridge that she sees, but a drawbridge.

On the left side of the print Nancy and her friends, Bess and George, cling to the cramped footings under the bridge retrieving their own cast-off frontispiece and drawings of three notable bridges in Hawaii.

The Mystery of the Tolling Bell

This artwork also puns extensively on its title. It is a conundrum involving tolling, or alluring or enticing, visual and aural clues. It engages the viewer. The print "rings a bell" as the frontispiece stuck in the drawing room door suggests, "'This is what I hoped to find!' exclaimed Nancy."

The bell shade of the lamp sheds light on the detective's discovery. This form is visually echoed in the euphonium bell and the speaking tube of Alexander Graham Bell's first telephone. The images on the wallpaper in the outer room are bell curves and the hanging artworks in the inner room are the Pythagoras bell tone system. The bell pepper on the table also plays on the title and refers to some famous photographs by Edward Weston and also to a sculpture of mine entitled *Bell Peppers*.

Charlie Chan and his Number-One Son, based in Honolulu in many books and films, solved countless mysteries. This particular Charlie Chan actor was Sidney Toler, referring again to the tolling title, while Number-One Son gestures with incredulity at Nancy's investigative powers.

I hope this discussion of these four prints indicates my concern with the nature of detection and the nature of art-making in the world. The scientist and artist and detective actively engage the

The Mystery of the Tolling Bell

world in order to comprehend its meanings. Within the highly enter-
taining popular literary context of the Nancy Drew books, serious
questions of meaning in art and meaning in the world can be addressed, even playfully. The Nancy Drew books provide an enormous
wealth of visual and verbal material; as an artist, I find them rich
resources for discovery, detection, and art-making.

Nancy Drew Titles, 1930–1994

24. The Clue in the Old Album, 1947, 1977.
25. The Ghost of Blackwood Hall, 1948, 1967.
26. The Clue of the Leaning Chimney, 1949, 1967.
27. The Secret of the Wooden Lady, 1950, 1967.
28. The Clue of the Black Keys, 1951, 1968.
29. The Mystery at the Ski Jump, 1952, 1968.
30. The Clue of the Velvet Mask, 1953, 1969.
31. The Ringmaster's Secret, 1953, 1974.
32. The Scarlet Slipper Mystery, 1954, 1974.
33. The Witch Tree Symbol, 1955, 1975.
34. The Hidden Window Mystery, 1956, 1975.
35. The Haunted Showboat, 1957.
36. The Secret of the Golden Pavilion, 1959.
37. The Clue in the Old Stagecoach, 1960.
38. The Mystery of the Fire Dragon, 1961.
39. The Clue of the Dancing Puppet, 1962.
40. The Moonstone Mystery, 1963.
41. The Clue of the Whistling Bagpipes, 1964.
42. The Phantom of Pine Hill, 1965.
43. The Mystery of the 99 Steps, 1966.
44. The Clue in the Crossword Cipher, 1967.
45. The Spider Sapphire Mystery, 1968.
46. The Invisible Intruder, 1969.
47. The Mysterious Mannequin, 1970.
48. The Crooked Banister, 1971.
49. The Secret of Mirror Bay, 1972.
50. The Double Jinx Mystery, 1973.
51. Mystery of the Glowing Eye, 1974.
52. The Secret of the Forgotten City, 1975.
53. The Sky Phantom, 1976.
54. The Strange Message in the Parchment, 1977.
55. Mystery of Crocodile Island, 1978.
56. The Thirteenth Pearl, 1979.

The Nancy Drew Cookbook: Clues to Good Cooking, 1973.
Mystery of the Lost Dogs [picture book], 1977.
The Secret of the Twin Puppets [picture book], 1977.
Nancy Drew Mystery Puzzles, 1977.
Nancy Drew Detective Logic Puzzles, 1977.
Nancy Drew Secret Scrambled Word Finds, 1977.
Nancy Drew Secret Codes, 1977.
Nancy Drew Mystery Activity Book 1 and 2, 1977.

Nancy Drew Mystery Activity Book 3, 1978.
The Hardy Boys and Nancy Drew Meet Dracula, 1978.
The Haunted House and Flight to Nowhere, 1978.
The Nancy Drew Sleuth Book: Clues to Good Sleuthing, 1979.
Nancy Drew Mystery Pictures to Color, 2 vols., 1979.

WANDERER BOOKS

Simon & Schuster

Nancy Drew Mystery Stories

57. The Triple Hoax, 1979.
58. The Flying Saucer Mystery, 1980.
59. The Secret in the Old Lace, 1980.
60. The Greek Symbol Mystery, 1981.
61. The Swami's Ring, 1981.
62. The Kachina Doll Mystery, 1981.
63. The Twin Dilemma, 1981.
64. Captive Witness, 1981.
65. Mystery of the Winged Lion, 1982.
66. Race against Time, 1982.
67. The Sinister Omen, 1982.
68. The Elusive Heiress, 1982.
69. Clue in the Ancient Disguise, 1982.
70. The Broken Anchor, 1983.
71. The Silver Cobweb, 1983.
72. The Haunted Carousel, 1983.
73. Enemy Match, 1984.
74. The Mysterious Image, 1984.
75. The Emerald-Eyed Cat Mystery, 1984.
76. The Eskimo's Secret, 1985.
77. The Bluebeard Room, 1985.
78. The Phantom of Venice, 1985.

MINSTREL BOOKS

Simon & Schuster

Nancy Drew Mystery Stories

79. The Double Horror of Fenley Place, 1987.
80. The Case of the Disappearing Diamonds, 1987.
81. The Mardi Gras Mystery, 1988.
82. The Clue in the Camera, 1988.
83. The Case of the Vanishing Veil, 1988.

84. The Joker's Revenge, 1988.
85. The Secret of Shady Glen, 1988.
86. The Mystery of Misty Canyon, 1988.
87. The Case of the Rising Stars, 1988.
88. The Search for Cindy Austin, 1988.
89. The Case of the Disappearing Deejay, 1989.
90. The Puzzle at Pineview School, 1989.
91. The Girl Who Couldn't Remember, 1989.
92. The Ghost of Craven Cove, 1989.
93. The Case of the Safecracker's Secret, 1990.
94. The Picture-Perfect Mystery, 1990.
95. The Silent Suspect, 1990.
96. The Case of the Photo Finish, 1990.
97. The Mystery at Magnolia Mansion, 1990.
98. The Haunting of Horse Island, 1990.
99. The Secret at Seven Rocks, 1991.
100. A Secret in Time, 1991.
101. The Mystery of the Missing Millionairess, 1991.
102. A Secret in Dark, 1991.
103. The Stranger in the Shadows, 1991.
104. The Mystery of the Jade Tiger, 1991.
105. The Clue in the Antique Trunk, 1992.
106. The Case of the Artful Crime, 1992.
107. The Legend of Miner's Creek, 1992.
108. The Secret of the Tibetan Treasure, 1992.
109. The Mystery of the Masked Rider, 1992.
110. The Nutcracker Ballet Mystery, 1992.
111. The Secret at Solaire, 1993.
112. Crime in the Queen's Court, 1993.
113. The Secret Lost at Sea, 1993.
114. The Search for the Silver Persian, 1993.
115. The Suspect in the Smoke, 1993.
116. The Case of the Twin Teddy Bears, 1993.
117. Mystery on the Menu, 1994.
118. Trouble at Lake Tahoe, 1994.
119. The Mystery of the Missing Mascot, 1994.
120. The Case of the Floating Crime, 1994.
121. The Fortune-teller's Secret, 1994.
122. The Message in the Haunted Mansion, 1994.

WANDERER BOOKS

Simon & Schuster

Nancy Drew and the Hardy Boys
Be a Detective Mystery Stories

1. The Secret of the Knight's Sword, 1984.
2. Danger on Ice, 1984.
3. The Feathered Serpent, 1984.
4. Secret Cargo, 1984.
5. The Alaskan Mystery, 1985.
6. The Missing Money Mystery, 1985.
7. Jungle of Evil, 1985.
8. Ticket to Intrigue, 1985.

Nancy Drew Book of Hidden Clues [activity book], 1980.
Nancy Drew and the Hardy Boys Super Sleuths: Seven New Mysteries, 1981.
Nancy Drew Ghost Stories, 1983.
Nancy Drew and the Hardy Boys Camp Fire Stories: Six New Mystery Stories, 1984.
Nancy Drew Ghost Stories, 1985.

ARCHWAY PAPERBACKS

Simon & Schuster

Nancy Drew Files

1. Secrets Can Kill, 1986.
2. Deadly Intent, 1986.
3. Murder on Ice, 1986.
4. Smile and Say Murder, 1986.
5. Hit and Run Holiday, 1986.
6. White Water Terror, 1986.
7. Deadly Doubles, 1986.
8. Two Points to Murder, 1986.
9. False Moves, 1986.
10. Buried Secrets, 1987.
11. Heart of Danger, 1987.
12. Fatal Ransom, 1987.
13. Wings of Fear, 1987.
14. This Side of Evil, 1987.
15. Trial by Fire, 1987.
16. Never Say Die, 1987.
17. Stay Tuned for Danger, 1987.
18. Circle of Evil, 1987.

19. Sisters in Crime, 1988.
20. Very Deadly Yours, 1988.
21. Recipe for Murder, 1988.
22. Fatal Attraction, 1988.
23. Sinister Paradise, 1988.
24. Till Death Do Us Part, 1988.
25. Rich and Dangerous, 1988.
26. Playing with Fire, 1988.
27. Most Likely to Die, 1988.
28. The Black Widow, 1988.
29. Pure Poison, 1988.
30. Death by Design, 1988.
31. Trouble in Tahiti, 1989.
32. High Marks for Malice, 1989.
33. Danger in Disguise, 1989.
34. Vanishing Act, 1989.
35. Bad Medicine, 1989.
36. Over the Edge, 1989.
37. Last Dance, 1989.
38. The Final Scene, 1989.
39. The Suspect Next Door, 1989.
40. Shadow of a Doubt, 1989.
41. Something to Hide, 1989.
42. The Wrong Chemistry, 1989.
43. False Impressions, 1990.
44. Scent of Danger, 1990.
45. Out of Bounds, 1990.
46. Win, Place, or Die, 1990.
47. Flirting with Danger, 1990.
48. A Date with Deception, 1990.
49. A Portrait in Crime, 1990.
50. Deep Secrets, 1990.
51. A Model Crime, 1990.
52. Danger for Hire, 1990.
53. Trail of Lies, 1990.
54. Cold as Ice, 1990.
55. Don't Look Twice, 1990.
56. Make No Mistake, 1990.
57. Into Thin Air, 1991.
58. Hot Pursuit, 1991.
59. High Risk, 1991.
60. Poison Pen, 1991.

61. Sweet Revenge, 1991.
62. Easy Marks, 1991.
63. Mixed Signals, 1991.
64. The Wrong Track, 1991.
65. Final Notes, 1991.
66. Tall, Dark, and Deadly, 1991.
67. Nobody's Business, 1992.
68. Crosscurrents, 1992.
69. Running Scared, 1992.
70. Cutting Edge, 1992.
71. Hot Tracks, 1992.
72. Swiss Secrets, 1992.
73. Rendezvous in Rome, 1992.
74. Greek Odyssey, 1992.
75. A Talent for Murder, 1992.
76. The Perfect Plot, 1992.
77. Danger on Parade, 1992.
78. Update on Crime, 1992.
79. No Laughing Matter, 1993.
80. Power of Suggestion, 1993.
81. Making Waves, 1993.
82. Dangerous Relations, 1993.
83. Diamond Deceit, 1993.
84. Choosing Sides, 1993.
85. Sea of Suspicion, 1993.
86. Let's Talk Terror, 1993.
87. Moving Target, 1993.
88. False Pretenses, 1993.
89. Designs in Crime, 1993.
90. Stage Fright, 1993.
91. If Looks Could Kill, 1994.
92. My Deadly Valentine, 1994.
93. Hotline to Danger, 1994.
94. Illusions of Evil, 1994.
95. An Instinct for Trouble, 1994.
96. The Runaway Bride, 1994.
97. Squeeze Play, 1994.
98. Island of Secrets, 1994.
99. The Cheating Heart, 1994.
100. Dance Till You Die, 1994.
101. The Picture of Guilt, 1994.
102. Counterfeit Christmas, 1994.

Nancy Drew Notebooks

1. The Slumber Party Secret, 1994.
2. The Lost Locket, 1994.
3. The Secret Santa, 1994.

Nancy Drew & Hardy Boys SuperMysteries

Double Crossing, 1988.
A Crime for Christmas, 1988.
Shock Waves, 1988.
Dangerous Games, 1989.
The Last Resort, 1989.
The Paris Connection, 1990.
Buried in Time, 1990.
Mystery Train, 1990.
Best of Enemies, 1991.
High Survival, 1991.
New Year's Evil, 1991.
Tour of Danger, 1992.
Spies and Lies, 1992.
Tropic of Fear, 1992.
Courting Disaster, 1993.
Hits and Misses, 1993.
Evil in Amsterdam, 1993.
Desperate Measures, 1994.
Passport to Danger, 1994.
Hollywood Horror, 1994.
Copper Canyon Conspiracy, 1994.

APPLEWOOD BOOKS

Facsimile Editions

1. The Secret of the Old Clock, 1930, 1991.
2. The Hidden Staircase, 1930, 1991.
3. The Bungalow Mystery, 1930, 1991.
4. The Mystery at Lilac Inn, 1930, 1994.
5. The Secret at Shadow Ranch, 1930, 1994.

SCHOLASTIC BOOK SERVICES

A Superboy, Supergirl Anthology: Selected Chapters from the Earlier
    Works of Victor Appleton, Franklin W. Dixon, and Carolyn Keene,
    1971.

Books by Mildred Wirt Benson

Reprinted in revised form from Geoffrey S. Lapin, "The Ghost of Nancy Drew," *Books at Iowa* 50 (April 1989). Used with permission of the Friends of the University of Iowa Libraries.

BELL, FRANK

Flash Evans Books

Flash Evans and the Darkroom Mystery, 1940.
Flash Evans, Camera News Hawk, 1940.

BENSON, MILDRED

Dangerous Deadline, 1957.
Quarry Ghost, 1959.
Kristie at College [Quarry Ghost], 1960.

CLARK, JOAN

Penny Nichols Mystery Stories

Penny Nichols Finds a Clue, 1936.
Penny Nichols and the Mystery of the Lost Key, 1936.
Penny Nichols and the Black Imp, 1936.
Penny Nichols and the Knob Hill Mystery, 1939.
Connie Carl at Rainbow Ranch, 1939.

DUNCAN, JULIA K.

Doris Force Mystery Stories

Doris Force at Locked Gates, 1931.
Doris Force at Cloudy Cove, 1931.

EMERSON, ALICE B.

The Ruth Fielding Series

Ruth Fielding and Her Great Scenario, 1927.
Ruth Fielding at Cameron Hall, 1928.
Ruth Fielding Clearing Her Name, 1929.
Ruth Fielding in Talking Pictures, 1930.
Ruth Fielding and Baby June, 1931.
Ruth Fielding and Her Double, 1932.
Ruth Fielding and Her Greatest Triumph, 1933.
Ruth Fielding and Her Crowning Victory, 1934.

JUDD, FRANCES K.

Kay Tracey Mystery Stories

The Mystery of the Swaying Curtains, 1935.
The Shadow at the Door, 1935.
The Six Fingered Glove Mystery, 1936.
The Green Cameo Mystery, 1936.
The Secret at the Windmill, 1937.
Beneath the Crimson Brier Bush, 1937.
The Message in the Sand Dunes, 1938.
The Murmuring Portrait, 1938.
When the Key Turned, 1939.
In the Sunken Garden, 1939.
The Forbidden Tower, 1940.
The Sacred Feather, 1940.

KEENE, CAROLYN

Mystery at the Lookout, 1942.

Dana Girls Mystery Stories

The Secret at the Hermitage, 1936.
The Circle of Footprints, 1937.
The Mystery of the Locked Room, 1938.
The Clue in the Cobweb, 1939.

The Secret at the Gatehouse, 1940.
The Mysterious Fireplace, 1941.
The Clue of the Rusty Key, 1942.
The Portrait in the Sand, 1943.
The Secret in the Old Well, 1944.
The Clue in the Ivy, 1952.
The Secret of the Jade Ring, 1953.
Mystery at the Crossroads, 1954.

Nancy Drew Mystery Stories

1. The Secret of the Old Clock, 1930.
2. The Hidden Staircase, 1930.
3. The Bungalow Mystery, 1930.
4. The Mystery at Lilac Inn, 1930.
5. The Secret at Shadow Ranch, 1930.
6. The Secret of Red Gate Farm, 1931.
7. The Clue in the Diary, 1932.

11. The Clue of the Broken Locket, 1934.
12. The Message in the Hollow Oak, 1935.
13. The Mystery of the Ivory Charm, 1936.
14. The Whispering Statue, 1937.
15. The Haunted Bridge, 1937.
16. The Clue of the Tapping Heels, 1939.
17. The Mystery of the Brass Bound Trunk, 1940.
18. The Mystery at the Moss-Covered Mansion, 1941.
19. The Quest of the Missing Map, 1942.
20. The Clue in the Jewel Box, 1943.
21. The Secret in the Old Attic, 1944.
22. The Clue in the Crumbling Wall, 1945.
23. The Mystery of the Tolling Bell, 1946.
24. The Clue in the Old Album, 1947.
25. The Ghost of Blackwood Hall, 1948.

30. The Clue of the Velvet Mask, 1953.

PALMER, DON

Boy Scout Explorer Series

Boy Scout Explorers at Emerald Valley, 1955.
Boy Scout Explorers at Treasure Mountain, 1955.
Boy Scout Explorers at Headless Hollow, 1957.

THORNDYKE, HELEN LOUISE

Honey Bunch Books

Honey Bunch, Her First Little Treasure Hunt, 1937.
Honey Bunch, Her First Little Club, 1938.
Honey Bunch, Her First Trip in a Trailer, 1939.
Honey Bunch, Her First Trip to a Big Fair, 1940.
Honey Bunch, Her First Twin Playmates, 1941.

WEST, DOROTHY

Dot and Dash Books

Dot and Dash at the Maple Sugar Camp, 1938.
Dot and Dash at Happy Hollow, 1938.
Dot and Dash in the North Woods, 1938.
Dot and Dash in the Pumpkin Patch, 1939.
Dot and Dash at the Seashore, 1940.

WIRT, ANN

Madge Sterling Series

The Missing Formula, 1932.
The Deserted Yacht, 1932.
The Secret of the Sundial, 1932.

WIRT, MILDRED A.

Sky Racers, 1935.
The Twin Ring Mystery, 1935.
Carolina Castle, 1936.
Courageous Wings, 1937.
Mystery of the Laughing Mask, 1940.
Linda, 1940.
Pirate Brig, 1950.

Brownie Scout Series

The Brownie Scouts at Snow Valley, 1949.
The Brownie Scouts in the Circus, 1949.
The Brownie Scouts in the Cherry Festival, 1950.
The Brownie Scouts and Their Tree House, 1951.

The Brownie Scouts at Silver Beach, 1952.
The Brownie Scouts at Windmill Farm, 1953.

Dan Carter, Cub Scout Series

Dan Carter, Cub Scout, 1949.
Dan Carter and the River Camp, 1949.
Dan Carter and the Money Box, 1950.
Dan Carter and the Haunted Castle, 1951.
Dan Carter and the Great Carved Face, 1952.
Dan Carter and the Cub Honor, 1953.

Girl Scout Series

The Girl Scouts at Penguin Pass, 1953.
The Girl Scouts at Singing Sands, 1955.
The Girl Scouts at Mystery Mansion, 1957.

Mildred A. Wirt Mystery Stories

The Clue at Crooked Lane, 1936.
The Hollow Wall Mystery, 1936.
The Shadow Stone, 1937.
The Wooden Shoe Mystery, 1938.
Through the Moon-Gate Door, 1938.
Ghost Gables, 1939.
The Painted Shield, 1939.

Penny Parker Mystery Stories

Tale of the Witch Doll, 1939.
The Vanishing Houseboat, 1939.
Danger at the Drawbridge, 1940.
Behind the Green Door, 1940.
Clue of the Silken Ladder, 1941.
The Secret Pact, 1941.
The Clock Strikes Thirteen, 1942.
The Wishing Well, 1942.
Ghost beyond the Gate, 1943.
Saboteurs on the River, 1943.
Hoofbeats on the Turnpike, 1944.
Voice from the Cave, 1944.
The Guilt of the Brass Thieves, 1945.
Signal in the Dark, 1946.
Whispering Walls, 1946.

Swamp Island, 1947.
The Cry at Midnight, 1947.

Ruth Darrow Flying Stories

Ruth Darrow in the Air Derby, 1930.
Ruth Darrow in the Fire Patrol, 1930.
Ruth Darrow in the Coast Guard, 1931.
Ruth Darrow in Yucatan, 1931.

Trailer Stories for Girls

The Runaway Caravan, 1937.
The Crimson Cruiser, 1937.
Timbered Treasure, 1937.
The Phantom Trailer, 1938.

Bibliography

The list includes works cited in the essays in this book and other sources of information about Nancy Drew, the Stratemeyer Syndicate, and Mildred Wirt Benson.

"1980s No Longer Mystery to Nancy Drew." *Chicago Tribune*, July 10, 1986, Tempo 7.

Abbott, Deborah. "Drew and the Hardys: Sleuths for a New Age." *Chicago Sun-Times Book Week*, June 8, 1980, 13.

Abrams, Alan. "Her Novels a 'Treasure.'" *Toledo (Ohio) Blade*, April 16, 1993, 1, 4.

Adams, Harriet. Letter to the editor. *New York Times*, November 23, 1975, sec. 6, 94.

——. "Their Success Is No Mystery." *TV Guide*, June 25, 1977, 13–16.

—— [Carolyn Keene]. "Nancy Drew." In *The Great Detectives*, edited by Otto Penzler, 79–86. Boston: Little, Brown, 1978.

"The Adventurous Millie Benson." *(Toledo, Ohio) People's Voice*, December 1974.

Ahrens, R. C. "Nancy Drew Was Downright Sexy." *AB Bookman's Weekly*, November 16, 1981, 3420–3424.

Allen, Barbara. "Personal Experience Narratives: Use and Meaning in Interaction." In *Folk Groups and Folklore Genres: A Reader*, edited by Oring Elliott, 236–243. Logan: Utah State University Press, 1986.

Allister, Jan. "The Bobbsey Twins 'Betrayal' Can't Crush Her Innocent Hope." *(Minneapolis) Star Tribune*, October 28, 1992, 19A.

American Library Association Council. Library Bill of Rights. Adopted June 18, 1948. Amended February 2, 1969; June 27, 1967; and January 23, 1980.

Anderson, James D. *The Education of Blacks in the South, 1860–1935.* Chapel Hill: University of North Carolina Press, 1988.

Anderson, Jon. "Drew Still Draws." *Chicago Tribune*, April 26, 1993, sec. 2, 1, 5.

Ash, Lee, and William G. Miller. *Subject Collections: A Guide to Special Book Collections and Subject Emphases as Reported by University, College, Public, and Special Libraries and Museums in the United States and Canada.* 6th ed. New York: R. R. Bowker, 1985.

Atkinson, Fred. "Keene, Carolyn." In *Dictionary of Literary Pseudonyms*, 221. 4th ed. Chicago: American Library Association, 1987.

Augustine, Mildred. "The Courtesy." *St. Nicholas* (June 1919): 762.

———. "Newspaper Illustration: A Study of the Metropolitan Daily, the Small City Daily and the Country Weekly." M.A. thesis, University of Iowa, 1927.

Bamberger, Florence. *The Effect of Physical Make-up of a Book upon Children's Selection.* Baltimore: Johns Hopkins University Press, 1922.

Barnes, Linda. "Lucky Penny." In *The Year's Best Mystery and Suspense Stories 1986*, edited by Edward D. Hoch. New York: Walker, 1986.

———. *Snapshot.* New York: Delacorte, 1993.

Basler, Barbara. "A Sleuth's Newest Venture." *New York Times*, October 26, 1986, sec. 3, 4.

Bedway, Barbara. "The Case of the Girl Detectives." *Ohio Magazine* (November 1989): 42–44, 89.

Beeson, Diana. "Translating Nancy Drew from Fiction to Film." *Lion and the Unicorn* 18:1 (1994): 37–47.

Beinecke Manuscript Collection, Yale University Library, New Haven, Conn.

Belenky, Mary Field, Blythe McVicker Clinchy, Nancy Rule Goldberger, and Jill Mattuck Tarule. *Women's Ways of Knowing: The Development of Self, Voice, and Mind.* New York: Basic Books, 1986.

Benson, Mildred Wirt. Papers, Iowa Women's Archives, University of Iowa Libraries, Iowa City.

———. *Quarry Ghost.* New York: Dodd, Mead and Co., 1959.

———. "Action Line." *Detroit Free Press*, June 8, 1969.

———. "The Ghost of Ladora." *Books at Iowa* 19 (November 1973): 24–29.

———. Letter to the editor. *Publishers Weekly*, September 26, 1986, 12.

————. Letter to the editor. *Yellowback Library* 36 (November/December 1986): 3–4.

————. Letter to the editor. *Yellowback Library* 55 (January 1989): 30.

————. "The Nancy I Knew." Introduction to Carolyn Keene, *The Mystery at Lilac Inn*. Reprint. Bedford, Mass.: Applewood Books, 1994.

————. "More About Nancy." Introduction to Carolyn Keene, *The Secret at Shadow Ranch*. Reprint. Bedford, Mass.: Applewood Books, 1994.

Berryman, Martha Ann. "Harriet Stratemeyer Adams and the Nancy Drew Mystery Stories: Feminist Gender Tales, 1930–1990: The Construction and Destruction of a Heroine." M.A. thesis, University of Texas at Austin, 1990.

Bibler, Cher. "Behind Nancy Drew; A Life of Mildred Benson." *Wastelands Review* (February 1993): 14–22.

Bierbaum, Esther Green. "Bad Books in Series: Nancy Drew in the Public Library." *Lion and the Unicorn* 18:1 (1994): 92–102.

Bilgewater, Cecil K. "The Secret of River Heights." *Yellowback Library* 83 (May 1991): 8–9.

Billman, Carol. *The Secret of the Stratemeyer Syndicate: Nancy Drew, the Hardy Boys and the Million Dollar Fiction Factory*. New York: Ungar, 1986.

Boise, R. D. "Be a Detective!" *Yellowback Library* 28 (July/August 1985): 12.

Bold, Rudolph. "Trash in the Library." *Library Journal* 115:9 (May 15, 1980): 1138–1139.

Bowman, Irene K. "Why the ALA Does Not Endorse Serials for Boys and Girls." *Iowa Library Quarterly* 9 (1921): 42.

Breen, Jon L. "The Jury Box." *Ellery Queen Mystery Magazine* (January 1993): 92–93.

Brock, Ira. "Author of Children's Books Works Out Endings First; Finds System Pays Off." *Toledo Times*, August 8, 1949.

Brooker-Gross, Susan. "Landscape and Social Values in Popular Children's Literature: Nancy Drew Mysteries." *Journal of Geography* 80 (1981): 59–64.

Brown, Ellen. "In Search of Nancy Drew, the Snow Queen and Room Nineteen: Cruising for Feminine Discourse." *Frontiers: A Journal of Women's Studies* 13 (1993): 1–25.

Brown, Patricia Leigh. "Nancy Drew: 30's Sleuth, 90's Role Model." *New York Times*, April 19, 1993, 1A.

————. "A Ghostwriter and Her Sleuth: 63 Years of Smarts and Gumption." *New York Times*, May 9, 1993, E7.

Bumiller, Elisabeth. "Squeaky-Clean and Still Eighteen: Nancy Drew,

Girl Detective, Marks Half a Century." *Washington Post*, April 17, 1980, D1.

Burke, W. J., and Will D. Howe, eds. "Wirt, Mildred." In *American Authors and Books, 1640 to the Present Day*, 704. 3rd rev. ed. New York: Crown Publishing, 1972.

Caprio, Betsy. "Nancy Drew, 'The Morning After.'" *Whispered Watchword* (April 1990): 18.

――――. *The Mystery of Nancy Drew: Girl Sleuth on the Couch*. Trabuco Canyon, Calif.: Source Books, 1992.

Cariou, Mavis Olive. "Syntax, Vocabulary and Metaphor in Three Groups of Novels for Children in Grades Four to Six." Ph.D. diss., University of Michigan, 1983.

Carlsen, G. Robert. *Books and the Teen-age Reader*. New York: Harper & Row, 1967.

Carlson, P. M. "Nancy and Me." Introduction to Carolyn Keene, *The Bungalow Mystery*. Reprint. Bedford, Mass.: Applewood Books, 1991.

Carrier, Esther Jane. *Fiction in Public Libraries 1886–1900*. New York: Scarecrow Press, 1965.

Carroll, Nicole. "The Case of Nancy Drew's Enduring Appeal." *USA Today*, April 14, 1993, 6D.

Chamberlain, Kathleen. Letter to the editor. *Ms*. (March/April 1993): 9.

――――. "The Secrets of Nancy Drew: Having Their Cake and Eating It Too." *Lion and the Unicorn* 18:1 (1994): 1–12.

Children's Express. "The Mystery of Nancy Drew." In *Murder Ink: The Mystery Readers' Companion*, edited by Dilys Winn, 116–118. New York: Workman, 1977.

Chorey, Carol. "'Nancy Drew' Still a Puzzler at City Library." *(Boulder, Colo.) Sunday Camera*, August 2, 1992, 1D–2D.

Commire, Anne, ed. "Adams, Harriet S." In *Something about the Author*, 1:1. Detroit and London: Gale Research, 1971.

Cooper, Ilene. "Children's Books: Sweet Are the Uses of Predictability." *New York Times*, November 8, 1992, sec. 7, 52.

Corr, John. "Updated for the 80s, Hardy Boys Fit to Interface with Valley Girls." *Des Moines Register*, April 28, 1987, 1T–5T.

Coyle, William, ed. "Benson, Mildred Wirt." In *Ohio Authors and Their Books: Bibliographical Data and Selective Bibliographies for Ohio Authors, Native and Resident, 1796–1950*, 50. Cleveland and New York: World Publishing Co., 1962.

Craig, Patricia, and Mary Cadogan. "A Sweet Girl Sleuth." In *The Lady Investigates: Women Detectives and Spies in Fiction*, 149–163. New York: St. Martin's, 1981.

Crawford, Robert L. "Rewriting the Past in Children's Literature: The Hardy Boys and Other Series." *Children's Literature Association Quarterly* (Spring 1993): 10–12.

Daigon, Arthur. "The Strange Case of Nancy Drew." *English Journal* 53 (1964): 666–669.

Daniels, Lee A. "Hardy Boys Named in Literary Suit." *New York Times*, June 10, 1980, A1, C9.

Davis, William. "Other Teen Sleuths Return in Original Form." *Boston Globe*, June 12, 1991, 78.

Deane, Paul. "Children's Fiction in America Since 1900: A Study of Books in Series." Ph.D. diss., Harvard University, 1966.

———. "The Persistence of Uncle Tom: An Examination of the Image of the Negro in Children's Fiction Series." In *The Black American in Books for Children: Readings in Racism*, edited by Donnarae Mac-Cann and Gloria Woodard, 116–123. Metuchen, N.J.: Scarecrow Press, 1985. Also published in *Journal of Negro Education* 37 (1968): 140–145.

———. "Black Characters in Children's Fiction Series since 1968." *Journal of Negro Education* 58:2 (Spring 1989): 153–162.

———. *Mirrors of American Culture: Children's Fiction Series in the Twentieth Century*. Metuchen, N.J.: Scarecrow Press, 1991.

DeWitt, Karen. "The Case of the Alter Egos." *Washington Post*, July 31, 1977, H1.

Dickinson, Peter. "A Defense of Rubbish." *Children's Literature in Education* 3 (1970): 7–10.

Dixon, Franklin W., pseud. *The Mystery of Cabin Island*. New York: Grosset & Dunlap, 1929.

Dizer, John T. "Stratemeyer and the Blacks." *Dime Novel Roundup* (October 1976): 90–117.

———. "So Who Wrote Tom, Swiftly?" *Newsboy* (May/June 1992): 9.

Donelson, Kenneth L. "Nancy, Tom and Assorted Friends in the Stratemeyer Syndicate Then and Now." *Children's Literature* 7 (1979): 17–43.

———. "History Rewritten: Nancy Drew and the Secret of the Old Clock." *Catholic Library World* 50 (1980): 220–225.

Donelson, Kenneth L., and Alleen Pace Nilsen. *Literature for Today's Young Adults*. 3rd ed. Glenview, Ill.: Scott, Foresman, 1989.

Doyle, Arthur Conan. *The Speckled Band*. London: French, 1912.

Drexler, Rosalyn. "The Real Nancy Drew." *New York Times Magazine*, October 19, 1975, 103.

Dyer, Carolyn Stewart. Letter to the editor. *Ms.* (March/April 1993): 9.

Editorial. *Library Journal* 30 (December 1905): 915–916.

Emburg, Kate. "Nancy Drew—Science Fiction Series?" *Whispered Watchword* (January 1990): 28–29.

———. *The Girls' Series Companion*. North Highlands, Calif.: Society of Phantom Friends, 1994.

Eng, Dinah. "Bridges." Gannett News Service, July 18, 1989.

———. "Bridges: Ties to the Past." Gannett News Service, June 4, 1991.

Farah, David. "Basic Nancy Drew." *Yellowback Library* 6 (December 1981): 6; 7 (January/February 1982): 5; 8 (March/April 1982): 7; 9 (May/June 1982): 10; 10 (July/August 1982): 12; 11 (September/October 1982): 18; 12 (November/December 1982): 7; 13 (January/February 1983): 7; 14 (March/April 1983): 16; 15 (May/June 1983): 13; 16 (July/August 1983): 19; 17 (September/October 1983): 7; 18 (November/December 1983): 9; 19 (January/February 1984): 18; 20 (March/April 1984): 6; 21 (May/June 1984): 12; 22 (July/August 1984): 13; 23 (September/October 1984): 16; 24 (November/December 1984): 11; 25 (January/Febrary 1985): 10; 26 (March/April 1985): 6; 28 (July/August 1985): 9; 29 (September/October 1985): 11; 30 (November/December 1985): 7.

———. *Farah's Guide*. 10 eds. Flint, Mich., and Newport Beach, Calif.: Farah's Books, 1985–1993.

———. "Collecting Nancy Drew Books." *Paper Collectors' Marketplace* (February 1990): 26–29.

Felder, Deborah. "Nancy Drew: Then and Now." *Publishers Weekly*, May 30, 1986, 30–34.

Fenner, Phyllis. *The Proof of the Pudding: What Children Read*. New York: John Day, 1957.

Ferraro, Susan. "Girl Talk." *New York Times Magazine*, December 6, 1992, 62–63+.

Fetterley, Judith. "Reading about Reading: 'A Jury of Her Peers,' 'The Murders in the Rue Morgue,' and 'The Yellow Wallpaper.'" In *Gender and Reading: Essays on Readers, Texts, and Contexts*, edited by Elizabeth A. Flynn and Patrocinio P. Schweickart, 164. Baltimore: Johns Hopkins University Press, 1986.

Field, Carolyn, ed. *Special Collections in Children's Literature*. Chicago: American Library Association, 1982.

Fisher, Anita. "Y[oung] A[dult] Detective Fiction: Nancy Drew and the Age of Technology." *ALAN Review: The Assembly on Literature for Adolescents, National Council of Teachers of English* 11 (1984): 8–10.

Fitzgerald, Frances. "Women, Success and Nancy Drew." *Vogue* (May 1980): 323–324.

Folsom, Mary Elting. Letter to the editor. "Censored Writer Praises Library." *(Boulder, Colo.) Camera*, July 16, 1991.

Foster, Catherine. "Slick New Image for Good Old Nancy Drew." *Christian Science Monitor*, September 11, 1986, 31.

Fredrickson, George. *The Black Image in the White Mind: The Debate on Afro-American Character and Destiny, 1817–1914*. New York: Harper & Row, 1971.

Gabin, Nancy F. "'They Have Placed a Penalty on Womanhood': Women's Reconversion Experience." In *Feminism in the Labor Movement: Women and the United Auto Workers, 1935–1975*, 11–42. Ithaca: Cornell University Press, 1990.

Gable, Mona. "The Real-Life Heroine Who Wrote Nancy Drew." *Los Angeles Times*, August 16, 1991, E6.

———. "The Way They Were." *Los Angeles Times*, August 16, 1991, E1.

Gardner, Emelyn E., and Eloise Ramsey. *A Handbook of Children's Literature: Methods and Materials*. Chicago: Scott, Foresman, 1927.

Gardner, Marilyn. "Teenager Taste Treat." *Christian Science Monitor*, July 19, 1991, 13.

Garis, Roger. *My Father Was "Uncle Wiggily."* New York: McGraw-Hill, 1966.

Garrison, Dee. *Apostles of Culture: The Public Libraries and American Society 1876–1920*. New York: Free Press, 1979.

Gehring, Wes D. *Screwball Comedy: Defining a Genre*. Ball State Monograph no. 31. Muncie, Ind.: Ball State University, 1983.

Geier, Thom. "She's Still Hardy Boys." *U.S. News & World Report*, April 19, 1993, 20.

Geller, Evelyn. *Forbidden Books in American Public Libraries, 1876–1939*. Westport, Conn.: Greenwood Press, 1984.

Ginsburg, Jane. "And Then There Is Good Old Nancy Drew." *Ms.* (January 1974): 93.

Girls Series Books: A Checklist of Hardback Books Published 1900–1975. Minneapolis: Children's Literature Research Collections, University of Minnesota Libraries, 1978.

Gluck, Sherna Berger. *Rosie the Riveter Revisited: Women, the War and Social Change*. Boston: Twayne Publishers, 1987.

Goldstein, Kenneth. *A Guide for Fieldworkers in Folklore*. Hatboro, Pa.: Folklore Associates, 1964.

Gould, Stephen Jay. *An Urchin in the Storm: Essays about Books and Ideas*. New York: W. W. Norton, 1987.

Greco, Gail. "Nancy Drew's New Look." *Americana* 14 (September/October 1986): 57–58.

Greenberg, Anne. Letter to the editor. *New York Times*, May 2, 1993, 18E.

Grosset & Dunlap, Inc. v. Gulf & Western Corp., and Stratemeyer Syn-

dicate. U.S. District Court, Southern District of New York, 79 Civ. 2242, 79 Civ. 3745 (1980). (Trial transcript.)

Grossman, Anita Susan. "Writings about Mildred Wirt Benson: An Annotated Bibliography." *Yellowback Library* 38 (March/April 1987): 11–15.

———. "The Ghost of Nancy Drew." *Ohio Magazine* (December 1987): 41.

———. "The Ghost of Nancy Drew: The Story behind the Teenage Sleuth." *San Francisco Chronicle*, August 21, 1988, 10–16.

Haitch, Richard. "At 83, Her Pen Is Far from Dry." *New York Times*, March 27, 1977, sec. 11, 19.

Hall, G. Stanley. "What Children Read and What They Ought to Read." *Addresses and Proceedings of the National Educational Association* (1905): 868–871.

Hardt,. Hanno. *Critical Communication Studies: Communication History and Theory in America*. London: Routledge, 1992.

"Hardy Once Again." *People*, August 5, 1991, 71.

"Harriet S. Adams, Nancy Drew Novelist, Dead at 89." United Press International, March 29, 1982.

Haycraft, Howard. *The Boys' Book of Great Detective Stories*. New York: Berkley Highland Books, 1940.

———. *The Boys' Second Book of Great Detective Stories*. New York: Berkley Highland Books, 1964.

Heffley, Lynne. "Young Adult Books: Nancy Drew Gets Thorough Makeover." *Los Angeles Times*, October 4, 1986, part 5, 10.

Heilbrun, Carolyn. *Writing a Woman's Life*. New York: W. W. Norton & Co., 1988.

Heines, Ethel L. "Brand Name Fiction." *Horn Book* 58:3 (June 1982): 25.

Helser, Linda. "Nancy Drew Girl Role Model." *Arizona Republic*, August 15, 1993, H1–2.

Herz, Peggy. *Nancy Drew and the Hardy Boys*. New York: Scholastic Book Services, 1977.

Hirsch, James. "Children's Books: Nancy Drew Gets Real." *New York Times*, October 9, 1988, sec. 7, 47.

Holt, Patricia. "In Between the Lines—The Updating of Nancy Drew." *San Francisco Chronicle*, October 19, 1986.

Hoover, C. Rusnock. "Nancy Drew, Hardy Boys a No-No." *(Boulder, Colo.) Daily Camera*, May 26, 1991.

———. "Boulder Library to Stock Series Such as Hardy Boys, Nancy Drew." *(Boulder, Colo.) Daily Camera*, July 11, 1991.

Howes, Durward, ed. "Wirt, Mildred." In *American Women: The Standard Biographical Dictionary of Notable Women*, vol. 3, 1939–1940, 998. Los Angeles: American Publications, 1939.

Hudson, Harry. *A Bibliography of Hard-cover Boys' Books.* Rev. ed. Tampa, Fla.: Data Print, 1977.

Jackson, Gregory, Jr. "'Spaceman's Luck!': An Interview with Frankie Thomas." *Yellowback Library* 42 (November/December 1987): 5–14.

Johnson, Deidre. *Stratemeyer Pseudonyms and Series Books: An Annotated Checklist of Stratemeyer and Stratemeyer Syndicate Publications.* Westport, Conn.: Greenwood Press, 1982.

————. "Child Labor in the Stratemeyer Syndicate Series Books: A Preliminary Study." *Dime Novel Roundup* (April 1983): 18–31.

————. "Continued Success: The Early Boys' Fiction of Edward Stratemeyer and the Stratemeyer Syndicate." Ph.D. diss., University of Minnesota, 1990.

————. *Edward Stratemeyer and the Stratemeyer Syndicate.* New York: Twayne Publishers, 1993.

————. "Nancy Drew—A Modern Elsie Dinsmore?" *Lion and the Unicorn* 18:1 (1994): 13–24.

Jones, James P. "Negro Stereotypes in Children's Literature: The Case of Nancy Drew." *Journal of Negro Education* 40 (1971): 121–125.

————. "Nancy Drew, WASP Super Girl of the 1930s." *Journal of Popular Culture* 6 (1973): 707–717.

"Jubilee for Nancy Drew." *New York Times,* April 10, 1980, 11, 15.

Kagan, Julie. "Nancy Drew—18 Going on 50." *McCall's* (July 1973): 15.

Kaplan, Deborah. "The Mysteries of the New Nancy Drew." *Detroit Free Press,* June 17, 1986, 1B.

Keeline, James. "The Mechanics of the Stratemeyer Syndicate as Related to Tom Swift." Paper distributed at the American Culture Association/Popular Culture Association Convention, Louisville, Ky., March 21, 1992.

————. "The Mechanics of the Stratemeyer Syndicate . . . as Related to the Tom Swift Series (Part I, 1910–1941)." *Newsboy* 30:6 (November/December 1992): 9–15.

————. "Who Wrote Nancy Drew? Secrets from the Syndicate Files Revealed." *Yellowback Library* 127 (January 1995): 5–12.

Kelly, Ernie. "The Tempest: Or, Writing Up a Storm." *Yellowback Library* 38 (March/April 1987): 19–22.

————. "Inside the Stratemeyer Syndicate, Part I," *Yellowback Library* 52 (October 1988): 5–11; "Part II," 54 (December 1988): 5–12.

Kensinger, Faye Riter. *Children of the Series and How They Grew, Or, A Century of Heroines and Heroes, Romantic, Comic, Moral.* Bowling Green, Ohio: Bowling Green State University Press, 1987.

Kinloch, Lucy M. "The Menace of the Series Book." *Ontario Library Review* 19:2 (May 1935): 74–76.

Klemesrud, Judy. "100 Books—Not a Hippie in Them." *New York Times*, April 4, 1968, 52.

Knight, Melanie. "Series on Film: Nancy Drew, Detective; Nancy Drew, Reporter; Nancy Drew, Troubleshooter; Nancy Drew and the Hidden Staircase." *Whispered Watchword* (October 1986): 20–21.

Koch, Katy. "Nancy Drew Devotees Praise, Critique Spunky Teen Sleuth." *(Riverside, Calif.) Press Enterprise*, April 25, 1993, 1E, 3E.

Kuskin, Karla. "Nancy Drew and Friends." *New York Times Book Review*, May 4, 1975, 20–21.

Laden, R. "Nancy Drew: 18 Going on 50." *Decatur (Ill.) Herald and Review*, August 10, 1980, C1.

Lake, Mary Louise. "What's Wrong with Series Books?" *Elementary English* 47 (1970): 1109–1111.

Lanes, Selma. *Down the Rabbit Hole: Adventures and Misadventures in the Realm of Children's Literature*. New York: Atheneum, 1971.

Lapin, Geoffrey S. Letter to the editor. *AB Bookman's Weekly* (December 1981): 21–28.

———. "The Mystery of Nancy Drew, or, The Clue in the Old Library." *Random Notes* 1 (Indianapolis, 1982): 1–5.

———. "Carolyn Keene—pseud." *Yellowback Library* 16 (July/August 1983): 3; 17 (September/October 1983): 16; 18 (November/December 1983): 9; 20 (March/April 1984): 13; 23 (September/October 1984): 18.

———. "Stratemeyer Syndicate Acquired by Simon & Schuster." *Yellowback Library* 24 (November/December 1984): 15.

———. "Madge Sterling, Penny Nichols, and Connie Carl and the Mystery of Ann Wirt." *Yellowback Library* 29 (September/October 1985): 15.

———. "Jim Lawrence and the Stratemeyer Syndicate." *Yellowback Library* 31 (January/February 1986): 5–10.

———. "Mildred Wirt: A Bibliography of Hardcover Juvenile Books." *Yellowback Library* 35 (September/October 1986): 26–30.

———. "The Ghost of Nancy Drew." *Books at Iowa* 50 (April 1989): 8–27.

———. "The Outline of a Ghost." *Lion and the Unicorn* 18:1 (1994): 60–69.

Lewis, Anthony. "TV Block Booking of Movies Barred." November 6, 1962. In *The New York Times Encyclopedia of Film*, vol. 7. New York: Times Books, 1984.

MacLeod, Anne Scott. "Secret in the Trash Bin: On the Perennial Popularity of Juvenile Series Books." *Children's Literature in Education* 15 (1984): 127–140.

———. "Nancy Drew and Her Rivals: No Contest." *Horn Book* 63:3 (May/June 1987): 314–322; 63:4 (July/August 1987): 422–450.

Maltin, Leonard, ed. *Hollywood Kids*. New York: Popular Library, 1978.

Maney, Mabel. *The Case of the Not-So-Nice Nurse*. Pittsburgh: Cleis Press, 1993.

———. *The Case of the Good-for-Nothing Girlfriend*. Pittsburgh: Cleis Press, 1994.

Marsh, Chuck. "Drawn to Drew." *Kansas Alumni Magazine* (August/September 1993): 28–31.

Maslekoff, Barbara. "Mildred Wirt Benson." *Ohioana Quarterly* (Fall 1989): S4.

Mason, Bobbie Ann. *The Girl Sleuth: A Feminist Guide*. New York: Feminist Press, 1975.

Mathiews, Franklin K. "Blowing Out the Boy's Brains." *New Outlook* 108 (November 1914): 652–654.

May, Roger B. "Durable Heroes: Nancy Drew and Kin Still Surmount Scrapes—and Critics' Slurs." *Wall Street Journal*, January 15, 1975, 1.

McCombs, Gillian M. "Nancy Drew Here to Stay?" *Acquisitions Librarian* 8 (Fall 1992): 47–58.

McCormack, Patricia. "Carolyn Keene Stars in 'Minor Mystery' at the Plaza Hotel." United Press International, May 8, 1981.

McDowell, Edwin. "Grosset & Dunlap Being Sold." *New York Times*, May 22, 1982, sec. 2, 33.

———. "Syndicator of Bobbsey Twins and Hardy Boys Purchased." *New York Times*, August 4, 1984, sec. 1, 9.

McFarlane, Leslie. *Ghost of the Hardy Boys*. New York: Methuen, 1976.

Mierau, Christina. "Much Ado about Nancy Drew." In *The Fine Art of Murder*, edited by Ed Gorman, Martin Greenberg, Larry Segriff, and Jon L. Breen, 254–258. New York: Carroll & Graf, 1993.

Miller, J. "A Study of Minority Roles in Nancy Drew Books: 1930–1940 and 1970–1980." Unpublished paper, Texas Woman's University, 1986.

Miller, Janet, and June H. Schlessinger, "Trends in the Portrayal of Minorities in the Nancy Drew Series." *Journal of Youth Services in Libraries* 1 (Spring 1988): 329–333.

Miller, Nancy K. "Representing Others: Gender and the Subjects of Autobiography." *Differences* (forthcoming).

Mitgang, Herbert. "Portrait of the Artist as Factory Employee." *New York Times*, April 4, 1982, sec. 4, 20.

Modleski, Tania. *Loving with a Vengeance: Mass-Produced Fantasies for Women*. New York: Methuen, 1982.

Monaghan, Charles. "Book Report: Girl Detective at 56." *Washington Post*, August 10, 1986, Book World 15.

Montague, Susan P. "How Nancy Got Her Man: An Investigation of

Success Models in American Adolescent Pulp Literature." In *The American Dimension: Cultural Myth and Social Realities*, edited by Susan P. Montague and W. Arens, 99–116. 2nd ed. Sherman Oaks, Calif.: Alfred Publishing Company, 1981.

Morris, Jan. *Conundrum*. New York: Holt, 1987.

Murphy, Cullen. "Starting Over." *Atlantic* (June 1991): 18–22.

"Mystery at Boulder Library." *(Boulder, Colo.) Daily Camera*, June 23, 1991.

"Nancy and the Professor." *Time*, May 3, 1993, 83.

"Nancy Drew, Other Stars of Children's Book Series Keep Rolling Along." *Wall Street Journal*, July 19, 1973.

"Nancy Drew Related Books." *Whispered Watchword* (April 1991): 23.

National Historical Publications and Records Commission. *Directory of Archives and Manuscript Repositories in the United States*. 2nd ed. New York: Orynx Press, 1988.

"Newark Author, Great Favorite with Young Folks, Talks of Stories for Boys." *Newark Sunday News*, ca. 1904. Reprinted in *Newsboy* 26:3 (November/December 1987): 75–77.

Newby, Idus A. *Jim Crow's Defense: Anti-Negro Thought in America, 1900–1930*. Baton Rouge: Louisiana State University Press, 1965.

Nichols, Marilyn A. "A Study of the Nancy Drew Mystery Books Series." Unpublished paper, School of Library Science, University of Minnesota, July 1975.

Nilsson, Maria. "Fallet Kitty Drew." *Göteborgs Posten* (Göteborg, Sweden), October 10, 1993, 14.

Nye, Russell. *The Unembarrassed Muse: The Popular Arts in America*. New York: Dial Press, 1970.

Odum, Howard W. *Social and Mental Traits of the Negro*. New York: Columbia University Press, 1910.

Olendorf, Donna, ed. "Benson, Mildred." In *Something about the Author*, 65:7–11. Detroit and London: Gale Research, 1991.

O'Toole, Patricia. "Passport to the Universe." *Reader's Digest* (January 1993): 78.

Paluka, Frank. ed. "Wirt, Mildred A." In *Iowa Authors: A Bio-Biography of Sixty Native Authors*, 197–208. Iowa City: Friends of the University of Iowa Libraries, 1967.

Parameswaran, Radhika. "Nancy Drew and Her Passage to India." *Lion and the Unicorn* 18:1 (1994): 78–80.

Paretsky, Sara. "Keeping Nancy Drew Alive." Introduction to Carolyn Keene, *The Secret of the Old Clock*. Reprint. Bedford, Mass.: Applewood Books, 1991.

Parish, James R., and Michael R. Pitts. *The Great Detective Pictures*. Metuchen, N.J.: Scarecrow Press, 1990.

Pave, Marvin. "Nancy Drew Banned in Newton? Not Quite, But . . ." *Boston Globe*, September 14, 1978.

Payne, Buchner H. *The Negro: What Is His Ethnological Status?* Cincinnati: n.p., 1872.

Pearson, Ann. "Merits of Drew, the Hardys and Bobbseys." *Auburn (Ala.) Bulletin*, March 14, 1979.

Pells, Richard H. *The Liberal Mind in a Conservative Age*. New York: Harper & Row, 1985.

"People." *Ohio Magazine* (August 1982): 13.

"People." *Time*, April 28, 1980, 85. (On the celebration of the fiftieth anniversary of Nancy Drew.)

Pickard, Nancy. *Dead Crazy*. New York: Pocket Books, 1988.

———. *Bum Steer*. New York: Pocket Books, 1990.

———. "I Owe It All to Nancy Drew." Introduction to Carolyn Keene, *The Hidden Staircase*. Reprint. Bedford, Mass.: Applewood Books, 1991.

———. *Twenty-seven Ingredient Chili Con Carne Murders*. New York: Delacorte, 1993.

Piehler, Harold. "Why Boys Like Nancy Drew." *Whispered Watchword* (November 1992): 2.

"Platitudes Every Child Should Know." *Scribner's Magazine* (January 1914): 130.

Plunkett-Powell, Karen. *The Nancy Drew Scrapbook: 60 Years of America's Favorite Teenage Sleuth*. New York: St. Martin's Press, 1993.

Polumbaum, Judy. "The Case of the Girl Detective." *Boston Globe Magazine*, June 6, 1993, 18–23.

Pother, Dick. "Nancy Drew's Back!" *Detroit Free Press*, October 10, 1975, C1.

Prager, Arthur. "The Secret of Nancy Drew—Pushing Forty and Going Strong." *Saturday Review of Literature*, January 25, 1969, 18, 34.

———. *Rascals at Large, Or the Clue in the Old Nostalgia*. New York: Doubleday, 1971.

———. "Edward Stratemeyer and His Book Machine." *Saturday Review of Literature*, July 10, 1971, 15–17, 52–53.

Quinby, Brie. "Nancy Drew, at 50, Is Still the Top Bubble Gumshoe." *Family Weekly*, August 3, 1980, 15.

Radway, Janice A. *Reading the Romance: Women, Patriarchy, and Popular Literature*. Chapel Hill: University of North Carolina Press, 1984, 1991.

Reuter, M. "Grosset Sues Simon & Schuster and Stratemeyer for $50 Million." *Publishers Weekly*, May 7, 1979, 25.

Review of *Dangerous Deadline*. *Booklist*, February 1, 1958, 306.

Review of *Dangerous Deadline*. *Kirkus Review*, November 1, 1957, 815.

Review of *Dangerous Deadline*. *Library Journal*, February 15, 1958, 654.

Rhys, Jean. *Wide Sargasso Sea*. New York: W. W. Norton, 1966, 1982.

Rich, Virginia. *The Cooking School Murders*. New York: Dutton, 1982.

Roberts, Nancy. "Nancy Drew Movies." *Whispered Watchword* (August 1991): 8–9.

———. "Nancy Drew Videos." *Whispered Watchword* (June 1992): 2–3.

Romalov, Nancy Tillman. "Editor's Note." *Lion and the Unicorn* 18:1 (1994): v–xi.

———. "Lady and the Tramps: The Cultural Work of Gypsies in Nancy Drew and Her Foremothers." *Lion and the Unicorn* 18:1 (1994): 25–36.

———. "Press Conference with Mildred Wirt Benson—April 17, 1993." *Lion and the Unicorn* 18:1 (1994): 81–91.

Rose, Lloyd. "Magical 'Nancy Drew.'" *Washington Post*, June 21, 1991, B2.

Rosenberg, Betty, and Diana Tixier Herald. *Genreflecting: A Guide to Reading Interests in Genre Fiction*. 3rd ed. Littleton, Colo.: Libraries Unlimited, 1991.

Rosenberg, Judith K., and Kenyon C. Rosenberg. *Young People's Literature in Series: Fiction—An Annotated Bibliographical Guide*. Littleton, Colo.: Libraries Unlimited, 1972.

Rosenblatt, Louise. *The Reader, the Text, the Poem*. Carbondale: Southern Illinois University Press, 1978.

Rouse, John. "In Defense of Trash." In *Challenge and Change in the Teaching of English*, edited by Arthur Daigon and Ronald T. Laconte, 170–176. Boston: Allyn & Bacon, 1971.

Sacharow, Fredda. "Speaking Personally: When Nancy Drew's 'Mother' Revealed the Secret of Cooking Up a Mystery." *New York Times*, April 11, 1982, sec. 11, 1.

Sayers, Dorothy L. *Gaudy Night*. London: Victor Gollancz, 1935.

———. *Clouds of Witness*. New York: Harper, 1955.

———. *Strong Poison*. New York: Harper, 1958.

Schatz, Thomas. *Hollywood Genres: Formulas, Filmmaking, and the Studio System*. Philadelphia: Temple University Press, 1981.

"The Secret of the Ghost(writer) of Ladora." *Iowa Alumni Review* (May/June 1985): 24.

Shale, Richard. *Academy Awards*. 4th ed. New York: Frederick Ungar Publishing Co., 1982.

Sikov, Ed. *Screwball: Hollywood's Madcap Romantic Comedies*. New York: Crown Publishers, 1989.

Skjonsberg, Kari. "Nancy, a.k.a. Kitty, Susanne, Alice—in Norway and Other European Countries." *Lion and the Unicorn* 18:1 (1994): 70–77.

Soderbergh, Peter A. "The Stratemeyer Strain: Educators and the Juvenile Series Book, 1900–1973." *Journal of Popular Culture* 7 (1973): 864–872.

———. "Edward Stratemeyer and the Juvenile Ethic, 1894–1930." *International Review of History and Political Science* 11 (1974): 61–71.

———. "Your Favorite (Unknown) Author." *Modern Maturity* (June/July 1975): 18–19.

Stefaniak, Mary Helen. "'An Affectionate Satire': Or, Roasting Nancy Drew." *Lion and the Unicorn* 18:1 (June 1994): 113–117.

Stillman, Terry A. "Edward Stratemeyer and His Boys and Girls Series." *AB Bookman's Weekly*, November 9, 1987, 1789–1796.

Stratemeyer, Edward, and Harriet Stratemeyer Adams Collection. University of Oregon Library, Eugene.

"Stratemeyer and S & S Call Grosset Suit Frivolous." *Publishers Weekly*, May 14, 1979, 124.

Streit, Everett A. "Started Here on Road to Fame." *Clinton (Ia.) Herald*, March 20, 1993, 4.

Suplee, Curt. "Nancy Drew's Story: Recalling the Woman behind the Adventure, the Woman behind Nancy Drew." *Washington Post*, March 30, 1982, Style B1.

Terman, Lewis M., and Margaret Lima. *Children's Reading: A Guide for Parents and Teachers*. New York: Appleton, 1926.

Thompson, Grace. "On the Selection of Books for Children." *Library Journal* 32 (October 1907): 427–433.

Thorndill, Christine Maltby. "A Critical Analysis of the Revision of Two Juvenile Fiction Series." M.A. paper, University of Chicago, 1976.

———. "The Skeleton in the Closet: Revision of Racial, Ethnic, and Sexual Stereotypes in Series Books." *Top O' the News* 34:3 (Spring 1978): 245–248.

"Toledoan's Prize Book Is Released to Stores." *Toledo Times*, November 6, 1957.

"Toledo Woman Is Author of Books for Young Folk: Mildred A. Wirt Works Daily Telling of Activities of Fictional Characters in Her Popular Stories." *Toledo Blade*, April 12, 1940.

"Tom, Jr." *New Yorker*, March 20, 1954, 26–27.

Treloar, James A. "The Artful Ways of Millie." *Detroit News Magazine*, August 13, 1971, 9B.

Tribby, Michael. "The Case of the Missing Authority File." Unpublished paper, School of Library and Information Science, University of Iowa, 1992.

Trotsky, Susan M., ed. "Benson, Mildred." In *Contemporary Authors*, 134:49–52. Detroit and London: Gale Research, 1992.

Vander Schaaf, Rachelle. "Timeless Teen." *Healthy Woman* (Winter 1993): 10.

Van Matre, Lynn. "Nancy Drew's Success Is Still a Mystery." *(Norfolk) Virginian Pilot*, February 20, 1980, B1.

———. "Nancy Drew Tingles Anew." *Chicago Tribune*, December 21, 1986, Tribune Books, 7.

Variety Film Reviews 1907–1980. "Nancy Drew—Reporter," March 1, 1939; "Nancy Drew—Troubleshooter," September 20, 1939; "Nancy Drew and the Hidden Staircase," November 8, 1939; "Nancy Drew—Detective," December 7, 1939. Vol. 6. New York: Garland Publishing, 1983.

Vivelo, Jackie. "The Mystery of Nancy Drew." *Ms.* (November/December 1992): 76–77.

Walther, Peter C. "Edward Stratemeyer's Appeal to Contemporary Young Readers." *Dime Novel Roundup* (February 1979): 2–5.

Ward, Martha E., and D. Marquardt, eds. "Benson, Mildred Wirt." In *Authors of Books for Young People*, 24–25. New York and London: Scarecrow, 1967.

Wartik, Nancy. "Nancy Drew, Yuppie Detective." *Ms.* (September 1986): 29.

Watson, Bruce. "Tom Swift, Nancy Drew and Pals All Had the Same Dad." *Smithsonian* (October 1991): 50–60.

Wawrzenski, Mark. "Nancy Drew, Detective." *Yellowback Library* 34 (July/August 1986): 5–9+.

———. "Nancy Drew, Troubleshooter." *Yellowback Library* 76 (September/October 1990): 5–11.

Wertheimer, Barbara S., and Carol Sands. "Nancy Drew Revisited." *Language Arts* 52 (November/December 1975): 1131–1134, 1161.

White, Jane See. "Nancy Drew Is Ageless." *Newsboy*, April 18, 1980, 13–14.

Wiley, Debora. "Conference Draws on Nancy Drew Reading Experience." *Des Moines Register*, April 16, 1993, 1–2T.

———. "Whodunnit?" *Des Moines Register*, April 16, 1993, 1–2T.

Winslow, Kent. "The Critic's Clew . . . to Miss Drew." *Mystery & Adventure Series Review* 7 (Winter 1981).

Wirt, Mildred Augustine. "Fog." *Lutheran Young Folks* (Philadelphia), March 23, 1935, 129–130, 136.

Women's Bureau. *Women's Occupations through Seven Decades*. Bulletin no. 232. Washington, D.C.: Women's Bureau, 1951.

Woodin, Heather Sloman. "Forum Gaining National Press." *Cedar Rapids (Ia.) Gazette*, April 16, 1993, 3B.

———. "Mysterious Popularity." *Cedar Rapids (Ia.) Gazette*, April 16, 1993, 1B, 3B.

Ybarra, I. R. "Series Books You Never Heard Of (Until Now)." *Mystery and Adventure Series Review* (Spring 1982).

Zacharias, Lee. "Nancy Drew, Ballbuster." *Journal of Popular Culture* 9 (1976): 1027–1038.

Zuckerman, Eileen Goudge. "Nancy Drew vs. Serious Fiction." *Publishers Weekly*, May 30, 1986, 74.

Contributors

LINDA BARNES, of Brookline, Massachusetts, is the author of Carlotta Carlyle and Michael Spraggue mysteries. Her first Carlotta novel, *A Trouble of Fools*, won the American Mystery Award in 1987. *Hardware* (1995) is her most recent Carlyle mystery.

DIANA BEESON is a Ph.D. candidate at the University of Iowa. She has been program director of University of Iowa Television since 1983 and has been an adjunct faculty member at Kirkwood Community College, Cedar Rapids, Iowa.

MILDRED WIRT BENSON was the original writer of the Nancy Drew books under the pseudonym Carolyn Keene. Using her own name and several others, she was author of more than 130 children's books. They include: Penny Parker, Dana Girls, Kay Tracey, and Mildred A. Wirt mysteries and books in the Ruth Fielding and Honey Bunch series among others. She is a reporter and columnist for the *Toledo Blade* where she has worked for more than 50 years.

ESTHER GREEN BIERBAUM is a professor in the School of Library and Information Science at the University of Iowa. Among her interests is the bibliographic and historical problem of determining and identifying authorship in ghostwritten books.

BARBARA BLACK is community and audiovisual services coordinator at the Iowa City Public Library. She was young adult librarian there from 1988 to 1993.

BONNIE BRENNEN is an assistant professor at the State University of New York at Geneseo. She has served as editor of the *Journal of Communication Inquiry*.

CAROLYN STEWART DYER is an associate professor in the School of Journalism and Mass Communication at the University of Iowa, where she teaches gender and mass communication and mass media law. She was coordinator of the Nancy Drew Project.

DINAH ENG, of Washington, D.C., is Special Sections editor and columnist for Gannett News Service. She was the founding president of the Multicultural Journalists Association.

DAVID FARAH, of Pasadena, California, publishes *Farah's Guide*, the reference book on Nancy Drew books and memorabilia. Farah, who is also a licensed doctor and optometrist, works as an attorney.

NJERI FULLER is a reporter at *Florida Today* in Melbourne. A 1993 graduate of the University of Iowa School of Journalism and Mass Communication, she was named one of twenty All-USA College Academic First Team members by *USA Today* in 1993.

ANNE GREENBERG is executive editor of Archway Paperbacks and Minstrel Books, the young readers imprints of Pocket Books. Her job includes managing the Stratemeyer Syndicate publishing program, including Nancy Drew and Hardy Boy books.

CAROLYN G. HEILBRUN retired in 1992 as Avalon Professor in the Humanities, Columbia University, where she had taught since 1960. A pioneering feminist literary scholar, Heilbrun is author of *Toward a Recognition of Androgyny* (1973), *Reinventing Womanhood* (1979), *Writing a Woman's Life* (1988), and *Hamlet's Mother and Other Women* (1990). As *Amanda Cross*, Heilbrun is author of the Kate Fansler mystery series begun in 1963. Heilbrun (Cross) won a Scroll from the Mystery Writers of America for *In the Last Analysis* (1964) and a Nero Wolfe Award for *Death in a Tenured Position* (1981).

KAREN NELSON HOYLE is professor and curator of the Children's Literature Research Collections, University of Minnesota Libraries. Hoyle has been president of the Children's Literature Association and chair of the Caldecott Award and Mildred L. Batchelder Award Committees of the Library Services to Children Division of the American Library Association.

DEIDRE JOHNSON is assistant professor of children's literature in the Department of English, West Chester University, West Chester, Pennsylvania. She compiled and wrote *Stratemeyer Pseudonyms and*

Series Books (1982) and wrote *Edward Stratemeyer and the Strate-meyer Syndicate* (1993).

CAROLYN KEENE, pseud., of Tucson, Arizona, has written five Nancy Drew Mysteries and, with Franklin Dixon, pseud., has written two Nancy Drew & Hardy Boys SuperMysteries, including *Evil in Amsterdam* (1993). She has also initiated a number of series under her own name.

GEOFFREY S. LAPIN "discovered" Mildred Benson as the author of early Nancy Drews and has written extensively on Stratemeyer Syndicate freelancers. He is a cellist with the Indianapolis Symphony Orchestra and an adjunct professor of cello at Purdue University.

DONNARAE MACCANN, a cultural historian and authority on racism in children's books, is visiting assistant professor in the African-American World Studies Program at the University of Iowa. She has written numerous articles and edited several books, including *Social Responsibility in Librarianship: Essays on Equality* (1989) and *The Black American in Books for Children*, 2nd ed. (1985).

KAREN M. MASON is curator of the Iowa Women's Archives at the University of Iowa, where some of Mildred Wirt Benson's papers are housed. She is the co-author of *Women's History Tour of the Twin Cities* (1982) and has written articles on women's history.

ROBERT A. MCCOWN is head of the Special Collections Department of the University of Iowa Libraries, which houses manuscripts and rare books, including all of Mildred Wirt Benson's books.

GIL O'GARA, of Des Moines, Iowa, began publishing the *Yellowback Library*, a magazine for collectors and enthusiasts of series books and dime novels, in 1981.

NANCY PICKARD, of Shawnee Mission, Kansas, is former president of Sisters in Crime, the women mystery writers' organization, and author of the Jenny Cain mystery series. She has won many awards for the series, including Agatha and MacCavity Awards for *I.O.U.* (1991). The most recent Cain mystery is *Confession* (1994).

NANCY TILLMAN ROMALOV has been involved with children's literature as teacher, researcher, librarian, and children's bookstore owner. She has taught children's literature at the University of Iowa, the University of Montana, and Pacific Lutheran University.

LAURA RUBY is a Honolulu artist and instructor of art at the University of Hawaii at Manoa. Her prints and sculptures have been shown in national and international exhibitions. Her Nancy Drew Series of serigraphs has been exhibited at the University of Nebraska at Kearney and will be exhibited at the Honolulu Art Museum.

JOEL SHOEMAKER has served as chair of the American Library Association's Young Adult Services Division Best Books for Young Adults Committee and is library media specialist at South East Junior High School in Iowa City.

BONNIE S. SUNSTEIN is assistant professor of English Education at the University of Iowa. She is the author of *Portfolio Portraits* (1992) and *Composing a Culture* (1994).

PHIL ZUCKERMAN, of Bedford, Massachusetts, is president of Applewood Books, which specializes in preserving American popular culture from the past. In 1991 Applewood began publishing reprints of the first editions of the Nancy Drew and Hardy Boys books.

Index